SLINGSBY

Norway:
the Northern
Playground

NORWAY: THE NORTHERN PLAYGROUND

by

W. CECIL SLINGSBY

"Norway: the Northern Playground" was first published in 1904 by David Douglas, Edinburgh.
Republished in 1941 by Basil Blackwell, Oxford.

2003 Edition published by Ripping Yarns.com, an imprint of Rockbuy Limited, Findon, Aberdeenshire, Scotland, 2003.

ISBN 1-904466-07-9

Website: www.RippingYarns.com

Cover Photographs

Front cover photograph: *Hamerøy shaft, Hamerøy.*
                                    © George McCallum / www.orca-tysfjord.com

Back cover photograph: *Trolltinder, near Åndalsnes.* © Ian Robertson

CONTENTS

Introduction to 2003 Edition

Slingsby's 'Northern Playground' is a tale of exploration, adventure and the exuberant joy of high endeavour. It was one of my earliest inspirations and I still have my 7/6d. 1941 edition on my bookshelf.

In the early 1950s, when climbing was far more esoteric than it is today, meeting anyone who knew anything about it was difficult. In the northern Peak District where I grew up, scrambling in my pre-teens on what were then famous gritstone cliffs such as Laddow and Dovestones, I only once saw 'real' climbers. For me, books like this were an introduction, temptation and escape to the climbing world. I read them avidly and dreamed of exploring wild mountains.

Slingsby and other early pioneers opened my eyes to the climbing world. Winthrop Young, another world class mountaineer of that period, describes the all consuming zest for adventure in high places which was at the core of Slingsby's life and which has played such a great part in my own: "his business instincts were not a little jeopardised by his picaresque sympathy for schemes and enterprises with names suggestive of forest and cañon and mountain fastness and far, sun-tinted lands and places". And why not!

Norway's mountains were Slingsby's consuming passion. Born in 1849, he visited the country over twenty times between 1872 and 1921 and is considered the 'Father of Norwegian mountaineering'. On his first visit, he saw the Hurrungane Massif in the Jotunheim, later writing, "I shall never, as long as I live, forget my first view of Skagastølstind, the grandest European mountain north of the Alps. Our guide told us that it was the highest mountain in Norway, that it had not yet been ascended, and that no doubt this was impracticable. Can it be wondered that I determined, if possible to make the first ascent?"

His routes were often made by preference with local mountain people. They will be found from Lyngen in the far north on peaks with "wild beauty and eerie forms" but plagued by "the musical mosquito and the bloodthirsty klegg", all the way beyond the Jotunheim, "the finest mountains in Scandinavia", to which much of this book is dedicated, to the ice cap and mountains above Hardangerfjord in the south. He writes about this golden age of pioneering and often bold mountain exploration with the same attention to detail and happy, unassuming style in which he made his climbs, both benefiting from the same joie de vivre.

It is hardly surprising therefore, that Norway was to be my own first experience of mountain exploration. We set out in the summer of 1962, armed with the 'Northern Playground' and some thin paperback guides to 'Rock Climbs in Norway' written in 1953. They were sprinkled with Slingsby's first ascents and his tantalising references to unclimbed walls. The Arctic islands of Lofoten were our destination. Slingsby had climbed there in 1903 and 1904 making first ascents, often with Norman Collie, of peaks that variously "rise precipitously out of the ocean", "resemble the Drus" and have "climbing of the very best Chamonix aiguille type".

Like Slingsby, we had a great time, climbing two or three known routes and adding numerous new climbs of our own. It was wild and remote. The weather was at times both glorious and foul. Almost penniless from the start, we eventually ran completely out of money despite the hospitality of fishermen and farmers who displayed to us, as they did to Slingsby, "the kindness and gentle attentions ... of a race that we are nearer akin than to any other in Europe". We finally hitched our way back to Bergen, working in farms and hotels for meals as we went. The die was cast. With the aid of Slingsby, mountains had indeed become a lifelong obsession.

On our way south, we passed through the magnificent Romsdal valley, tempted there by Slingsby's tales of "good sport" on the many peaks. The visit was to play an important role in my life. From Åndalsnes at the head of the fjord, the truncated tower of the Romsdalshorn dominates the view. Slingsby climbed it in 1884 with his wife Alizon, the first woman to reach the top, commenting "The mountain is more difficult than the Matterhorn when in good condition". Beyond, the partially concealed alpine ridge of Vengetind instantly attracts. Obviously Slingsby felt likewise, making the first ascent of both its summits where "the scenery is too grand to describe" in 1881 and 1884, returning in 1885 for the first ascent of the neighbouring fang of Kvandalstind. He described the latter rather enthusiastically as "the steepest mountain in Europe".

Travelling up Romsdal, by the swift waters of the Rauma, the blue-black plunge of the Troll Wall then comes into view. In the early sixties, it was considered Europe's greatest unclimbed rock wall. This awesome vision gnawed at us for three more years until, in 1965, we climbed it. Rumours of our plan were leaked to the Norwegians by Arne Randers Heen, the ageing doyen of Romsdal rock, resulting in what the media portrayed as "a race between British and Norwegian climbers to be the first up Trollveggen". If it was a race, they won, as they topped out by their route a day before us – perhaps Norwegian honour had been at stake, as it was when Slingsby summited alone on Skagastølstind, but we celebrated together as a gathering storm swallowed up the wall.

When in Romsdal, Slingsby stayed at Hotel Aak, now a deservedly popular Mountain Centre but then an idyllic small farm and inn that had been used by climbers since the 1860s. His route descriptions can still be found in the guest book. We stayed there twice in the1990s, enjoying the company of old friends and familiar mountains before returning south, past another haunt of Slingsby's, the delightful Hotel Union at Øye in Sunnmøre. There, he and others including Raeburn and Patchell, climbed peaks like Slogen, "Norway's prettiest peak" with, according to his entry in the hotel guest book, "the proudest view in Europe". He was also active in Nordmøre, where he attempted "the fearsome-looking" 3,500 feet Furuveita Ghyll in 1906, only to be halted by a waterfall near the top of "the grandest ghyll it has ever been my good fortune to enter". He found the neighbouring alpine peaks rather more attractive, writing, "there is an air of mystery and romance about Vinnufjell and its great snowfields". Unsurprisingly, it was Slingsby that made the first ascent, climbing by two different routes, just four days apart in July 1906.

I have not yet had time to explore these peaks, nor those of Europe's great ice cap, Jostedalsbræn, whose "snow solitudes, glaciers and ice-fields were a joy" to Slingsby. To their east is the great Jotunheim Massif "Home of the Giants" and beneath is Turtagrø Hotel, still one of Norway's pre-eminent centres for mountaineering. Slingsby spent many happy days there and mementoes remain though tragically, the old hotel burnt down recently. "What a jolly time we spent at Turtagrø!" he wrote. "Is it heresy to say that the 'off days' picnicking were as enjoyable as the days spent on the mountains?" Here are the most alpine peaks in Norway. In the distance is Galdhøppigen, at 8095 feet, Norway's highest but, in fair weather, nothing more than an enjoyable glacier trek compared with

Slingsby's favourites, the Hurrungane Group, "with great glaciers and dramatic peaks, none more so than Skagastølstind".

For me, this alpine spire has remained elusive but Slingsby considered it "Norway's crowning glory", epitomising, like the Matterhorn, all that is most appealing about mountain architecture. He made its first ascent in July 1876, four years after first seeing it and two years after making the first traverse of the range, to get better acquainted with his ultimate objective. This traverse was itself considered of great significance to Norwegian mountaineering, crossing the only region of the Jotunheim still unexplored. When he finally succeeded on the mountain itself, he climbed the last five hundred feet alone, leaving his companions over-awed at the head of the glacier, asking him "Should we declare it inaccessible?". Its north summit is still named *Slingsby's Fortopp* in his honour. My 1953 guidebook says "The ascent made climbing history in Norway ... it is still a first rate climb with a splendid variety of ice and rock".

We are planning another trip to Norway this summer, maybe this time we will get a chance to climb it and tread once more in Slingsby's footsteps. If not, you can be sure of one thing, we will continue to enjoy Slingsby's 'Northern Playground'.

I trust this book will give others equal inspiration.

Tony Howard, Greenman's Farm, Greenfield, Oldham.

Editor's Note:

Tony Howard, was a member of "The Rimmon Group", English climbers who were active in the Romsdal area, and who operated as guides. He climbed numerous new routes in the region, including the first ascent of the Rimmon Route (English Route) Wall. This became the classic Big Wall route in the country. Tony produced the first Romsdal climbing guide book, a contributing factor to the growth of popularity for the area. He was a founding member of Troll Climbing Products Ltd, and over the last twenty years has been very active in desert climbing in Jordan, especially in Wadi Rum.

His guidebook on Romsdal is well worth getting hold of – it covers walks or scrambles in the area as well as climbs (see *Links* later in the book).

Notes on Cover Photographs

Hamerøy shaft, Hamerøy, Nordland, Norway.

Photograph © George McCallum / www.orca-tysfjord.com

The following information was supplied by George McCallum:

The "shaft" lies on Hamerøy on the south side of Vestfjord – the view from the top looks over to Lofoten.

A few details – it's 612m high – first climbed by Martin Ekroll from Skrova on the 8th of August 1888. There is a book on the plateau on the summit – where you can enter your name and details etc. – it's a popular climb that needs some respect. The resemblance to the dorsal fin of a killer whale makes it all the more interesting as the area has the largest concentration of killer whales in the world every winter.

Trolltinder, near Åndalsnes

Photograph © Ian Robertson

These lie on the south side of Romsdal, near Åndalsnes. The famous Troll Wall lies on the north side of these mountains. They are somewhat easier from the back!

Photographs Inside the Book

The photographs inside the book were supplied by John Baddeley, with the exception of "Bodalsbreen" and the "Romsdalhorn", both by Krystina Lotoczko.

Two of the line drawings are by W.C. Slingsby himself.

The third line drawing, "Figure 7: Store Skagastölstind" is reproduced with the kind permission of the artist's children.

Norwegian Names and Spelling

In the 2003 edition, we have retained Slingsby's original (and sometimes inconsistent…) 1903 spelling. A glance through a modern map will show that many of the spellings are now different – one obvious example is the current use of "ø" rather than "ö". However, to have "corrected" these would have been to spoil the flow of many passages of the book, and we have left them as Slingsby originally recorded them.

Maps

Many of Slingsby's adventures in the book take place in the Jotenheim and on the Jostedalsbreen. Tourist "walking maps" of these areas are published by Statens kartverk (the Norwegian Mapping Authority). They can be obtained in Britain from Stanfords map shop, www.stanfords.co.uk

Notes

The original footnotes from the book are included in an Appendix at the end. The notes are indicated by angle brackets, e.g. [1].

Disclaimer/Warning

On the basis that "there's always someone", I thought I'd better add the following paragraph:

Whilst the spirit and thrill of mountaineering is as enthralling today as it was in Slingsby's time, rope techniques have changed and improved dramatically. I would therefore suggest that any novices who are inspired by "Norway: the Northern Playground" should also read a modern book on rope technique, or better still go on a course of expert instruction.

Another point which must be emphasised is that on many Norse mountains, the glaciers have now shrunk considerably. The diagram on the back of the Jostedalsbreen 1:100,000 map shows that the Nigardsbreen glacier tongue has shrunk by over 2km since Slingsby's day... Hence even though Slingsby's book is still relevant to many of the Norwegian areas, route descriptions of glacier descents/ascents should be treated with considerable caution. Rockfalls also occur in high mountains, and the difficulty of rock routes can change from one year to the next.

As an example, the original approach that Slingsby followed up the glacier to Skagastølstind is more difficult now that the glacier has receded. The slabs leading up to Mohns Skar are smooth and difficult to protect, so require some care.

Slingsby himself found out what it is like to have an awkward way down off the ice cap without the benefit of either a local guide – or of himself having previously fully reconnoitred his descent route. If you want a first hand account of what it's like to descend a shrunken glacier amidst séracs, ice falls and precipices; Slingsby's epic when he descended the Kjenndalsbreen (see Chapter 11) makes particularly exciting reading!

"Hill-sense" and experience are as important today as they were in Slingsby's time. Ripping Yarns.com can accept no responsibility for anyone having a mishap through reading this book, directly or indirectly.

Ian Robertson, Findon, Aberdeenshire, 2003.

Preface to First Edition

"For to myself, mountains are the beginning and the end of all natural scenery; in them, and in the forms of inferior landscape that lead to them, my affections are wholly bound up."

Modern Painters: "The Mountain Glory."
RUSKIN.

For over twenty years I have received letters regularly every spring from persons desirous of obtaining information about the mountains in Norway, the answering of which has afforded me much pleasure. On their return, my friends invariably wrote to tell me of their doings, and thus I have had an almost unique opportunity of noting the growth of the sport of mountaineering in the country and of realising that it is now established on a firm and an enduring basis, and that Norway has become recognised amongst mountaineers all the world over as one of our great playgrounds.

Many have asked me to write a book on general climbing in the country; at last I yielded to the temptation, the result of which is embodied in this volume. Some friends wished me to keep well above the snow-line and to leave the fjords alone. This advice I have ignored, and have tried instead to interest the general tourist.

Copious notes, enlarged from pocket-book memoranda soon after my return from each campaign, formed the foundation of the book, and to these I have added some papers which have seen the light before, but which are all, more or less, dressed in a fresh garb. For leave to use these, I thank the Editors of *The Alpine Journal, The Yorkshire Ramblers' Journal, The Yorkshire Post, the Norwegian Club's Year-Book, The Craven Pioneer, The Proceedings of the Burnley Literary and Scientific Society*, and *Den Norske Turist Forening's Aarboger.*

To me the great feature connected with this book is the exceptional kindness which has been literally showered down upon me by my friends. I express my indebtedness to Herr H. Bache, Mr. G.P. Baker, the Rev. D.G. Cowan, Mr. Frank Ellis, Herr Carl Hall, Mr. Geoffrey Hastings, Mr. T.C. Porter, Mr.

Howard Priestman, Mr. C.H. Todd, Mr. W.N. Tribe, Miss Ecroyd, Mr. Thomas Gray, Mr. Eric Greenwood, and Mr. Colin B. Phillip.

Many Norse friends have given me much assistance, for which I am very grateful; but most of all my thanks are due to the leading Norse lady mountaineer, Fröken Therese Bertheau, who has given me much valuable help and advice.

All but one of the excellent maps which so much enhance the value of this book have been drawn and corrected by Mr. Howard Priestman from the best existing maps. The one is the result of a remarkable photo-topographical survey of the Horungtinder made by the same gentleman during several summers. This arduous work demanded the carrying of a half-plate camera up to the summit of many a rugged mountain and the taking of numerous photographs in bitter cold and with numbed fingers, followed by much close work at home. By the courtesy of Mr. Priestman, I am privileged to use for the first time this, the best map yet existing, of the finest range of mountains in Scandinavia. I need hardly say that I thank Mr. Priestman. My thanks are also due to my publisher for the invariable courtesy and attention which he has shown to me at all times since the MSS. were placed in his hands.

I make no apology for any probable misspelling of Norse place or personal names for an obvious reason, viz., that the Norse folk themselves are constantly changing their mode of spelling. The words Norse and Norseman are used throughout the book, though personally I prefer Norsk and Norskman, as I think they are more in harmony with the rugged nature of the country. The word Norwegian is wholly unsuitable for an Englishman to use; and as for Norway used as an adjective, which one sees only too often, no expression of condemnation is here necessary. For the most part, I have tried to use English mountaineering words, but as we have in our language no equivalent of the French word *col*, for which we cannot always use pass or gap, I have brought into service the Norse word *skar*, which has the same meaning as col. Ridge, gully, or ghyll, being English, are preferable to *arête* and *couloir*.

There are many friends who have given me much willing assistance in the preparation of the book, whom I have not named in this preface. To them, one and all, I tender my heartfelt thanks.

Wm. Cecil Slingsby.

Carleton, near Skipton-in-Craven,
November 5, 1903.

DEDICATED TO MY WIFE.

Chapter 1: General Remarks On Norway

If thou wouldst read a lesson that will keep
Thy heart from fainting, and thy soul from sleep,
Go to the woods and hills."
　　LONGFELLOW.

Once upon a time, a long, long while ago, soon after most of the world had been created, the Evil One wandered round and round, over land and sea, and when he saw that all was fair and beautiful he became very spiteful, and seizing an immense mass of rock, in his anger he threw it into the Northern Seas. It was so large that for many hundreds of miles it stood out of the waters – a terrible region of dark cliffs, sharp peaks, narrow ridges, and stony valleys, without one single blade of green grass or any sign of vegetation whatever.

Then the good God looked down with pity upon the waste, and threw here and there a little of the good soil which, fortunately, still remained. This caused fertile valleys, dark forests, and green uplands to appear. Moreover, He commanded huge shoals of fish to come yearly to the far north, where the sea cliffs and crags were the wildest and most forbidding. Thus has man been enabled to dwell in peace, happiness, and plenty in this land which is now called Norway.

Whether this origin, which is told in an old saga in picturesque and glowing language, be the true version or not matters but little nowadays, but the fact remains that Norway is one of the most mountainous countries in the world, and is to-day recognised as being one of the most delightful of our Alpine playgrounds. True it is that the height of no peak, when represented in feet, requires the use of five figures. What of that? Does it matter? Not a halfpenny, in a country where in some cases continuous ice-falls of nearly 6000 feet and rock ridges and faces of 5000 feet await the climbers who have the hardihood to tackle them.

Few Englishmen are aware of the size of Norway. Its total length along an axis which runs from N.N.E. to S.S.W. is 1100 miles, through 13 degrees of latitude. In breadth, at first sight the extent of over 26½ degrees would appear to be very great, and indeed, longitudinally, or in its time equivalent it is similar to the difference between Marseilles and Odessa, but it must not be forgotten that at a latitude of 70 degrees a very few miles represent one degree of longitude. The country, therefore, is relatively narrow.

All geologists testify to the great geological age of the country. Primary rocks probably occupy as large an area, comparatively, as in any portion of the globe. Gneiss is a prevailing formation, and to its presence are due the square-cut walls of so many fjords and deep valleys of the west coast and the vast snow-clad uplands and mighty waterfalls. Fortunately for the poet, the artist, and for us mountaineers, there are large areas where volcanic rocks, in most cases capped by gabbro, have been upheaved through the adjoining strata, whether primary or silurian, and now appear in the form of horns, serrated ridges, and sharp sky-piercing peaks.

Ancient glaciers, as great as, if not greater than, those of the present day in Greenland, have left their imprint almost everywhere in Norway. The luxurious tripper of to-day can see from his deck-chair on the tourist steamer crags rounded and polished hundreds of feet above the water. Moraines, large and small, are numerous; but the "raised beaches," which tell us that the land has risen out of the waters, and which may be seen in so many places, must not be mistaken for the former. Striated rocks and the signs of glacier erosion are frequently visible, and strangely perched erratic blocks may often be noticed on the rounded sea crags near the coast. Nay further, today we may find boulders in Yorkshire which have been transported from their parent beds in Norway by ice, but whether in the form of glaciers or icebergs I leave others to determine.

The whole of the Scandinavian peninsula has been covered by ice, as most of Greenland is to-day. Even now, the Justedalsbræ consists of one connected ice-sheet of nearly 400 square miles, and there is an aggregation of neighbouring but disconnected snow-fields of an even larger extent. There are also other large ice-caps, such as the Folgefond and Svartisen, but these are mere baby glaciers when compared with those of the "great ice age."

There is no doubt that in Norway the glaciers have been mighty workers, but whether they have done all that is attributed to them is open to doubt. The ice-plough of old is credited with the excavation of most of the fjords and the valleys which head them, and even many of the glaciers of to-day are said to be gouging out, as well as clearing out, "botner" or "cirques" in Jotunheim and elsewhere. The extreme case and noblest example worked by Nature's graving tools is probably that of the Sognefjord, which has been sounded to a depth of 600 Norse fathoms, or over 4000 English feet, whilst the neighbouring mountains are nearly 4000 feet above sea-level, or 8000 feet above the bed of the fjord. Many scientists of the present day wish us to believe that the principal portion of this 8000 feet has been dug and carved out by ancient glaciers. Why should they not also declare that the basin of the Mediterranean has been formed in a similar manner, as in many respects it resembles a huge fjord?

The greatest friend of Norway, as well as of Great Britain and Ireland, is the Gulf Stream, whose warm waters temper the severity of the Northern climate, with the result that, dotted here and there amongst the barren mountains on the whole wind-swept coast of Norway, may be seen green oases, where are comfortable homesteads, inhabited by thriving merchants, blue-eyed fishermen, and sturdy farmers; while on the sheltered shores of the fjords the population is numerous in harmony with the luxuriance of the vegetation.

Along the whole coast, including 4 degrees of latitude within the Arctic Circle, there is never a block of drift-ice to be seen except perhaps the little bergs which are calved from the Jökulsbræ, the only glacier in Scandinavia which actually bathes its feet in the sea, the séracs which fall from an arm of Frostisen into the Ofotenfjord, and the small blocks which are washed down the rivers.

When one sees the fertility, the pretty gardens, and fields of oats, at a place like Lyngseidet, very near the 70th parallel, one is apt to forget the conditions which prevail elsewhere at that latitude. In order to correct this forgetfulness it is well to follow that parallel in an atlas through the Kara Sea, North Siberia, a bit of Alaska, and the ice-bound islands north of Canada, where Sir John Franklin lost his life, then to Disco Bay and Greenland, and by doing so, one can faintly realise what would happen to Norway, if the threat of the facetious American to cut off the Gulf Stream from Europe could become an accomplished fact.

Christiania [2] does not get the benefit of the Gulf Stream, and consequently the blue waters of its great fjord are frozen over every winter, though the harbours of Trondhjem, Tromsö, and Hammerfest, which latter is nearly 1000 miles farther north, are always open. As may naturally be expected, the heads of the longest fjords, which contain a large proportion of fresh water, are usually frozen in winter, I myself having seen the Lysterfjord – the innermost part of the Sognefjord – covered with a film of ice from Dosen to Skjolden. The Osefjord in Hardanger is usually ice-clad. The Nordfjord is often frozen as far down as Faleide, and sometimes even farther. Oddly enough the Lake Stryn above rarely freezes.

Purely for want of sufficiently good corroborative evidence, I will not ask my readers to believe in the legend that the Ark rested on Molden, a mountain near the head of the Sognefjord. Had this been the case, the annals of mountaineering, if only by water, in Norway, would have gone considerably further back than they do. It is, however, undoubtedly true that the sport of mountaineering was followed by the Vikings nine hundred years ago, as we can see by referring to "King Olaf Tryggvesson's Saga" in the *Heimskringla*, where we read the following:-

"King Olaf was more expert in all exercises than any man in Norway whose memory is preserved to us in sagas; and he was stronger and more agile than most men, and many stories are written down about it. One is that he ascended the Smalsarhorn (Hornelen or probably a spur of that grand sea-cliff) and fixed his shield on the very peak. Another is that one of his followers had climbed up the peak after him, until he came to where he could neither get up nor down, but the king came to his help, climbed up to him, took him under his arm, and bore him to the flat ground."

Was there ever a more picturesque mountaineering scene than this? We can almost imagine that we see the great sea-king scrambling up those gaunt sea-cliffs, with his scarlet robe fluttering in the breeze; that we can hear the deafening cheers of the thousands of Vikings in their boats below, as their hero picks up his living burden, toys with it, and returns step by step down to the shore. Yes; cannot we also hear the answering echoes bandied about from cliff to cliff, from Gulen to Bremanger Land?

Though the ancient Icelandic historian, Snorro Sturleson, did not mention it, I believe that in King Olaf's days an Alpine Club was founded, that the climbing qualification was a very stiff one, and that the doughty king himself was the first president. Perhaps, too, he was the last. Who knows? Whether there was an Alpine Club winter dinner or not I cannot tell, but I am certain that there were plenty of speeches, much skaal drinking and emptying of many flagons of mead.

When the Viking days were ended, the spirit of active enterprise in great measure died out in Norway, or possibly lay dormant. As a proof that this adventurous spirit has again entered in full measure into the breasts of the hardy Norsemen of to-day, I need only write the name of the hero – Fridtjof Nansen.

In the year 1820 there was a notable reawakening of the sport of mountaineering in the country. Two parties were afield, and Norse climbers have every reason to point to this year with especial pride. Professors Keilhau and Boeck discovered Jotunheim, where they ascended the beautiful mountain well named Falkenæbbe – falcon's beak. They made plucky, though, unfortunately, unsuccessful attempts to ascend Skagastölstind, Galdhöpiggen and the Lodals Kaupe. On the last named they were nearly killed by an avalanche; one of them was indeed only saved by carrying a large barometer. This was broken by a falling stone, which would otherwise have crushed his spine. On this expedition ice-axes were used to good purpose. At this period ice-axes were barely known in the Alps, though hatchets were often used.

The second party consisted of Lektor Bohr, of Bergen, and three others. They made a plucky attempt to ascend Lodals Kaupe, and the question whether they reached the top or not still forms a favourite topic for an after-dinner argument amongst Norse mountaineers.

After this, one would naturally have expected that the Norsemen would have continued to practise and to develop the sport up to the present day. Such, however, was not the case, and during the space of at least half a century ice-axes were not used by the natives as implements of snow craft, and in practice the sport died out.

It is true that peasants made the first ascent of certain prominently situated mountains, such as Galdhöpiggen, the Gausta Fjeld, Kviteggen, Slogen, Lodals Kaupe, and the Romsdalshorn. Still, mountaineering, as a noble sport, was not recognised until it was reintroduced by our countrymen, upon whom the good fortune has fallen of ascending very many of the finest mountains in Norway, of making many grand new glacier passes, and of reopening others, which, though not new, were quite forgotten.

The British pioneers were Lieutenant Breton, R.N., whose book, *Scandinavian Sketches*, published in 1835, describes, with the modesty nearly always associated with naval men, a remarkably adventurous journey made in 1834 through Jotunheim and other wild regions. Then came Mr. Thomas Forester and his companion, Lieutenant M.S. Biddulph, whose joint book, *Norway in 1848 and 1849*, introduced Englishmen to the Horungtinder, i.e. at a respectful distance. Next, and of most importance, was Professor J.D. Forbes, whose work, *Norway and its Glaciers visited in 1851* undoubtedly one of the greatest mountain classics, and is much the best book ever yet written on Norway. Mr. F.M. Wyndham in 1861 brought out an excellent sporting book about reindeer-stalking in East Jotunheim, which was followed by those of other sportsmen and travellers, good, bad, and indifferent. Next came my old friend Lieut.-Colonel J.R. Campbell, whose papers in the sixth volume of *The Alpine Journal* were subsequently published in book form under the name *How to see Norway*, a book which ought to be found in the library of every lover of that land.

These men were the real pioneers. With the exception of the last named, who climbed Horningdalsrokken and St. Cecilia's Krone, they did not make any actual ascents, yet they paved the way for us, who came later in the field and in some measure benefited by their experience.

In the late sixties and early seventies the hardy Norsemen began mountain exploration in earnest. Foremost amongst them was Emanuel Mohn, with whom it was my privilege and pleasure to have a long and very successful campaign in 1876. There were also Dr. Yngvar Nielsen, Konsul T.J. Heftye, Prof. E. Sars, the poet Vinje, Herr Martens, Herr Thorgeir Sulheim, and a few others. These men, in addition to English sportsmen, with laudable persistency unravelled the secrets of Jotunheim so far as the deep valleys, wild glens, and snowy uplands are concerned.

Alpine climbers in general did not believe that any first-rate climbing could be found in Norway. Indeed, this is not to be wondered at, as in most cases the real mountains themselves are hidden from the sight of the ordinary traveller, whose journey so often is confined to the bottom of a deeply cut groove-like valley, whether he be on land or sea. The usual hog-backed fjelde, of the Helvellyn type, which represent most of the mountain forms of Norway, do not offer many attractions to the adventure-loving climber, and, though I have been on scores of them; and have had much enjoyment out of them, I had usually some ulterior object in view other than that of making the ascent of the highest point. I generally wanted to see how the land lay, and what there was at the other side.

The most notable district for mountaineers is that of the Jotun Fjelde, which includes the Horungtinder with their crowning glory, Skagastölsind the finest mountain in Norway, which for many years was also considered to be the highest in Northern Europe.

Then there are the snow solitudes of the Justedalsbræ, whose many glaciers and ice-falls are the joy of those who, by dint of much practice, have gained considerable experience, and have become adepts in the science of snow and ice craft.

Farther west is the Gjegnalund glacier region where the strangely tilted strata of rounded conglomerate form man regular escarpments and little blue lakes.

A little to the north are the rugged spires, which are beautifully reflected on the placid waters of the Hjörund and Sökkelv fjords. These "Söndmöre Alps," as the Norse folk now designate them, are bewitching, and are like glorified Coolins of Skye with glaciers in the corries. They have a similar geological formation.

In Romsdal, some of the gneiss and metamorphic ranges afford good sport to the mountaineer. Notably Mjölnir, the Voengetinder, the Romsdalshorn, and Troldtinder.

In the north there are the Oxtinder, which however, have disappointed those who have visited them. The ice-cap of Svartisen, the rugged ranges about Sulitelma, some in Norway and others in Sweden, already have their devotees. The aiguilles of Lofoten have an uncanny atmosphere about them in addition to their great beauty, and some stiff climbing problems still await solution here.

Last, but by no means of least importance, are the sharp peaked ranges and mysterious haunts of the frost giants about Lyngenfjord, where Nature has, apparently, developed her wildest and most eerie forms. These are lighted up with a brilliance and beauty of colouring which I have never seen equalled anywhere else. Jæggevarre the Mont Blanc of the north, is the snow-crowned monarch of the peaks of Lyngen, and is a very fine aggregation of rolling mountain snow-fields. Fornoestind is the Romsdalshorn of the north; whilst the Jægervandtinder and their neighbours form a group of fine peaks the grandeur of which is only second to the Horungtinder, whilst they excel the latter range in beauty. One peak of the Jægervandinter the Stortind, is almost as beautiful as Slogen in Söndmöre. What can I say more in its praise?

I have now had fifteen mountain campaigns in Norway, which have irregularly alternated with visits to the Alps. [3] As my principal object was mountain climbing and exploration, a large number of maiden ascents and new glacier passes have fallen to my lot in the company both of Norse and English climbers. Though I have made above fifty good new expeditions, I could easily have doubled the number if I had adopted the principle of making headquarters, and of making ascents from and returning to these places. However this method never much commended itself to my taste, at least when I could carry well, and I always flitted about where fancy led. Other reasons which prevented centralisation arose from the discomforts of sæter life [1], and the pangs of hunger, which have driven us scores of times away from the high fjelde to seek the soft luxury and the flesh-pots of the valleys.

For some years I had the field, so far as the sport of mountaineering was concerned, almost to myself, as English climbers had not yet recognised the value of this northern playground, and consequently much of my early mountaineering was done in company with Norsemen. As at first I knew little of the technicalities of the sport from actual experience, and found that my companions as a rule knew still less, we went warily and treated the glaciers with a respect which I regret is not shown by all young climbers of the present day. Our successes were not numerous, neither were our failures. We walked before we ran, and gained experience step by step. For the most part the leading was left to me, and I fear that I was very often autocratic.

The ascent of Skagastölstind in the year 1876 reawakened the dormant interest in mountaineering, and after an unsuccessful attempt on this mountain in 1877 the artist, Herr Harald Petersen, succeeded in making the second ascent the following year, and as on the first occasion he had to climb the last 500 feet entirely alone.

Then came Herr Carl Hall, a Dane, who had climbed a little in the Alps, and great success crowned his efforts on the Romsdalshorn, amongst the Horungtinder, the Smörstabtinder and elsewhere. A little army of Englishmen and one English lady, Miss Green, then came on the scene, and it followed as a matter of course that victory greeted them all along the line. Then Mr. Patchell began, and his record of grand and new expeditions is very large. Later a gallant French scientist, M. Charles Rabot, explored many wild mountain regions, hitherto almost unknown.

During the eighties and nineties, friends and I practically completed the mountain exploration of the Söndmöre Alps which Mohn and I had begun in 1876. We also climbed the peaks of the Voengetinder, which had fascinated Lieutenant Breton sixty-seven years ago so much that his sketch of this rugged range was introduced as a frontispiece into his book. The Justedalsbræ which even now provides a field for detailed exploration, and affords unrivalled scope for the attainment of proficiency in snow-craft, occupied us for many seasons. Neither were the Aalfotenbræ and the Gjegnalund glaciers overlooked.

For many years it has been known that in the far north in general, and about Lyngenfjord in particular, there were grand mountain ranges which invited exploration. The great distance and the impossibility of getting suitable companions saved these mountains from desecration by the hobnailed boot until quite recently

So far back as the year 1851 Professor Forbes wished to explore a glacier on the peninsula of Lyngen, but had no opportunity of doing so. Subsequently the German Emperor and Dr. von Gussfeldt were so fascinated by the weird peaks of Lyngen, that they engaged the services of Émile Rey of Courmayeur, at that time one of the three best guides in Europe, for the following year. However, political or other reasons prevented the fulfilment of this dream of the Imperial mind, and, in consequence, the regiments of rock Trolds which guard the many mountain crests were denied the honour of an imperial review.

Since then Mr. Hastings initiated serious mountaineering in Lyngen by his ascent of Jæggevarre, the Mont Blanc of the north, and had four campaigns there. Mrs. Aubrey le Blond, with the two Swiss guides, Joseph Imboden and his son, also scored well there. Mr. W.P. Haskett-Smith and I joined Mr. Hastings in his second campaign, and it proved to be one of the very best and most enjoyable holidays I have ever had. I refer my readers to a paper which I read on the subject before the Alpine Club, and which is to be found in *The Alpine Journal, vol. xix.*

I will merely say how that in the mountains of Lyngen Nature has developed her wildest and most eerie forms, and that from the climbing point of view the best of Jotunheim, the best of the Justedalsbræ, the best of the Söndmöre Alps and the best of Romsdal have in these far northern latitudes worthy rivals.

What delightful memories we have stored away of our camp life on the shores of the Jægervand and of the brilliance and beauty of colouring when at midnight we saw the sun's disk rolling or gliding over the subtle lines of that most beautiful island – the Fuglö.

However I must not allow the attractiveness of this theme to tempt me further, but will leave others to write in detail about the charms of climbing in Lyngen. There is no rose without a thorn. But let us forget the musical mosquito, and the blood-thirsty klegg.

The first serious climb on the flame-coloured peaks of the Lofoten Islands was that of the Troldtind above the icy Troldfjordvatn, which was made in 1890 by an English lady, Miss Jeffrey. The next campaign was organised by Mr.

Priestman, whose paper on the subject can be found in *The Alpine Journal, vol. xix,* as well as an excellent view of the Troldtind. A third was undertaken by a strong party in 1901, and the paper read on it by Professor Collie before the Alpine Club shows that the weird granite peaks of Lofoten afford rock-climbing of quite as difficult a character as the aiguilles of Chamouni. This is much to say of mountains of such comparatively low stature, but I believe it to be quite true, though I have only seen the mountains from the deck of a steamer.[4]

The regions of Frostisen, Sulitelma, and Svartisen, all within the Arctic Circle and now, thanks to the admirable coasting steamboat service, easily reached, will well repay the visit of mountaineers, but apparently the Oxtinder just outside the Circle are a disappointing range of mountains.

The gallant French scientist and explorer, H. Charles Rabot, has introduced us by his book, *Au Cap Nord,* to much hitherto unknown grand mountain scenery in Arctic Norway and Sweden, including the snow-crowned, glacier-girt Kebnekaisse. Still, I cannot think that they can be so grand or so beautiful as the mountains of Lyngen which bathe their feet in the green waters of Lyngen, Ulfsfjord, Kjosen, and Sorfjord.

There is much to tempt the mountaineer to the far north. There he will see some of the best which Nature can offer in the form of ice, snow, and rock scenery, and what is probably the most weirdly beautiful coast in the world.

To prove the popularity of mountaineering in Norway at the present day, it is only necessary to pay a visit to Turtegrö the Riffleberg of Norway, to Fjærland or Øie, and to read in the climbers' books of the many ascents which are annually made from these centres by mountaineers of various nationalities. As a rule, however, I must say that most of those who frequent these resorts do not show, by the feats which they accomplish, much originality. There are, however, notable exceptions, whom it would be invidious for me to name, who are admirable mountaineers, who have done much first-rate new work, and who do not keep slavishly to old tracks.

Though the scenery of the skerries is occasionally monotonous, a voyage up the coast is very enjoyable in fine weather; and if not pressed for time, there is more fun to be got out of the slower boats, which make many stoppages, than on the express steamers. The interchange of passengers and cargo is always interesting, especially, perhaps to the snapshot photographer; and when the traveller knows sufficient Norse to be able to converse freely with the sturdy farmers who come on board, the interest of the voyage is much increased. To have to lie to for hours in a fog off Hornelen, or near the promontory of Stadt, as I have done on several occasions, is not pleasant, but even then there is some fun. Perhaps a fishing-boat comes alongside, and its occupants, who have entirely lost their bearings, are told in which direction their home lies, only half a mile away, or a sportive whale or a school of porpoises may pop up close to.

After one tour has been made in Norway, the desire to revisit the romantic Northland in most cases is irresistible. This is not surprising, because when we go to Norway we feel that we are visiting the land of our remote ancestors, the country from whence the Vikings of the ninth and tenth centuries set sail to harry the coasts, not only of Great Britain, but also of France and the Mediterranean as well. These Vikings pushed their skiffs up our navigable rivers and, struck by the fertility of the country, in many cases settled on the land, intermarried with the Saxon maidens, and became the progenitors of the finest race in the world.

Most of the qualities which are especially cherished in the north of England today, the sturdy independence, dogged endurance and self-reliance, to name no others, and the best blood which we possess, we have derived from our "for-elders," the Vikings of Scandinavia. We must remember, too, that the Normans themselves were, in the main, of Norse race, and that Ganger Rolf, or Rollo the Sea-King as we call him, who sailed from Aalesund to conquer Normandy, was the great-great-great-grandfather of William the Conqueror.

From our Viking ancestry we have also derived the most interesting portion of the rich dialect of our Northern Counties. Especially is this the case in Cumberland, which has probably more Norse blood and general Norse characteristics than any other portion of the British Isles with the exception of Orkney and Shetland.

The study of place-names is always interesting, and to a lover of Norway it is delightful to recognise the Norse name of an English farm such as Braida Garth, broad enclosure; or of a river, as the Rothay, the Red River; a lake, as Wasdale, or lake valley; a hill, as Kirkby Fell, or Church town mountain. It is equally interesting to recognise Norse in our rich dialects. In my own village, the bairns still laike, the joiner rears his stee, the blacksmith hammers on his stiddy, the cowman rives his hay from the baulk stead in the laithe, takes it along the fodder gang and ligs it in the boos, and then gets meal frae the kist; and the sensible man still eats havver bread.

The statesmen or yeomen of our north country dales, whose holdings one after another unfortunately so often become absorbed by the neighbouring squire, or worse still by some rich townsman, very closely resemble the Norse "bonder" of the present day, and none who know the types of both can doubt for one moment that they have a common ancestry. They possess a similar sturdiness of character, the same virtues, and, if you will, the same weaknesses. They are bluntly hospitable, and are as honest and truthful as the day. At the bottom they are essentially religious and are invariably patriotic. A vein of picturesque superstition still lingers in their minds, and long may it do so! They are simple in their habits; they get up early, and go early to bed. They take their porridge and eat their havver bread, and, until a wicked licensing bill became law in England, enjoyed their wholesome home-brewed ale. They have constitutions like cast-iron. The one has his farm "Garth" in the dale, and his sheep on the "fell "; the other has his "gaard" in the "dal," and his cattle, sheep, or goats on the "fjeld." It is true that the bonde, on account of his greater isolation, is now more of a Jack-of-all-trades than his English cousin, but improved communication is depriving the former of his individuality, and every year sees him buy more of the commodities which were formerly made better at home.

Physically, the statesman and the bonde bear a close resemblance. They are fairly tall, broad shouldered, ruddy complexioned, with light brown hair and grey eyes. The women folk and children are also often alike and often good-looking. In fine, the statesmen of the English dales and the bonder of Norway are as fine a body of men as can be found in the world.

By travelling alone, as I have often done in Norway, I have had much better opportunities of getting to know the home-life of the people than when travelling with English friends, and have received kindness and gentle attentions to which the ordinary tourist is a complete stranger. I have travelled hundreds of miles too in the company of peasants, and at other times with ladies and gentlemen, and have invariably met with courtesy and consideration on the part of the Norse folk.

Many a day have I spent weather-bound in some lonely farmhouse in an out-of-the-way valley, where the folk still live in the simple manner in which I imagine that their remote "for-elders" and ours in England were wont to pass their lives. Many an old-fashioned house has sheltered me, where, in lieu of a chimney, the smoke from the fire on the "peis" had to escape through the trap-door in the roof, to which is attached a long pole, by which it is raised, and though the smoke from a log fire is trying to the eyes, I firmly believe that these lofty old rooms are more healthy than the modern form, and smoke is an excellent disinfectant. I have often sat down at the long table and shared in the simple family meal where we all ate out of one bowl of porridge. This we scooped out with wooden spoons, which we then dipped into the general bowl of milk. Then we had "speget köjd" – smoked and salted mutton or kid, nearly a year old – and very good it is when one is hungry. Fladbröd, butter and cheese, completed the repast. Could we not have seen the same in England had we lived a few centuries ago?

At other farms I have drunk with many a hearty skaal out of beautiful silver tankards or quaintly carved wooden bowls. Once, in a remote farm-house where no foreigner had ever been seen before, my hostess honoured me by giving me an ancient bed to sleep in where the coverlet was a remarkable and aged piece of tapestry. The subject was "The Adoration of the Magi." There were six kings, three of whom were riding horses, blue, pink, and red. All had golden crowns. One king was gaping with open mouth, throwing up his arms and evidently much astonished. The Virgin and Child were pink. There were many grotesque animals, strangely coloured, and altogether the quilt was a curiosity. When I spoke of it to our hostess, she offered to exchange it for my Scotch plaid. However, each was better in its own place.

Very often at farms or merchants' houses, I have been ushered into the pretty white-painted parlour, where the piano, pictures, and numerous pots of beautiful flowering-plants testified to the presence of refined women, and the embroidered pipe-rack on the wall told its own tale of contentment at home. Then, with great solemnity, I have been invited to sit in the place of honour at the right-hand end of the sofa, and when sherry and delicious red currant wine and sweet biscuits have been brought in and placed on the white mat in the centre of the round table, I have been invited to drink "et glas viin" and have clinked glasses with all present.

As I have stayed at all sorts of farm-houses and with many of the Norse gentry and merchants, I have got to know and I hope to appreciate fully the characteristics and sterling good qualities of a race to which I am proud to believe that we are nearer akin than to any other in Europe.

Chapter 2: My First Visit To Norway In 1872

"To travel hopefully is a better thing than to arrive."
        R. L. STEVENSON

"A plague on your languages, German and Norse!
Let me have the song of the kettle."
        WORDSWORTH

From earliest childhood when, under the guidance of a governess, I acquired some inaccurate information about the Dovre Fjeld, to the advanced period of existence when Miss Martineau's charming little book, *Feats on the Fjord*, lay open before me, I longed to go to Norway more than to any other country. In the year 1872 this wish was first realised. Before starting, I went to a bookseller's shop in our neighbouring town. Behind the counter stood a jolly old Yorkshire woman whom I asked for a guide-book to Norway. She looked at me, and said quite innocently, "Norway! Well, I think not; but 'ere's *Black's Guide to t' English Lakes*. It'll 'appen do as weel."

Eventually my companion, Mr. Chris. Sidgwick, and I provided ourselves with a little suitable literature, including a magazine article about a visit to the Vöring and Skjæggedal fosses and a journey to the "neighbourhood of the midnight sun." The difficulties and dangers attending a visit to Vöringfos were enormously exaggerated, and the picturesque beauty of the whole expedition to the Skjæggedalsfos was so grandly described, that we determined to see the two waterfalls, and to make a journey up to the North Cape, in order I suppose principally to burn holes in our hats with burning glasses at midnight. Then we were to try the fishing and to follow the dictates of fancy as far as we liked, and to return home – some time. But that was not all. I knew something about rock-climbing, and had already made a few climbs on the Yorkshire and Cumberland fells. With my brothers and sisters I had tried standing, sitting, and shall I say rolling, glissades? But I had never seen a glacier. There were glaciers in plenty in Norway. Yes. We would climb too.

On June 20th, on the *Argo*, we first became acquainted with the discomforts of a clammy fog-bank, a slow speed and the abominable steam-whistle, and in due course with all the pleasures too of a passage over a rippleless sea. This was followed by a stiff gale, which upset the equilibrium of most of the passengers. However, peace was completely restored by the entrance into still water near Stavanger. We all ate the next meal with the voracity of tigers, and what was stranger still, we all seemed to think it quite natural to do so.

Since this time the steamboat service from Hull to Norway has been much improved, and a very successful Norse line has for some years plied between Newcastle and Norway, and the number of tourists has increased at least a hundredfold. Still, the North Sea is as wayward, as fickle, and as treacherous as ever, and I for one long for the time when the voyage between Newcastle or Hull on this side, and Bergen on the other, can be accomplished under twenty-four hours.

As this first tour introduced us to some of the most charming districts in Norway, I will give a general outline of it.

The clearness of the water and the number of jellyfish – "manæt" or sea-nettles in Norse – perhaps are noticed by most people in the harbour at Stavanger. Along the coast, on bleak headlands on the various skerries, the gaily painted wooden lighthouses and the numerous little white targets with black centres, painted on the rocks to indicate safe mooring-places for boats, testify to the fact that even between the islands which guard nearly the whole of the coast of Norway and the mainland, there can be foul as well as fair weather.

Bergen, Björgvin – the mountain pastures – of old, overlooked by its seven hills, is, even yet, in spite of the ruthless substitution of prosaic stucco buildings for picturesque wooden houses each with its gable end towards the front, one of the most beautiful cities in the world. Let him who doubts this statement walk up Lövstaken on a fine day, and see indescribable beauties close at hand, and far away, on one side the snows of the Folgefond, and to the north the mountain Alden, north of the entrance to the Sognefjord.

The day after our arrival proved to be St. John's Eve, a great festival in Norway, more, however, a relic of paganism than a Christian feast. The burning of the god Balder on his funeral pyre in his boat *Hringhorn* is in fact yearly commemorated on St. John's Eve by "Balder's bale fires" being lighted on the hillsides all over the country. Old boats are often requisitioned for this purpose. I am glad to say that in out-of-the-way valleys, where the almost ubiquitous telephone has not yet appeared, much superstition still remains, and will, I hope, long continue to do so.

From Bergen we steamed for six enjoyable hours on the little boat *Vos* to Bolstadören. The last ten or eleven miles are absorbingly interesting; everything is weird, suggestive of elves, fairies, water-nymphs, mermaids, and I know not what besides. The fjord is everywhere narrow, and it is well to bear in mind this fact, that in Norway generally the narrower the fjord and the farther it pierces into the heart of the country, the finer is the scenery. In some places the Bolstadfjord is little over fifty yards wide. The cliffs, though never very high, rise like walls out of the water. Dark Scotch firs, apparently glorying in their power of growing out of mere chinks in the rocks, raise their proud crests in many an inaccessible position, boldly defying time, the elements, unfavourable situations and, worst of all, the dread woodman's axe. Here and there graceful birches or clumps of immense white saxifrages and the greenest of mosses add beauty to the scene. Little oases of cultivated land at the foot of lateral glens appear where we stop and have an interchange of merchandise with the boats.

At one place, an Amazonian red-haired girl in a green bodice with red sleeves and the usual blue wadmel skirt is the rower. At another, three boats manned by white-haired old veterans come alongside; their boats are quickly laden with full and empty casks and coils of rope, and then, after many struggles, a cow is craned up and slung over the side, and soon lowered into one of the boats. The discharging and taking in cargo upcountry is always an amusing scene. On one occasion on the Hjörundfjord I saw a pony lowered into the sea, as there was no suitable boat for it alongside. It puffed and snorted for a few seconds, and then swam merrily ashore.

Gorges and arms of fjords keep appearing as we pass, where perhaps they are least expected, and disappear again as quickly as they come into sight. In one place the fjord appears to be terminated by a high cliff, towards which we seem to be steering. When within a few yards of it another reach discovers itself on the right, and we turn sharp round, and pull up close to a collection of little houses, whose grass-covered roofs appear to be the most fertile meadows of the place. Then the fjord partakes of the nature of a river, and as it is low tide we see some rapids ahead where the navigation is difficult. We stop to get up steam, and then make a charge. The course is shown by posts on shore and by floating buoys on the water. As the latter have to be steered over, the idea of "kicking the bucket" is suggested. Sharp-toothed rocks not very far below the surface show plainly that it is not a place to be trifled with.

This Bolstadfjord is certainly very pretty. It reminds one of Scotland, alas! without the heather, and it has many a counterpart in Norway. It is not by any means famous, but it is a most fitting preparation for grander scenes in store.

The river at the head is well known to salmon-fishers, and a few years ago one of the English lessees had the good luck to land a fifty-two pound fish after a three hours' fight in the river. Three years later my sister and I rowed down the rapids in this river, some two miles in length, and much enjoyed the fun.

At Evanger we were fortunate enough to see two bridal parties, a most picturesque sight, as most of those concerned arrived, donned in their brightly-coloured costumes, in gaily decorated boats. A few days later we saw three weddings at Odde. June, and early in July, are favourite times for weddings, as it is rather a slack time before the hay and corn harvest. The Norse peasantry are by nature gregarious, as far as they well can be. They are christened in batches, married in batches, and, what is stranger still, they are occasionally buried together when, after a hard winter, the frozen corpses of a remote district are brought, on the melting of the snows, to their last resting-place, and are buried at the same time. I knew a lad who was killed in a sledge accident in the winter in the north of Norway, and whose body was not buried until the following June, because until that time the ground was all covered with snow and frozen as hard as iron.

We pushed on the same day to Eide, and drove our first carioles. The distance from Evanger is about thirty-two miles, and the country is very varied and pretty. We saw many strange things on the road: a hatless ruffian in a cariole dashing madly downhill, and using his new whip unmercifully. We passed dozens of pretty little wooden corn-mills driven by water. The roofs are invariably covered with turf, and very often birch-trees may be seen growing on the top. At that time each farmer had his own mill, and each grew his own corn. Nowadays dairy-farming and grazing are displacing husbandry in most parts of Norway, and in consequence, these most picturesque mills are disappearing slowly but surely, and the importation of grain from Russia and other countries is yearly increasing.

Near the beautiful lake, Gravens Vand, we first saw the "jern streng," or iron wire, a capital invention. One end is attached to a rock or a tree in the valley, the other far up on the mountain above. It is merely a novel kind of hay-cart. As grass is scarce and valuable in Norway, the most has to be made of what there is, as horses and cattle do not thrive well either on fishes' heads or dried foliage.

Grass is therefore cut on the little ledges and steep slopes in almost inaccessible places. Cutting is one thing, carrying is another, a difficult and dangerous matter on tree-clad crags; hence some inventive genius, a public benefactor hit upon the wire method. The grass is bound into a bundle with birch or hemp ropes, a hook is fixed to it, then it is put on the wire. A shove at starting and in a few seconds the cargo is at the farm, perhaps 1500 feet below, and then made into hay. Wood and birch bark, or "noever" which is used in roofing buildings and as kindling for the fires, and which burns when dry almost like paper, are also sent down. In some places grass is sent down fully 3000 feet in this manner. At Hansen's cosy little inn at Eide we first saw ivy trained round the inner walls of the rooms.

At this time there were very few steamboats on what is now the most tourist-ridden fjord – the Hardanger – in Norway, and long boating expeditions were inevitable. In order to avoid a very long one to Vik, we determined to cross the mountain to Ulvik. As my companion wished to ride and try the merits of a Norse pony, we hired a couple, an experiment I have never repeated. Norse saddles are usually horrible instruments of torture, high pommelled, and with the stirrups too far back, so that the rider is forced forward. A bridle is often a mere rope to which is attached a straight piece of round rusty iron with a ring at each end, which does duty for a bit. I have seen metal entirely dispensed with, and in its place either a rope bit, or a rope nose-band and head-piece. Of course there is not much power in such bits, but the customary pur-r-r-r-r will almost always stop a horse even down the steepest hill.

Three hours' ride brought the two lazy fellows to Ulvik, the loveliest place in Hardanger. The wolves which give the Vik or bay its name are happily not existing now.

For us, Ulvik was merely a resting-place on the way to the Vöringfos a grand waterfall now very well known, but formerly surrounded by an air of mystery, as the early visitors could only see it from above by leaning over the edge of a precipice. On our visit there was a party of ladies who had three horses. In the gorge above, several frail bridges had to be crossed. When a horse came to one it first sniffed at it and put its nose close to the ground, then it moved on a few paces, and where any plank more rotten than usual appeared, the horse put out one foot slowly and deliberately and gently pressed the wood, and, in fact, felt whether it was safe or not before trusting its weight on it, and when reassured, he walked ahead. Each horse did exactly the same. We were almost the first to see the fall from the bottom, and, indeed, I was actually the first tourist to cross the river below the fos by a bridge which had only been slung across the river within an hour of our arrival.

Our next visit was to Odde, now a popular resort. Here my friend and I tried a little bottom fishing, which I soon tired of, and resolved to walk up to a patch of snow above the fjord. I said I would reach it in an hour's time. My friend said it would take two. I raced up an ancient avalanche track, in one-and-a-quarter hour's rush from the fjord. It was my first scramble in Norway, and showed me once and for all on what a grand scale the Hardanger mountains are built.

A visit to the Skjæggedalsfos was next undertaken. This is one of the most interesting tourist expeditions in Europe, and the old path on the north side of the Tyssedal is the most enjoyable mountain path that I have ever traversed. I will not attempt to describe the great waterfall, but merely say that, in my opinion, in grandeur it has no rival in Norway, and hence none in Europe.

From Odde we made our first glacier pass over the Folgefond and back again. Like the greater portion of the Justedalsbræ, the Folgefond has no peaks. The top, seen in the distance, forms a horizon of wavy graceful lines; when on the snowfield itself, it is seen to consist of a series of huge white and sparkling domes of great beauty. No crevasses are usually seen on the route across, but they are there, and to my mind it is quite within the limits of probability that in some year of great snow denudation one of the sledges which carry merry parties of tourists across may disappear with all its occupants into some hitherto unsuspected crevasse.

A few years ago arrangements had been made for the inauguration of reindeer sledging, and many notables came from Bergen and elsewhere to see the start. However, the solitary reindeer supplied for the purpose, disliking publicity, spoiled the fun by running away. Let us hope that ultimately it joined some of its wilder brethren on Hardanger Vidden across the fjord.

In the early seventies, even in Odde, huge hotels were unknown, but two cosy inns existed where good and wholesome Norse fare could be had in plenty, and where the linen was spotless, and the beds rough but clean.

In places where there is no hotel proper, the "landhandler," or country shopkeeper, if there be one, in virtue of his calling is obliged to entertain travellers, as if he were an innkeeper. Speaking generally he likes this, as it adds variety to the life of his wife and himself, and brings a little more grist to the mill, but at the same time the considerate traveller will do well to remember that he is in some measure receiving a favour. I have stayed at several merchants' houses where I could see that the entertainment of strangers was a burden not at all relished by the owners, and in such cases I have always endeavoured to make as short a stay as I could, and to give as little trouble as possible. As a rule, however, a well-behaved Englishman receives a hearty welcome at the house of any "landhandler" whose house he may visit, and usually he feels on taking his departure, that he is leaving real friends behind him.

After exploring the Hardanger pretty thoroughly we returned to Bergen and set off for the North Cape in earnest on *S.S. Michael Krohn*. We were told that the boat would start at "Klokken Eet," i.e one o'clock. This was a veritable trap and nearly caught us, as the word "eet" is pronounced like our English "eight." As the steward's English was, if possible, even worse than our Norse, we aired the latter, and at breakfast I distinguished myself by using the word "strax" which meant immediately, instead of "lax" or salmon, and asked for "fiske strax," or for fish immediately.

Nothing in its way can be much easier or more pleasant than a journey up the island-guarded coast of Norway on a good clean and comfortable ship in fine weather. A halo of romance seems to cling to every bold headland, sheltered bay, or deep fjord, and solid historical facts of great interest are identified with hundreds of picturesque corners on this most weird western coast.

See how many places are associated with Harold Haarfager. Haugesund, where he died, and where, in 1872 a large obelisk was erected to commemorate the thousandth anniversary of his victory over other kings. See Hornelen, that grandest of all sea-cliffs, rising 3000 feet into the clouds out of the blue sea waves, and think of King Olaf Tryggvesson.

At Molde we got our first view of the Romsdal peaks, and even then I felt attracted by the Voengetinder, whose grisly summits I was to scale some years later.

Long before reaching Trondhjem we resolved to abandon our intention of going to the North Cape and to go inland instead. Even when cruising through the very finest scenery I always find the confinement of a steamboat to be oppressive after a couple of days, in fact much more so than when far out of sight of land. The scenery is no doubt very grand, the mountains are weird, the colouring is exquisite, but – it lacks something. You cannot get hold of it with your hands, or put your feet upon it, and that means a great deal.

Shortly after rounding the tempestuous Cape of Stadt, the ancient kingdom of Söndmöre is entered, and, unless a southwest wind is blowing, in all probability the deck-tied passenger will have some lovely though distant peeps of the sharply serrated Söndmöre peaks which beckon him in a most tantalising manner and make him long for freedom.

Still, for people who need rest, nothing is much easier or more pleasant in its way than a journey up to the North Cape, along the romantic west coast of Norway, on the well-ordered, clean, and comfortable mail steamboats of to-day. Early last century, it was far different, and the few travellers who visited Hammerfest and Tromsö usually went in winter by way of the Gulf of Bothnia to Tornea, and from thence over to Alten by sleighs. Sir A. de Capell Brooke, in 1820, was probably the first Englishman who travelled from Trondhjem to the North Cape by the western coast. This part of his journey occupied forty days.

Trondhjem, the Nidaros of old, is well known, and I will pass it by quickly. It has figured prominently on scores of thrilling occasions. Here it was that Thor's immense jewel-bedecked image was destroyed by Kolbein the Strong, at the order of King Olaf, in the presence of thousands of heathens who had brought out the great idol to enable them the better to outweigh the king's arguments in favour of Christianity. Here it was also that St. Olaf's silver shrine for many a long age attracted hundreds of pilgrims from all over Europe. The cathedral, by far the most interesting building in Scandinavia, is well worth a visit. The city is clean-looking, and possesses many interesting wooden buildings. The scenery around is pretty but not grand. Some of the neighbouring hills, as is the case about Bergen, have within recent years been wisely planted with Scotch firs and deciduous trees, which are a great improvement.

We made our way by the usual pass over the Dovre Fjelde to Gudbrandsdal, travelling very slowly by cariole, and stopping at many places for trout-fishing. In one river the fish were absurdly innocent. Sidgwick was using a cast of four flies and once hooked four fish at a time, which I landed for him, and on thirteen separate times he landed two trout together. The unhooking soon became a nuisance, and even I, almost a novice in the gentle art, wished that the fish were less greedy but rather bigger.

At Kongsvold we found an invasion of the impudent and most pugnacious little creatures, the lemmings. A visitation of these pretty guinea-pig-like pests is a great scourge, and they eat up the herbage almost like a flight of locusts. A lemming will not allow a man to pass within a couple of yards of the hummock of grass under which he is lurking, without giving a shrill challenge and showing his teeth.

Some of the popular myths concerning the migration of the lemmings are now discredited; still, many extraordinary statements concerning their wonderful gregarious marching habits are told which are undoubtedly true. I have myself found hundreds of dead and a few living lemmings on the snowy domes of the Justedalsbræ miles away from any sort of herbage. I once saw a poor little creature running up and down on the surface of a large rectangular mass of névé on an icefall of a glacier in the Horungtinder, and apparently without any chance of escape, as deep crevasses surrounded the mass. On the same day some of our party found a living lemming on the top of a mountain over 7000 feet in height. Undoubtedly, thousands of them get drowned in attempting to swim across swift-flowing rivers. On rare occasions, the screws of steamboats have been stopped by the bodies of countless lemmings which have attempted to swim across the fjord. To some extent it is probably true that they journey westwards, but we need hardly now believe that when they get to the western sea they swim out and commit suicide.

At Dombaas we met with mosquitoes for the first time. In south and central Norway as a rule they are not very troublesome, though I was once nearly devoured by them during two days of elk-stalking in a boggy pine forest in Hallingdal. In arctic Norway they are in some places terrible pests, though not a tenth part so bad as on the uplands in Lapland. It has often struck me in connection with mosquitoes, midges, and other flies that, in the places where they most abound, Providence has fortunately provided an antidote in the form of innumerable insectivorous plants, the *Drosera rotundifolia* and *longifola* and the *Pinguicula*, thousands of which voracious vegetable fly-eaters may be seen growing side by side on the boggy ground alongside most roads in Norway.

Down the grand Rusten gorge we drove to Laurgaard, where we fished and caught many grayling. Then "Westward Ho" to Vaage along the tree-bereft shores of the Vaage Vand. Here and at Skiaker, and on the wild uplands, towards Raudal in one direction and Grothid in another, may be seen the evil effects of the ruthless disforesting of the country in the sixties and seventies, where farms such as Mörk, once fertile clearings in the forest, have gone back to sterility, there being now nothing to break the strong and icy winds which blow furiously over the western glaciers. When a forest of Scotch pines is cut down young pines do not take the place of their sires, but, instead, the ground soon becomes covered with useless juniper bushes. Wise forestry laws now prevent such wholesale devastation as that which I hint at here.

At Lom we turned south and followed the course of the river Boever, named after the beavers which, in times not so long past, frequented the river, and made our way to Rödsheim the northern gate of Jotunheim.

Rödsheim is a gaard (hence our north country word "garth") or a group of picturesquely situated farm-buildings at the base of the mountain Galdhö, which separates two fine alpine valleys, Bœverdal and Visdal. It is a capital instance of a large mountain farm-house, and its owner, Ole Rödsheim at the time of my first visit in 1872 and for many a long year afterwards, was a good type of a bold mountaineer and an experienced guide through the wilds of Jotunheim. Rödsheim is, and always will be, the favourite starting-place for the ascent of Galdhöpiggen, which is now universally recognised as the highest mountain in northern Europe. I have spent many happy and lazy days there, so I know it well. The house and its many outbuildings are perched on the rocks just above a wild, narrow, water-worn gorge, through which the Bœver rushes furiously along. There are dozens of large, round, water-worn holes in the rocks, technically termed "jette gryder," or witches' cauldrons.[7] An old wooden bridge adds a picturesque element to the scene, and on one of its handrails is a spout which conveys water to a large wooden trough, where the family washing is done.

Across the river, several acres are sown with potatoes, which are nearly always being watered. Wooden spouts bring the water to channels which radiate in every direction downhill. At intervals there are pools, and here stand the waterers, each armed with a wooden shovel, with which, even during a thunderstorm, they shovel out the water over the crops.

Every evening a herd of sixty or seventy goats come to the farm. From whence they come seems to be a mystery. The milkmaids give them salt, and then there is always a little tournament amongst them on the rocks in the farmyard. It is probably only friendly banter, but they butt each other with rare good-will and on scientific principles too. After a time, the Nanny goats are cooped up for milking, and the rest disperse.

Like many other persons, our first journey in Jotunheim was from Rödsheim to Skjolden, about fifty-two miles, and our first sæter was Bœverthun which is beautifully situated at the head of a large lake.

A few miles above the sæter we came near a large broad glacier, out of which arise six fine peaks – the Smörstabbræ and tinder – which prepare the traveller for the glories of the Horungtinder. This range suddenly and quite unexpectedly bursts upon the view when near the top of the pass.

The Horungtinder, is undoubtedly the finest mountain range in Norway. We had heard practically nothing about it so our delight was probably the greater and I shall never forget as long as I live my first view of Skagastölstind, the grandest European mountain north of the Alps. Our guide told us that it was the highest mountain in Norway, that it had not yet been ascended, and that no doubt it was impracticable. Can it be wondered at that, when I saw the weird form of this mighty mountain in bright summer sunlight towering head and shoulders above her fellows – a score of sharp aiguilles of fantastic shape – I determined if possible, on some future occasion, to make the first ascent?

Up to a dozen years ago, in spite of the fact that the height of most Jotunheim peaks had been accurately measured trigonometrically, and the fact established that the Galdhöpig and the Glittertind were the two highest mountains in Norway, many farmers of Fortun and Aardal still insisted that Skagastölstind was the highest. In old geography books and atlases the mountain is spoken of as being "the culminating point of the Scandinavian mountains." In the Aarbog of the *Turist Forening* for 1870 Herr T. Dahl says that "Skagastölstind, about 8000 feet high, comes between Galdhöpiggen and Glittertind," whilst in the Aarbog for 1874 the mountain is called only the eighth highest mountain in the country. In former years, like so many "highest mountains," Skagastölstind had great rivals. The earliest was perhaps Snehættan then Sulitelma. Then came its successful rival, the Galdhöpig 8399 feet, and later appeared the ambitious but beautiful Knutshultind, whose pretensions were never very formidable. Now it is pretty well known that Store or – the Great – Skagastölstind is 7874 feet above sea-level, and is only the eighth mountain in height in Norway.

From a height near where we first saw the Horungtinder, which is now called Oscarshaug or the hill of King Oscar, who crossed the Sognefjeld in 1860, the gentler beauties of Nature, represented by the green Helgedal, blend most harmoniously with the sterner works around.

Though this view is very grand, it is not comparable to the views of the same range from the plateaus or from mountains rising out of the plateau, of Vettismarken on the other side. From Oscarshaug the Horungtinder are seen to consist of three clusters or groups of more or less detached peaks, each cluster being separated from the others by a much crevassed glacier. The central group, opposites contains the Dryhougstinder, the Midt Maradals, and eastern Riingstinder. The western consists of the Riings – Stöls Maradal-, Solei-, and Austabottinder. The eastern, and by far the finest group, contains the Gjertvas Styggedals-, Maradals-, and the three Skagastöls-tinder.

When we first saw these score of fine aiguilles I believe I am right in saying that not one of them had yet been ascended, and that no glacier pass in the range had been crossed, though in the year 1821 professor C.F. Naumann climbed the northern buttress of Skagastölind. Three fine glacier passes of prime importance evidently invited an exploration and when I pointed them out to our guide, his face, long and thin to start with, lengthened visibly, and the word "umueligt" (impossible) was all that we could hear.

A lovely descent brought us down to the cosy inn at Fortun. The head of Fortunsdal is so narrow and its mountain walls are so high and steep that there is an old saying existing to the effect that "If a man of Fortun wishes to see the sun, he must lie on his back on the ground."

As fishing and general touring were our principal objects, we left the Horungtinder, but, for my part, with regret. However, I made four little ascents, three of them alone, in order to find out how the land lay generally, and to add to my slender stock of orographical knowledge.

First, I climbed a hill a little north of Skjolden. Then I ascended a fine little peak called Okken from Husurn, whilst my friend caught a creel of grand trout below. Then together we climbed Stugunöset from Nystuen on the Fillefjeld, where we had a fine distant view of Jotunheim.

Lastly, whilst staying for some days at a charming little inn on the shores of Vangsmjösen, I was attracted by a steep mountain whose crags tower above the farm of Berge and the lovely lake below. I soon found myself walking quickly through fields, then a birch-clad slope led me to high pasturage where, amongst the stones, holly, and parsley ferns and the long-stalked white Ranunculus luxuriated. After this came bare micaceous rocks and snow, a short steep gully, and a broad ridge, where I found under a rock an ancient moss-covered skeleton of a reindeer. Who can tell how many years it is since this noble animal lay down there to die alone and quite hidden from his companions?

In three hours of very quick walking from the inn I reached the point I had intended to gain, a corner of Skjoldfjeld, where a tiny cairn showed traces of an earlier visitor.

The view was doubtless the most varied that I had as yet seen in Norway, and for some hours I enjoyed myself to the full. Nearly thirty miles off, the Horungtinder stood, towering above the nearer mountains of Koldedal. Uranaastind, seen as it were end on, was grand and sharp. The ice-bound summits beyond Lake Bygdin, gilded by the setting sun, were most lovely, and many peaks whose rugged crests afforded friends, and myself, grand sport in later years, had, when the afterglow was followed by the cold greens and faint purples, a "noli me tangere" look about them, which, however, fascinated me. Range beyond range appeared, and fleecy clouds added much beauty to the scene, but the beauteous maiden Skagastölstind was the great attraction, and I found myself still deeper in love with her.

Immediately below me, 3000 feet or more, lay one of the loveliest lakes in Norway, and to the south were the fair lands of Valders. I will not describe their beauties. As on many Norse fells, I found a bed of deep and elastic reindeer moss [6] of which I gladly availed myself. Whilst comfortably lying at full length and only half-awake, I thought I heard a little noise up aloft. Looking up, I saw one of those wretched drab and black crows hovering forty or fifty feet above me and evidently meditating an onslaught. Impudent rascal to mistake an alive Briton for carrion! My signs of life showed the disappointed bird his mistake and away he flew.

As was the case on the road from Trondhjem over the Dovre Fjeld, we stopped at every inviting station between Lærdal and Christiania, so we got to know Valders pretty well. At one place we gathered a lot of bilberries and were determined to have bilberry tart, because my friend said he knew how to make pastry and would give the necessary directions. Our host was summoned. "Flour, water, eggs, etc." "Are you certain about the eggs?" "Yes, of course." After the foundation was laid, the affair was brought for us to inspect. "Yes, it is all right so far, but it wants a roof on it." Our host replied: "If it has a roof you cannot eat it." In due course our "middag" was ready. The meat was eaten; now for the tart. In came a luke-warmed paste with the uncooked berries laid on the top. A batter pudding with bilberries, a variety to the ordinary fare, but hardly pastry. Did not the wild strawberries and cream which appeared next taste delicious?

Of the three routes connecting Valders with Christiania I can recommend that by Lake Spirillen as being the prettiest, but towards the middle of August the river Bægna becomes too low to be navigated even by the little toy steamer which earlier in the summer, after steam-pressure is raised to 125 lbs., charges the rapids so pluckily and so successfully.

Our first tour in Norway naturally ended at Christiania. It had been a very lazy and a very pleasant one. We had seen a great deal of the country and had our first introduction to Jotunheim, or rather to the borderland of that wild terrain. It was not to be wondered at that one of the two of us made up his mind to explore, at the earliest opportunity, its glens, gorges, and glaciers, and to attempt the ascents of the finest peaks which rise so abruptly from the glaciers at their bases.

Chapter 3: Aardal – The First Crossing Of A Glacier In The Horungtinder – Galdhöppigen And Three New Ascents

"Thou, Nature, art my goddess…

To northern climes my happier course I steer,
Climes where the goddess reigns throughout the year."
　　　　　　　CHURCHILL

Who remembers the frost in the winter of 1872–73? I do; because I sprained my ankle badly when trying to skate the outside edge backwards, and was not able to go to Norway the following summer as I had intended to do.

In 1874 my friend Dewhurst and I set out well equipped with mountaineering necessaries, including a Whymper tent, cooking utensils, soup squares, tinned meats, and a considerable amount of the needless articles with which young climbers so often hamper their movements and increase their cares.

On the steamer *Argo* we met the Rev. A.G. Girdlestone and the Rev. E. Worsley, each armed with an ice-axe. They were intending to hurry through the country, but to climb Galdhöpiggen on the way. It was soon arranged that we should travel together part of the time. We scampered through Hardanger, then by Vos and Noerödal Here we met a Norseman engaged on the Government survey in the Sognefjord. He asked me to guess the height of the top of the Keelfos. I said "fully 3500 feet." His sextant showed it to be 4200 N. feet above the fjord, and the first leap of the fall to be over 800 feet. The white wall of cliffs farther up the valley is considerably higher; in fact it is nearly a mile high. There are still higher cliffs at the head of Fortunsdal, some miles beyond the little inn at Fortun, but few tourists have seen them.

Aardal was the gate by which we were to enter Jotunheim, and here we left a portion of our luggage. As I had been here and to the Vettisfos before, I was for the nonce made chief guide.

I cannot mention Aardal without naming my old friend Jens Klingenberg, who kept the little shop and inn, rowed tourists over the Aardalsvand, and occasionally acted as guide over the mountains. Store Jens, or Big Jens, as he was called, and Thorgeir Sulheim (a local landowner and farmer) were the only two natives living near the Horungtinder who would allow for a moment that there was the slightest chance of ascending Skagastölstind, though it is true that the way by which Jens suggested it should be approached, by Gravdal, was about as suitable as the Val de Bagnes would be for the Aiguille de la Za. Still, he believed that mountains were made to be climbed, which is a very wholesome faith to hold. Once I told Jens that I thought the view of the fjord and mountains from his house was very fine. He shook his head, and said philosophically, "Ikke saa frugtbar" – not so fertile. He was right; the mountain I was admiring in the evening light had hardly a particle of vegetation to be seen on it.

Aardal, or Aurdal, means the valley of "ur," or "aar," that is, of rocks and stones, or more correctly of screes or avalanche debris. Uradal and Aurland have a similar meaning. The Aardal, Vettisgjæl – or Ghyll of Vetti – and Store Utladal, different lengths of the same valley, show probably the grandest gorge scenery in Norway, and the portion of the Utladal from Vormelid upwards is so completely cut off from the Aardal, into which the river Utla flows, that all the sæters in it belong to the valley of Fortun on the north side of the Horungtinder, and, in consequence, the cattle have to be driven over the high Keiser pass to get to their summer pasturage. The Aardalsvand is one of the grandest lakes in Norway, and is worthy to rank with the great quartette at the head of the Nordfjord. It is about six miles long, and consists of three reaches nearly equal in length. A fine massive mountain – the Stigeberg – rises with a huge black precipice straight out of the water to a height of about eight hundred feet.

The path up to Vetti is now suitable for horses, but for several years after I first knew it, it was only a very rough and more or less dangerous footpath. Above the pool, the gorge opens gradually, until at Vetti there is room for perhaps twenty acres of meadow land. The lonely farm-house of Vetti itself stands about two hundred and thirty feet above the Utla on the top of a green hill. Above this, the true crags reappear in their old grandeur.

Even now comparatively few tourists visit Vetti, and some idea of its former isolation may be formed when it is told that little more than thirty years ago a party of five or six English reindeer hunters surprised Anfind Vetti and some of his family up in the forest, and that the latter ran away and hid amongst the rocks, supposing the sportsmen to be robbers. Anfind told me this himself. In a whole lifetime, only one visitor, a Bergen man, had been known to arrive at Vetti. Whether Anfind Vetti and his predecessors had been able to evade the payment of taxes by virtue of the apparent inaccessibility of his domain or not, I do not know.

Here we held a grand council of war whilst quaffing mugs of black beer. One of our party had to take duty the following Sunday at the Consular Chapel in Christiania, and now it was Monday evening, and we all wished to attempt the ascent of Skagastölstind and also to climb Galdhöpiggen. We had no map, but luckily we found at Vetti the *Turist Forening's Aarbog* for 1871, in which was that most useful map of the Horungtinder by Lieutenant Lund. As it was loose, we "requisitioned" or "commandeered" it, and returned it a few weeks later. By this map we made out that we could cross the chain by a glacier pass, get at least a near view of Skagastölstind and at any rate strike the path from Skjolden to Rödsheim.

We then told our scheme to Anfind, and he and three Norse tourists gave us much valuable information, but said decidedly that our projected route was impracticable, that there was a large glacier, full of crevasses, and that it never could be crossed by man. What greater encouragement could be given to Englishmen fond of adventure, "sound in wind and limb and warranted not to jib." ?

As some local knowledge was necessary to enable us to tackle the rock wall which faces Vetti across the Utla, we engaged a stalwart young fellow named Thomas, now unfortunately gone to America, to guide us as far as the glacier, and to carry two knapsacks. We left our tent and heavy baggage behind.

Next morning we set off at 7.40 and soon crossed the river by a picturesque but most rickety bridge. Then, beyond the wild-strawberry beds, where a handful of delicious fruit could be plucked at once, the real tug-of-war began. The cliff is called Brænd-stigen and it had been climbed before. I have now been three times up it. The 2200 and odd feet are mounted by loose stony gullies amongst decayed branches and living birches which grow out horizontally instead of vertically, having been beaten down by winter snows. Truly this route does not form the choicest staircase in the world.

From a moss-covered rock, 1700 feet above the river, where we had a well-earned rest, we had a grand view of the Vettisfos just opposite, and of Uranaastind and other fine mountains.

At the top we entered a level valley crowned by grand peaks, the Stöls-Maradal. Four main valleys drain the Horungtinder on the south-east side. Three of them bear the name Maradal (the valley of mares), which seems to indicate a strange want of the inventive faculty on the part of those responsible for the nomenclature of this region. In order to distinguish them, the most eastern valley, which contains the largest glacier, is termed the Maradal; the middle one is called the Midt or middle Maradal; the third is termed Stöls-Maradal, or the Maradal with a "stöl" or "sæter". The fourth main valley is the Afdal.

When looking at the Horungtinder and neighbouring ranges on each side of Utladal it will be noticed that each little range has one principal feature, and that is its "Naasi." As a rule this "naasi" or buttress or bastion of Gothic castles, is a flattish-topped, round-ended, snow-sprinkled mountain mass running almost to the verge of the mural precipices which rise out of the Utla. Every "naasi" can be ascended near its blunt end from a lateral valley, but few can be reached by their sides, and avalanches may often be seen falling over their crags.

In some few cases the peaks rise directly out of these buttresses, but very frequently they are severed from them by deep gaps or glacier belts. In some cases these buttresses and the glaciers at the heads of the secondary valleys offer routes to the peaks. Almost invariably the native will choose the buttress, whilst an Englishman will follow up the valley to the glacier. This is because one dislikes snow and ice, and will struggle for hours over loose rocks, if by doing so he can avoid a glacier, whilst the British mountaineer looks upon a glacier as the natural highway to lead him to the summit.

We reached the sæter in two hours from Vetti, and stopped a quarter of an hour there brewing Liebig. Three miles' flat walk brought us to the foot of the ice-fall which terminates the Stöls- Maradalsbræ. We began our climb up some steep snow at the side of the ice-fall, and a shower of stones fell on our track a few minutes after we had passed the place. Thomas kept with us for two or three hundred feet, in fact, until he smelt crevasses, when he glissaded madly down the snow and watched us from below.

We soon put on the rope and went to work with our ice-axes. The crevasses, in no place difficult to cross, were numerous, the slope was steep, and the way was intricate enough to afford interest without being one of danger. In due course the ice gave place to snow and the slope eased off.

Rain came on, and the highest peaks were invisible. By the map two routes were open to us, one on each side of the eastern Riingstind. That to the west seemed to promise best, so we turned to it, and in three and a half hours from the foot of the glacier we reached the top of the Riingsskar – the first glacier pass that – so far as is known – had ever been crossed in the Horungtinder. By my aneroid I made the height to be 5757 feet.

Two pretty peaks guard the pass, and had we been sure about our future route we should no doubt have climbed that to the east; as it was, we built a cairn at the foot of it instead of on its head. We had fleeting glimpses of the highest peaks, and left them with reluctance, and I did not visit the pass again until almost exactly twenty years later.

After a well-earned rest and a meal we set off *prestissimo*, and soon managed to get a good glissade down the snow in the centre of an ice-fall, which brought us to a flat portion of the glacier.

The Riingsbræ lies in a wild amphitheatre of jet-black crags, capped with pure white snow or frost-riven rock, which, in the case of the highest Riingstind, rise many hundred feet in vertical precipices, contrasting and yet harmonising with the rugged faces and jagged skyline of the beautiful Soleitinder. There is more moraine on this glacier than is generally the case in Norway.

In two and three-quarter hours from the top we sat down on the sun-dried grass above the Riings sæter and talked over our plans. At 6.15 we entered the sæter and were most hospitably regaled with sæter produce by the girls and men whom we found there, and noticed at the time that the good folk were exceptionally kind and polite. Some few years later I was told that when we were seen emerging from the dark portals of the Riingsbræ where no human being had ever been known to enter or emerge from before, we were supposed to be "Huldre folk" or elves, who live in the heart of the mountains, are enormously rich, and amongst other possessions are blessed with tails; the latter as a rule, are carefully hidden under their clothes, which usually are blue. Huldre folk are supposed now and then to intermarry with ordinary human beings. On this occasion I suppose that the inducements to enter into matrimonial alliances must have been too slight, though at that time each of the four strangers was a bachelor. Certain it is that we all passed on quite heart-whole. Ah! these delightful days of picturesque superstition have vanished, and the people have become prosaic and prosperous. Ice-axes and ropes, which formerly created such an amount of curiosity and interest, are now at this same sæter looked upon as necessary articles of travel, and the English tourist in Jotunheim can indulge in any eccentricities which he likes without exciting much remark.

An hour and a half's walking found us at Optun, where ended the adventures of a very enjoyable day.

This pass makes an interesting day's march between Vetti and the north. It involves a severe climb of two hours' quick going to the Stols- Maradal sæter where milk can be had; then an hour's walk up the valley; a climb of 2787 feet up the glacier to the pass, or four and a half hours from the sæter; then 1890 feet of glacier to descend. The Riings sæter can be reached in seven and a half hours from Stöls-Maradal sæter or in nine and a half hours from Vetti; or from Vetti to Optun in eleven hours, or from Vetti to Turtegrö in ten hours. A still shorter route from Vetti to Turtegrö is by way of Midt Maradal.

The day following our passage of the Riingsskar, we crossed the Sognefjeld to Rödsheim. When on the top of the pass, the clouds blew away and revealed the Smörstabbræ and the fantastic peaks at the head of this fine glacier. Had we known what I learned a few years later, we would have made a glacier pass between two of the peaks and have descended to the semi-luxurious Yttredal sæter and then have climbed Galdhöpiggen from thence the following day. Instead of doing this we went to Rusten sæter and stopped the night there, huddled together like sheep in a pen. When we asked for milk and used the proper word "melk," we were not at first understood. Then light dawned upon a man who was present, and he said: "Oh! murak, ja."

At Rödsheim we met an English lady with a Norse lady friend who had come with the intention of crossing the mountains to Skjolden. The latter lady was great of stature and by no means light in weight, and, alas, the way was long and the path rough. After a few equestrian experiments of short distance had been made, it became apparent that Ole had no horse in his stud sufficiently strong to convey the tall lady across the snowy mountain uplands, whilst it was equally certain that she could not walk so far. Hence the project was abandoned and they resolved to go round, a journey at that time of some 300 miles.

Our parson friends left us at Rödsheim so Dewhurst and I asked the veteran Ole Rödsheim to accompany us for a week or two amongst the mountains, and he soon agreed. He admired our ice-axes, both home made and most lovely weapons to look at; indeed the handle of one of them was French polished, and the adze end was nearly sharp enough to shave with.<8> Ole tried to climb up the walls of his house with a pair of Tryrolean crampons which formed part of our outfit, but did not get very far.

It was agreed that we should first climb Galdhöpiggen and descend to Spiterstul, the highest sæter in Visdal, sleep there, attack some unascended peak next day, and descend to the Tourist Club's comfortable hut at Gjendin. Then we were to attack one of the Gjendin giants and soon after this we were to return to Vetti, pick up our tent and stores and go to the Horungtinder.

Doubtful weather kept us idle for a day, but during a short walk Ole showed us the place where a spring avalanche had carried away a house some distance up the snow-covered river, and had caused the death of eight people.

Ole got together some provisions for us, rye bread, bacon, and cheese, and as the weather looked better we decided to start next morning. As he had some business at home, and was not feeling well, it was arranged that he should join us at the sæter in the evening, with the provisions, whilst the old guide Eilif should take us up Galdhöpiggen.

Next morning in perfect weather we were up at 5, but did not get off until 6.15. Tempted by the bright weather, a lanky native who had not yet made the ascent asked if he might join us, which we allowed him to do, as we heard that it was easy. He had a swallow-tailed coat, and wore a red woollen cap.

At eleven o'clock, and about 2000 feet from the top, we set foot on the Styggebræ, i.e. the ugly glacier, and put on the rope. We had here a fine view of the summit, a beautiful cone of snow which crowns a black triangular precipice of considerable height. A snow ridge of lovely outline leads from the east to the very summit. The usual route is along this ridge, which is reached by a rocky buttress from the Styggebræ. Our guide wished to take off the rope when we gained the ridge, but as there was a snow cornice and as it was still glacier, we insisted on retaining the rope. A few years later a Norse friend of mine fell into a crevasse on this very ridge, and though he was roped he had an extremely narrow escape from death.

At 1 p.m. we reached the top in perfect but not absolutely cloudless weather. As to the view, which was magnificent, all I will say is that every one who sees it is struck with the vastness of the Norse snow-fields, the utter absence of vegetation and of all traces of mankind.

On the summit, and dotted over the snow-fields below, we saw the dead bodies of thousands of the red-spotted Burnet moths, those with five red spots on each black upper wing. How or why they had come up there to be frozen to death, as they were, we could not say. A few days previously we had seen a great number in Leirdal. Four years after this I found a very sprightly spider on the top of Aletschhorn. He was apparently well and enjoying himself, and as no recent human ascent had been made, we must assume that he made it without guides. Had he been blown across from Æggischhorn and retained his silken connecting link all the time? Who can say?

The first ascent of Galdhöpiggen was made from Spiterstul, in July 1854, by Herr Steinar Sulheim and two schoolmasters. Two years later this heroic descendant of ancient Norse kings, led his son Thorgeir (my friend) and several undergraduates to the summit by the same route. Ole Rödsheim was probably the first man who climbed the peak from Rödsheim.

Galdhöpiggen is the highest mountain in Europe north of the Alps. The height is now called 2560 metres, or 8399 English feet above sea-level, and as Rödsheim is 1870 English feet, the height to be ascended is 6529 feet.

Whilst admiring the view we did not neglect to pick out a suitable mountain for our next adventure, which we found later to be one of the Memurutinder, though our guide gave it another name.

There is now a hut on the top of the Galdhöpig, and the ascent is made by scores of patriotic Norsemen and their lady friends every year. In the summer of 1899, fortunately in this case an exceptionally snowy year, an enthusiast from Christiania took a horse up to the top, and, I suppose, gained notoriety and "established a record" by doing so; but, though a Norse pony can and does go willingly over very rough and stony ground, I cannot think that it is fair thus to take such an advantage of his willingness to oblige his master.

Dewhurst and I suggested a descent by the Svelnaasbræ which we could have easily gained either down a rib of rock or by means of a snow gully, but the faces of our two companions expressed such horror at the bare notion of such a course that we meekly abandoned the project and followed the ordinary route to Spiterstul.

Near the bed of the valley – the Visdal – the flowers were very numerous, varied, and beautiful, and butterflies in great numbers and variety were flitting about from flower to flower, principally Small Tortoise-shells, Red Admirals, and Peacocks. In Norway they are called "Sommer fugle" – summer birds – also "fri vil," which in this case may be interpreted as – liberty.

Spiterstul at that time consisted of a two-roomed hut, where were a man and his wife and little girl. This poor little child would have to stop there for some two months from their first coming, without either playmates or toys. The only things that I could see for her amusement were two catechisms, and in them a few carefully preserved advertisement pictures which had been cut out of the Bergen papers. We much regretted that we had nothing to give to amuse her, and I mentally resolved that in future I would never travel in Norway without having some little pictures, story-books, or small trinkets to leave at sæters and out-of-the-way farms. In consequence, I have made many adult friends by merely recognising in some trivial manner their children, and have received numberless and wholly unexpected favours where I little expected them.

There is now a small tourist hut at Spiterstul which is a great boon to mountaineers, as there is a group of interesting mountains within easy reach. A very casual glance at the excellent new Amtskart will corroborate this statement.

All who have walked up the head of Visdal in fine weather have noticed on the south side the Uladalstinder, a group of four or five pretty aiguilles rising out of small glaciers with steep ice-falls. Towards the centre of these – the pretty Visbræ – we bent our steps. We easily found our way through the ice-fall, and in process of time reached the skar at the top. A pretty peak on the east gave us half an hour's excellent rock-climbing up a steep face and along a narrow crest until the top was reached. Here we built the usual cairn and then enjoyed the view.

This peak may be safely styled the central Uladalstind. In a deep cirque just below us was a blue tarn in which a small glacier bathed its icy foot. This cirque is to my mind now wrongly called Semmelholet. The real Simlehullet, as it was formerly called and spelt, is undoubtedly the grand glacier-filled hollow under the eastern wall of the Simletind. The Semmelholstind is a pretty but minor peak of the Uladalstinder, and had probably led to the misnaming of the little cirque.

As is the case with many another fine mountain seen in full face across a narrow valley, Heilstuguhö appeared to us then to be utterly inaccessible. We then climbed the highest Uladalstind, where I think there was a cairn already in possession. Good glissades took us to the Langevand, and thence our walk to Gjendin was straightforward.

Late in the evening came the gallant Ole, and great was our disappointment when he told us that he was unwell, had hurt his knee, and was quite incapable of undertaking hard mountaineering work. He regretted his inability very keenly, as he was, and I believe is still, very fond of adventure. He had, however, done his best by bringing as a substitute Rolf Alfsen, "who knew all the mountain-paths, and was more or less used to glaciers." He would either act as guide or porter, and we were to pay him about two-and-sevenpence a day. In the circumstances, we engaged him.

Next morning there was a little rain. So whilst we waited for weather, Rolf finished cutting a young tree which he had brought with him, to his entire satisfaction. It was his alpenstock, and had a fork at the top. Forked sticks are often very useful when fording rivers.

Ole gave Rolf and us many directions, and we parted from him with great regret with the intention of climbing the peak we had selected the day before, one of the Memurutinder.

For two or three miles we walked up Visdal over a carpet of gentians (*Gentiana nivalis*), and had lovely views of the fine aiguilles which head this somewhat dreary valley. In an hour from the sæter we reached the foot of the great glacier, the Heilstuguhöbræ. A convenient snow-stripe on one side gave us a path on to the ice. Dewhurst led, as it was his turn, and I went last. Being a year of much snow, we soon left the ice for its tender sister – snow – and had to go on with great care.

Contrary to what was shown on the old maps, the glacier is divided into two distinct portions by a line of precipices. The greater portion, that on the west, is invisible from the Galdhöpig but the eastern branch, a lateral or tributary glacier, is plainly seen from there, and has, I imagine, been mistaken for the main one. Our route lay up the eastern arm, and very steep we found it, and for our leader at least it was hard work, as he had to kick out steps in the snow for several hundred feet. Above us on our left were frowning crags, which sent us some warning messengers in the form of rocks and stones, so we discreetly kept out of their way.

Near the top of this Steilebræ we came to a savage-looking bergschrund, where we were fortunate enough to find a convenient snow-bridge; otherwise we should have had much trouble, as at that time we were only novices in snow-craft. After crossing a few easy crevasses we reached a gentle slope of névé and at 2 p.m. we gained the top of a gap from which an arm of ice, corresponding to that up which we had come, led directly down to the immense eastern portion of the Memurubræ.

I am told that this glacier is locally called the Hesteskobræ or Horseshoe glacier, and we therefore named the col the Hesteskoskar. It forms an interesting connecting link between Visdal and the little-visited peaks in eastern Jotunheim. It is 3354 feet above Spiterstul.

After lunch we turned up a steep rock ridge, and half an hour's excellent climbing brought us to the top of our peak, where we found a clump of the lovely "rensblomst," or reindeer flower – the *Ranunculus glacialis* – in full flower.

Our peak was at the south-western end of a narrow and precipitous ridge shaped like a horseshoe, which bounds the Hesteskobræ. We were not above an English mile from the northwest corner, where there was another peak about the same height. Another point farther on the ridge and across the glacier seemed then to us to be a little higher than ours, but as it looked lower when we saw it from Galdhöpiggen we thought then, and for several years afterwards, that we had climbed the highest Memurutind, and the third highest mountain in Norway. However, in 1881 the ridge was traversed by Herr Johannes Heftye, with Knut Vole as guide, and our pretty peak was deposed from its assumed superiority, as the eastern peak was found to be a few feet higher. This was our first maiden peak, and, to say the least, we felt mightily proud of our success.

After considerable experience, I have come to the conclusion that there are two weak points connected with the making of new ascents. First, one considers it to be one's bounden duty to turn oneself for the time being into a stone-mason, and to build a cairn. What funny builders and flabby cairns I have seen! Some men will pile up a dozen stones, and never notice that on one side they are covered with a cake of ice which will melt and let down the cairn; or they will place two or three, end up, in some reindeer moss or lichen, and then with great labour they place a heavy flat stone across the top, when down they all fall over the precipice. Others will devote the whole of their attention to leaving a hole where the empty jam-tin which is to contain their cards can be placed. Some will build on a foundation of snow. But others will carefully prepare the ground, and build in a most workmanlike manner a cairn seven or eight feet high, and with a mean diameter of 3 feet 6 inches. These latter are terrible companions on a mountain-top, because one cannot see a man work like a galley-slave without wanting to give him substantial help.

The second weak point, surely the weaker of the two, is this. One conceives it to be necessary to write a note recording the ascent in the pages of *The Alpine Journal*, and goodness knows in how many more climbing journals nowadays. This must be done, for have we not the authority of Sir Martin Conway that "an unrecorded ascent does not count"? [At least a dozen maiden ascents which I have made are not recorded in *The Alpine Journal*.] I may say in passing, that in writing these notes, many men seem to imagine that the use of pronouns is almost, if not entirely, unnecessary, and that terseness, combined oddly enough with a needless use of French words and an absolute fidelity to the "times," are the only desirable features. The following is not a quotation, but will serve as a sample: ... Same party left gîte 5.30... crossed bergschrund 8.7, difficult, first-rate climb up rocks to arête ... top 12.24... foot of glacier 2.49, arrived hut 4.28.

Our view was wonderfully grand, wilder and more picturesque than that from Galdhöpiggen. On all sides the mountains formed a sky-line of rugged and weather-worn peaks with serrated ridges, the finest being Heilstuguhö, the Uladalstinder, and the Simletind just across the glacier. From no standpoint does the regal Galdhöpig look better than from here, towering above the mighty ice-fields. In every direction the view was grand, and everywhere too it was beautiful. In the far distance the Horungtinder and the Koldedalstinder, partly wreathed in shrouds of mist, seemed to beckon us to visit their wild ridges and icy glens, and we felt that we must obey the call.

We had a great wish to explore the whole ridge of the Memurutinder, but could not afford the time. A walk of five or six English miles on a narrow ridge of firm rocks covered with reindeer moss with a precipice of several hundreds of feet and views of blue gaping crevasses on the one hand, and no doubt much the same on the other side, would have been a good mountaineering adventure. A small black cloud in the north warned us to be off, and at four o'clock we faced for Gjendin.

When we regained our bags at the Hesteskoskar, Dewhurst and I wished to descend by the eastern glacier, but Rolf who, as we subsequently found knew nothing about it, said it was not possible. So we made the mistake of following his advice, which was a great pity, and crossed the little Steilebræ to a line of crags which separates it from the upper portion of the western Memurubræ. I was now the leader, and, as the storm seemed to be brewing, we hurried along at a quick pace.

After some hunting about on the top of the crags we found a wet gully and had a steep and unpleasant descent of 300 or 400 feet. The rope was both a nuisance and a necessary safeguard, and we had a good deal of holding fast and removing of loose rocks until near the bottom, when a tongue of snow afforded us a good glissade. When too late to be of service to us, we discovered some capital snow gullies farther south. We struck the Memurubræ at about its highest point. It is, however, very nearly flat, and slopes very gently towards the rolling uplands of Memurudal, for which we were making. There were very few crevasses, but for all that, the dead body of an excellent glacier wanderer – to wit, a reindeer – was once found in a crevasse on this portion of the glacier. As this fine glacier pass connecting Visdal and Memurudal has apparently no recognised name, I ventured to call it the Rensdyrskar, or reindeer's pass.

At 6.10 we left the ice, and soon after, when rounding a crag, we came suddenly within a stone's-throw of a herd of forty to fifty reindeer, most of them on the ice of a frozen tarn, the rest browsing on the scanty herbage on the shore. It certainly was a grand sight. Rolf set up a great screech, and for some moments the whole herd gazed at us in mute astonishment, as if petrified. At last, a grand old buck, the monarch of the mountain, gave the alarm by a sonorous bellowing, and some of the herd collected on the ice; two young disobedients going the wrong way he bullied quite savagely and used his antlers pretty freely upon them. When his little army was marshalled, they galloped madly away over the ice, which to our astonishment did not break through, and they soon disappeared. The storm meanwhile had veered round from north to south, and after a time vanished entirely without ever breaking upon our heads. Rolf managed to take us to the top of the cliffs of Memurutungen overlooking Gjendin, whose clear green waters, 1400 feet below us, and yet almost within a stone's-throw, we then saw for the first time. As I now know, we were in turn close to the top of each of those giddy paths, Bukkelægeret and Ramstigen, but we could not find them, so instead we went miles round and descended into the Store Aadal as best we could, through foot-tripping junipers, rain-wetted ferns, and mosses or loose screes, and arrived at the cosy Tourist Club's hut in the silent midnight hour.

Gjendin is a fascinating place and a first-rate centre for mountaineers. The lake is eleven miles long in two reaches of nearly equal length, the breadth is a little over half a mile. It runs from west to east, and is 3247 feet above sea-level. The trout are the most beautiful I have ever seen, and are exactly the colour of the blue-green water. The group of mountains on the south side contains some very grand and rugged peaks, which are perhaps best seen from Memurutungen. The finest is Knutshultind, which has a most jagged and narrow northern ridge. A deep glen, a dark chasm cut by time through the range between the lakes of Gjendin and Bygdin, is well named Svartdal – the Black Valley – and it is overlooked on both sides by fine rocky peaks.

In some respects the most interesting features about Gjendin are the great cirques, culs-de-sac or botner, Knutshullet, Skarflyen, and Kjærnhullet. The glaciers in these grim sanctuaries of the lordly buck are of a size and grandeur not believed in but by the few, who, like myself, have made their close acquaintance. Each of these amphitheatres is difficult to get into, but a visit well repays those whose love of adventure leads them to forsake the usual mountain-paths and to strike new ground. Nor must I omit the Leirungsdal, a wild glen which runs at the back of the mountain-walls of the three botner I have named, and into which, most interesting glacier passes may be made by those who possess the necessary snow-craft. From Gjendin a pretty five hours' walk brought us to Eidsbod, on Lake Bygdin.

Chapter 4: The Passage of Morka-Koldedal. A frozen lake. Skagastölstind, or not?

"Our doubts are traitors,
And make us lose the good we oft might win,
By fearing to attempt."
                    SHAKESPEARE.

It was a lovely day in the last week of July when Dewhurst, Rolf, and I arrived at Eidsbod. In the evening, with three Norse gentlemen I walked up Skineggen, 1400 feet above the lake, to admire the view generally, and particularly to study the Horungtinder in the distance.

A few minutes after we reached the top the sun began to set. But where? Behind the grandest of Norway's icy mountains, the Horungtinder. Never did they look more bewitching, more inaccessible, and more proudly defiant. Only fourteen miles away, their dark forms stood out with the clearest lines in the golden evening light, and cast dark and lengthy shadows on the cold glaciers which guarded their bases. The group of the Koldedalstinder, though nearer, seemed almost a continuation to the west. Across the Koldedal, my eyes were attracted towards a pretty glacier-girded range at the head of Lake Tyin, the Gjeldedalstinder. As the highest peak seemed to offer an interesting and easy climb, I made a sketch of it, dotted out the route, and resolved that we would try to climb it the next day on our way to Vetti.

Though I have seen many finer and more beautiful views than that from Skineggen, I shall never forget the beauty of that sunset. The day's breezes were lulled to rest, there was not a single jarring note, nor a sound to disturb the breathless silence; no peak was obscured by clouds, not a ripple could be seen on either Lake Bygdin or Lake Tyin, and upon the glassy surface of the latter quite a large fleet of little icebergs was floating. Such an evening often preceded stormy weather, and unfortunately this was no exception. At this time only one of the proud peaks north of Tyin had been climbed.

At Eidsbod several old reindeer-hunters were passing the night. I asked them about the route to Vetti through Morka-Koldedal, which by the map was undoubtedly the shortest. All of them said that this route was impracticable.

When asked where the impracticability lay, they could not tell; they only said that no one had tried it. Early in the season cattle-drovers now occasionally make use of this short-cut.

In these circumstances Dewhurst and I of course resolved to climb Gjeldedalstind, to descend to Morka-Koldedal, and to force our way through the gorge if it were at all possible. We did not know whether the difficulties would be caused by a glacier or by water.

Next morning, after a cold bath in the lake and some warm coffee in the hut, we set off soon after four o'clock. The ground was crisp and hard, the weather all that could be desired, and we soon got into Koldedal. Keilhau wrote of the valley as follows: – "Koldedal is about 4000 feet above the sea, and has hardly any vegetation; only moss and the hardiest Alpine plants can brave the severe climate. One is encircled by five or six tottering glaciers. Two indescribably sharp peaks stand boldly at the head of the valley, and look down on a lake still covered with blueish-green ice-masses" (*N.T.F.'s Aarbog*, 1872, p. 62).

The only thing we feared in connection with the ascent of Gjeldedalstind was the crossing of the Koldedöla, which in the summer time is very large and rapid, and which we could neither wade nor swim, and the peak rose precipitously from its farther side. We soon reached the river, walked along its banks for a mile or two, and saw ahead immense masses of snow apparently over the river, and our hopes of finding a natural bridge grew bright. Above some rapids where the river was split up into several streams, we found a splendid snow bridge thirteen or fourteen feet thick and about the same width. This was fortunate, and it was the only way over the river. Without this kind provision of Nature we should thus early have suffered defeat.

Well is this valley named Koldedal. A snow-bridged river; an ice-bound lake, great peaks with blue and white glaciers descending from them, here and there a dark precipice which makes the ice and snow look whiter by contrast, all combine to make it a most weird Arctic scene, a real cold valley.

The bridge was exactly at the proper place, and after having put on the rope we set foot on the glacier which we had selected for our highway. The glacier was steep and covered with hard snow, which gave us a good deal of work for our ice-axes, but there were very few open crevasses. We crossed it obliquely to a rib of rock separating this glacier from another which descends almost from the top of the mountain, and finally tumbles its avalanches over a perpendicular cliff on to the shores of the lake below. By this time the peak, with the coyness of maidenhood, had drawn a thin gauze veil over her lovely face, but we felt sure that if we wooed her boldly she would withdraw it again.

Before gaining the rib of rock we had a wide bergschrund to cross. At the place to which we first came it was impracticable, and we had some difficulty in finding a suitable crossing. The blue depths and the icicles hanging from the lips of the schrund did not please Rolf; indeed it was rather an uncanny place. After an interesting rock-scramble of 150 to 200 feet we reached the upper glacier. The rocky cone-shaped summit was still in clouds, but with my sketch and observations made with the compass our way could easily be found. We intended to reach a rock ridge a few hundred feet below the summit, to lunch there, and to wait for the clouds to blow away, which we felt certain would be the case before very long.

The second glacier was much more crevassed than the first, but there was neither difficulty nor danger. The crevasses, as a rule, were very deep, but not more than five or six feet wide, and there were good and substantial snow-bridges wherever they were required. We plodded along, and success seemed almost within our grasp, when, much to our surprise, Rolf solemnly unroped, said he would go no farther, and asked us to pay him on the spot. After a little gentle persuasion we convinced him that there was no danger, and we went on again. Soon the clouds obscured the rock ridge, and after making many dramatic gesticulations our friend untied himself again, and said that he would descend to the valley alone, which indeed would have been madness, as we were at that time in a somewhat intricate maze of crevasses. We all sat down on the snow, and though Dewhurst and I argued in bad Norse for half an hour, our friend was inexorable. He had a wife and family at home and would not further endanger his life with two crazy Englishmen, but would return and leave them to their miserable fate. We then had a meal of fladbröd cheese, and cold tea, and tried to admire the view.

Though there was not the least danger for us, we could not conscientiously leave Rolf alone on the snow whilst we went forward to make a quick ascent of the peak because we were afraid that he would set off alone, descend by our track, and thus incur, through gross ignorance of snow-craft, a real danger unsuspected by him. After our frugal meal we inscribed indelibly in our memories the word defeat, and astonished our friend by going at a tremendous pace down the steep snowslopes. Near the base of the lower glacier we made a short-cut which, like many short-cuts, lost time, as we had to cut a staircase down a steep slope of ice about one hundred feet high.

We reached the shore of the icy Koldedalsvand at 9.35. It is perhaps one and a half or two English miles long and half a mile broad, and was then almost covered with ice and snow. The view was indescribably grand. The shore was thickly strewn with the ruins of some of the icy turrets which guarded the base of the second glacier, up which we had climbed, and which had toppled down over the crags. Across the lake were the gloomy portals of Uradal – the valley of "ur" or debris and that of the Morka-Koldedal, which are separated by the Falkenæbbe (Falcon's beak). This rises with terrible precipices to a height of nearly 3000 feet above, and almost out of, the icy surface itself. The height of these cliffs was much enhanced by a mantle of thin gauzy clouds enshrouding the lower portions. To the right of Uradal we could see an arm of the great Melkedalsbræ. The snout of this projects into a little tarn which few men have seen. Above this glacier the knife-edged ridge of Uranaastind appeared and disappeared from time to time through the clouds, and its ghastly precipices frowned down upon the valley and a tarn below. The portal of Morka-Koldedal is still grander, more forbidding, deeper, and narrower than that of Uradal.

In order to avoid the possibility of an avalanche from the ice-towers of the "Tilbagegangsbræ," as we may be allowed to call this glacier, I walked over the ice on the lake, whilst the others ran the gauntlet on the shore. The ice was crevassed just like a glacier, and the colour of the water was the most beautiful sky-blue imaginable. The crevasses were generally parallel with the shore, as the ice had followed, at the time of fracture, the line of least resistance towards some open water near the opposite shore, and had thus left great and little gaps.

In due course we arrived at the portal of Koldedal. Here we had a quarter of an hour's rough walking, and then came to a second lake or tarn only a trifle smaller than the first, and like it still frozen. As we considered the northern shore to be impassable, and the southern to be dangerous on account of avalanches and smooth ice-glazed rocks, we took to the ice at once. The stream which falls over the Vettisfos has its birthplace here. The ice was all covered with snow, and had a wavy surface, but was quite safe. We kept near the southern shore. Near the western outlet the ice was crevassed, and was formed into large cubes. Here we had to be most careful not to overbalance any block of ice by standing too near an edge.

After regaining the shore we had another short scramble over rocks, and soon to our great astonishment a third frozen tarn appeared. It was an oval-shaped, glacier-surrounded, cliff-locked tarn, awe-inspiring to look at, and about the size of the second lake. Stern inaccessibility seemed to us to be the ruling feature of all the surrounding peaks.

It was then 11.30 and the day was rapidly improving. We glissaded down a steep snow-slope straight to the ice on the lake, to which we now took as a matter of course. Indeed, the shores appeared to be anything but inviting. We passed some high rocky islets, where we found the ice rather thin. I suggested putting on the rope, but as the others thought it to be unnecessary, we made our way without it down the middle of the lake. The lower end was much crevassed, and for safety, I prodded about a good deal with my ice-axe. In one place it suddenly went through the thin covering, and I barely escaped accompanying it. Then we brought the rope into use, and had to alter our course. A black towering rock prevented our landing where the ice was the best, and we were forced to jump from one disconnected iceberg to another over apparently fathomless blue water.

At 12.10 we were again on terra firma and had a most charming retrospective view over the arctic region we had just traversed. Beyond the lake a beautiful sugar-loaf mountain rose out of a dark precipitous mass. To this, three or four small steep glaciers clung with a death-like embrace, and liberally contributed to the collection of debris below with ice and rocks. Falling stones and ice must at all times make the passage along the southern shore one of danger. A fine cataract on the same side and an eagle soaring above us added interest to the scene. The sugar-loaf, apparently inaccessible from this side, was the victorious Gjeldedalstind. She looked triumphant being quite free from mists and clouds, and though we had made a most delightful pass we could not help regretting that we had been so easily defeated. The mountains on the north and south were very grand, though their mural precipices hid the peaks above them.

Having unroped we followed the course of the river, which however was rarely visible, being generally roofed over by deep snow. As we advanced the rocky walls diminished in height, and the gorge widened. On rounding a corner the Horungtinder unfettered by clouds came one by one into view. The striking individuality of this, the grandest chain of mountains in Norway, is best seen from this, the south side. The grimness and sharpness of the peaks coupled with terrific precipices bounding deep and dark defiles, the wild glaciers, cataracts, rivers, forest land, green clearings, and picturesque sæters combine to form a view of exceptional beauty and grandeur.

When we reached the forest our progress became slower, as we had left the snow, and in its place encountered decaying tree trunks and juniper bushes. As we descended the trees became bigger and bigger and many immense giants appeared. They are, unfortunately quickly disappearing under the wood-man's axe. Every tree that is felled has to be thrown over a vertical precipice close to the Vettisfos, 1100 feet deep, and many, though thrown in winter on the snow, are broken with the fall.

We reached Vettismark sæter at 2.15, where Rolf charmed the ears of a few eager listeners with an account of his week's adventures. On the plateau near where the Koldedal river takes its wonderful leap at the Vettisfos, fair Flora smiles most benignly, and lovely *andromedas, ericas, comarum, pyrola*, and many other floral gems abound.

Half an hour sufficed for us to descend the zigzag mountain-path to the farm Vetti far below, and here, welcomed by old friends, we ended one of the wildest and most interesting scrambles we ever had in Norway or elsewhere, in spite of the fact that it was a day of defeat. Though some years later we learned that Dr. Yngvar Nielsen had traversed the icy Morka-Koldedal the previous year, we had all the fun of believing at the time that it was entirely new.

After failing on Gjeldedalstind, Dewhurst and I were agreeably surprised by Rolf's consent to accompany us on our attempt to ascend Skagastölstind provided that we could engage another man to assist in carrying our tent and provisions, left at Vetti a fortnight earlier, up the precipice Brændstigen to Midt-Maradal. This we soon arranged, and the following morning at 5.30 a.m. we bid adieu to Anfind and his wife. At the best Brændstigen is a barbarous ascent, and our heavy burdens made it appear worse than ever. We saw, as is usually the case on the wooded heights above Utladal, plenty of fresh traces of a bear. At 8.5 we reached the sæter in Stöls-Maradal and then the weather began to look very bad.

We had intended to cross over a high mountain spur by a little gap and so to get into the parallel valley, Midt-Maradal, and there to pitch our tent. We thought, but were by no means sure, that the great ascent would have to be made from that valley. At this period there was a strange ignorance of the position of Skagastölstind which cannot easily be appreciated by the tourists of to-day who find a comfortable hut wherever one is needed, guides who can at least lead them to the foot of any mountain which they may wish to climb, and last, but not least, improved maps and most excellent guide-books. Some idea of the difficulty of getting into Midt-Maradal, and of the imperfect knowledge of the positions of the small lateral valleys of the Horungtinder, may be gathered when I say that, although a great portion of Midt-Maradal abounds in rich grass, and although it is only half a Norse mile from Vetti and only half that distance from the sæter in Stols-Maradal, and although it is perfectly visible from the pastures above Fleskenaasdal, yet the owner of the valley, Anfind Vetti, a good climber, had at that time never been into the valley. Indeed a few years later, he asked me to guide him into it. Thorgeir Sulheim, who owned Vormelid not half a Norse mile distant, had never been into it until he went with me some years after this time when bear-hunting. Old Jens Klingenberg of Aardal, who was one of the few men who believed that Skagastölstind could be ascended, thought that the route to the mountain lay up Gravdal; and even so late as in 1876, Emmanuel Mohn thought that the way might probably be through Maradal rather than through Midt-Maradal.

Pelting rain and heavy clouds prevented us from attempting to cross the mountain spur. It was fortunate for us that this was the case, since I subsequently discovered that the route we intended to have taken would have landed us upon the top of an impracticable wall of rock about 1500 feet high. In order to descend we should have been forced to make a long detour, and wearied ourselves out in vain on account of the storms which soon broke upon the mountains.

As we had no intention of running away just yet, we got a supply of butter and fuel, marched off up Stöls-Maradal and, a short distance below the glacier which we had ascended when we crossed the Riingsskar, we chose a suitable place for our tent, and with twigs of dwarf willow and birch and plenty of reindeer moss, covered by a waterproof sheet, we made a most luxurious couch. By exercising a little engineering skill we made capital shelter and most excellent drainage. When our tent was quite ready our porter Thomas bade us farewell, and left us to enjoy our camp life among the Horungtinder. Rolf now appeared to the best advantage. He proved to be an excellent cook, and as he had a fisherman's oilskin coat and leggings and was perfectly weather-proof, we had no hesitation in allowing him to do the cooking outside, whilst we sheltered inside the tent, read books, and watched the avalanches falling from a dark cliff just opposite. As night came on, the wind and rain increased; occasionally, but very rarely, a silvery drop came through our canvas, but this did not prevent us from sleeping most soundly.

When the rain did at last stop, we set off on a tour of exploration on the glacier, intending, if possible, to climb one of the Dyrhougstinder, and from thence to study the route to Skagastölstind and to discover some feasible pass over the first-named range by which we could gain the foot of the great peak.

The fine warm weather of the eight days which had intervened between our first and second visit to this glacier had materially altered its character. Where we had before gone with great ease over the snow, we now found the intricacies of most interesting crevasses. On our first visit there was a broad belt of snow up the ice-fall at the foot of the glacier. Now it was completely bare, and we had plenty of work for our ice-axes. We had one delightful snow-bridge to cross, very narrow and not too strong; and as numerous icicles hung from its under side, it seemed like a portcullis guarding the gateway of a palace of the Trolds. We had to creep very carefully over the bridge one by one, whilst the others were fast anchored. Both here and in many other places we had some really interesting ice-work, and to our delight Rolf went most pluckily, and seemed for the nonce to have forgotten the existence of the wife and children who had given him, and us too for that matter, so much trouble on Gjeldedalstind. At any rate he expressed no fear, though the dangers were much more apparent than those on the Koldedal mountain.

When we had ascended about 2000 feet the rain came on most pitilessly; the clouds obscured everything; and though we persevered for a short time, as we knew that there would be no great difficulty in climbing one of the Dyrhougstinder, or at least in reaching some portion of their narrow crest, we were obliged to beat a retreat.

We did nothing more with the peaks so near to us. The vilest weather succeeded; there were storms, avalanches, and everlasting wet. To make a long story short we were thoroughly beaten. We did not remain the fourteen days in camp which were ascribed to us by a well-known writer in the *Nor. Tur. For. Aarbog*, but, yearning for civilisation, dry clothes, and other scenes, we struck camp at a much earlier date.

We had a very enjoyable walk to Aardal by way of Afdal, in spite of the rain. The path follows the tops of the cliffs which bound the northern side of Utladal, and from it we got most wonderful views of the gorge below.

As we trudged along, the lower sea of clouds ascended, and after a time completely enveloped us. Here Rolf's pathfinding instinct became extremely useful. Although he was on new ground his previous experience taught him better where to look for the little heaps of stones, foot-worn rocks and old foot-prints which determined the path, than novices like ourselves.

Just above the most contracted part of the gorge we had a sharp rise over a mountain-spur to a height of 3200 feet above the river, and from this a steep descent brought us to Afdal, a high sæter valley. When we reached its swollen glacier river we found it quite impassable, so we followed its course through a tangle of rain-wetted birch and juniper to the Afdal gaard.

Here the sun beamed forth most graciously, and revealed to us in all its grandeur the situation of this farm, the beauties of the Gjeldefos, and the peaceful grassy valley far below us. We had been three hours on the way from Stols-Maradal sæter; but in fine weather, and without heavy burdens, the walk along these most romantic cliffs could be done easily in two hours, and is an expedition which I can recommend to all good walkers.

At the farm, a talkative cripple evinced great astonishment at the sight of foreigners, never having seen such animals before.

We hastened on, as we were anxious to catch the one weekly steamer which was to call at Aardal that day. At the lake we lost much time in finding rowers. At last we got one man and two little boys. Dewhurst and I helped at the oars, but Rolf, though he tried manfully, failed utterly, and is the only Norseman I have yet met who could not handle an oar.

"Ah! What is that?" "Dampen piber." (Steamer whistle.) "Ja ja." We reached the little pier at Aardal just five minutes too late. The steamer was gracefully turning round. We halloed and signalled vigorously, but all in vain, as the boat very sensibly kept on her course and gently glided out of sight, whilst we, half-drowned by the rain, made our way to Jens Klingenberg's hospitable inn amidst the smiles and titters of the bystanders.

It was with genuine feelings of regret that soon after this we parted from Rolf who had acted as our guide, porter, cook, valet, and friend for some ten days. He was most obliging, and was always ready to put up with discomfort provided that we benefited by it. He recited many old sagas which unfortunately we could not understand; he was quick at expedients, and like most sons of the mountains could improvise much that was useful in emergencies.

Our next move was to Amble, where a land-locked bay of gentlest beauty, well-tilled meadows, fruitful orchards, a picturesque church and prosperous-looking homesteads formed a most welcome change from the sterile scenes which we had just left behind us.

Chapter 5: An English Lady In Jotunheim

"Ye are bound for the mountains!
Ah! with you let me go
Where your cold, distant barrier,
The vast range of snow,
Through the loose clouds lifts dimly
Its white peaks in air –
How deep in their stillness!
Ah, would I were there!"
    MATTHEW ARNOLD

"In a well-found vessel, with a good pilot, we have none of that mixture
of danger which gives dignity to the traveller."
    SCOTT.

Another year rolled by, and in lovely weather early in July 1875, my sister [9] and I found ourselves in Bergen. On the Sunday morning we went to the Lutheran service at the Nykirke. The singing at that time, and I suppose also now, was purely congregational, where all sing the air. The hymns were sung very slowly, at not more than a third of the pace we sing them in England, and eight verses of Luther's hymn left one quite breathless. The organ, which had a Posaune on the pedals, was always one or two seconds before the voices.

In the afternoon we went to the Domkirke, or cathedral, where we saw the christening of several infants. A large golden-winged angel was suspended in front of the altar holding in her outstretched hands a basin of water. It was a pretty sight to see the mothers carrying their wee treasures to the angel. The priests dipped their heads three times and blessed them. During the service the organ was played now and then, and we admired the tone of it. I mentioned it to the apparitor who took us upstairs and introduced us to the organist. He very politely pointed to his seat saying, "væer saa god," and almost before I knew where I was I found myself playing the instrument. The organ had three manuals of short compass and about forty stops, of which ten belonged to the pedals. The choir organ, with its stop knobs too, was in front of the rest of the organ or behind the organist's back. The diapasons had a beautiful and full mellow tone, and the organ was evidently very old.

In large churches up country where they have a precentor, "kirke sanger," or "klokker" as he is also called, as well as an organ, three distinct times are followed. The organist gives "tum," then the "klokker" takes it up and gives his "tum," after which come the congregation, each of whom sings what he conceives to be the tune. Even if the latter be all on the right note, they are pretty certain not to be in harmony with the organ, which is one good note ahead of them. I have often been to church in Norway, and it is excellent discipline, but I have always felt that I should like to train the choir for a few weeks.

The Nordfjord with its glorious lakes and grand glaciers was to be our first stopping place. On board the *Fjalir* we met a charming whale-fisher who was going to be married, and was enjoying the first summer which he had spent in habitable latitudes for sixteen years, as during that time he had always been on board his thirty-ton schooner. He told me many adventures. Once in Spitsbergen a polar bear attacked his iron-sheathed boat, and after a long struggle he harpooned it. He once shot seven reindeer out of a herd of eight. However, so far as I can judge, in some parts of Spitsbergen shooting reindeer is more like shooting cows in a pasture than anything else. A Tromsö – sportsman, shall I say? – once asked me to go with him to Spitsbergen, telling me that he had himself shot forty-two reindeer in one day; and, on my questioning him, he told me that as his party could not possibly make use of them, he had left the carcases on the ground for the bears and foxes. Our whale-fishing friend however was a true sportsman. He said that with ordinary care whale-fishing was not at all dangerous, but was very exciting. This was before the days of harpoon guns.

As this was my third coasting voyage I began to feel at home, and took an increased interest in the history of the various places which we passed, as well as in their rich legendary lore.

A little north of the mouth of the Sognefjord, not very far from Florö, may be seen a curious rock islet whose one mountain seems to have been cut almost in two by some giant's sword. On this island is a church, which was built in the tenth century during the reign of King Olaf Tryggvesson, and is the oldest but one in the country.

We spent a delightful week at Olden, and then went to Hellesylt. Near Indre Haugen we met at different places children carrying a "lure" a wooden horn seven to nine feet in length, formed by two hollowed pieces of wood bound firmly together by birch bark. The bell mouth, five or six inches in diameter, is formed of the same material. The boys blew these "lurer" most vigorously in order to frighten away the bears which had just killed two cows at Haugen. I heard afterwards that about the time we passed through this bear-infested region, in the immediate neighbourhood of Haugen sixteen cows had been killed in eight days by bears. This I can readily believe. I have often seen bear "skræmmer" or horns with which to "skræmme" or scare away the troublesome beasts. After seeing the Geirangerfjord, we went to Romsdal and stayed some little time at Aak, which at that time was an inn. We carioled to Holset, then crossed the mountains with a stolkjærre – how I hardly know – to Svee, and were welcomed at Rödsheim by the gallant Ole On July 29th.

At this time I think I am right in saying that no English lady had ever crossed the heart of the Jotun Fjelde, and that very few members of the fair sex of any nationality had been much beyond the mere gates of Jotunheim. When I told Ole that we wished to make our way across the mountains to the Vettisfos and Aardal he was much astonished, but did everything in his power to help us. We had a small portmanteau. Could Ole accompany us with a horse, or send a man with one, to carry all the impedimenta? He was unable to come himself; the man and horse he could only send as far as Eidsbod by one route, or Muradn sæter by another; farther than those two places he did not like to send a horse, nor would it have been reasonable to have expected it. He suggested that my old friend of the previous year, Rolf Alfsen, if fairly paid, would gladly go with us and could carry the portmanteau. A bargain was soon made with him, and it was decided that we should take the direct route through the very heart of Jotunheim by way of Visdal, Gravdal and Utladal to Vetti, and that we were to sleep at Spiterstul, Skogadalsböen sæter and at Vetti. He provided us with an ample stock of provisions, which made my knapsack very heavy.

The walk to Spiterstul alone would have made a very short day's work, so as the weather was perfect, we decided to ascend Galdhöpiggen or Glitretind on the way.

As I had ascended the former, and as it had already been climbed by ladies, we decided that it would be much the best fun to storm the snow-crowned Glitretind, which no lady had yet attempted, and indeed very few men.

For many reasons, perfectly obvious in Norway, but not so in the Alps, we could not get off early, do as we would, and we only got under weigh at 8.20. Ole Rödsheim and a party of four charming Danes accompanied us until ten o'clock through lovely forest and river scenes on the walk up Visdal. At midday we reached the junction of the Glitra and the river Visa. Here we lunched, hung up our luggage on a pine-tree, and started to ascend the steep hillside. We were much interested with the climatic series of the trees and the plant life. At first the noble *Pinus sylvestris*, that most characteristic of all European trees, was our companion, but it disappeared entirely at a height of 3720 feet above sea-level. Next came the turn of the graceful spruce (*Abies communis*), which forsook us at 3800 feet. The mountain gem, the birch (*Betula pendula*), only maintained a foothold 400 feet higher than the spruce, or 4280 feet above sea-level. Beyond that, the dwarf *salix* and *betula* were to be found for a considerable height. This was on the west slopes of the mountain.

After crossing a moorland track carpeted with bright Alpine flowers, we entered a shallow gully north of the Glitterhö, and at 2.45 reached the top of the "hö" itself. Here a beautiful white cone came suddenly into view. Upon seeing this I called out, "Der ligger toppen," and thought our climb nearly at an end. However, I remembered that when I had seen the mountain from the Galdhöpig the cone-shaped apex crowned a precipice of dark rock, and now we could see no precipice. "Well! there is the top, and the sooner we are on it the better." The snow was very soft and steep too, and we went very slowly. When close to the top of the cone, the real summit appeared for the first time, and consisted of two lovely domes of snow, which, like that we were on, stood on the top of a curving ridge of rock. Below us on the north and to the west of the real summit, was one of the most notable "botner," or "cirques," in Jotunheim; in which, many hundreds of feet below us, was a well-crevassed glacier and a yawning bergschrund at the base of the mighty perpendicular cliff.

The snow on the two highest domes appeared to be about ninety feet deep, and great threatening cornices overhung the precipice almost everywhere. Rolf was quite satisfied with the point we had reached, but my sister and I were determined to reach the actual top. We put on the rope and kept well round to the east, where we crossed the top of a large glacier – the Glitterbræ – the surface of which was hard frozen, and as it was steep, great care was needed. In order to make quite sure of the top we climbed both cones. When on the first we satisfied ourselves that the farther one was the higher, so we struck off boldly for it. A good many steps had to be cut in the icy shroud, which lent additional interest to the climb. When close to the top, I stopped, as I had done at the other cone, and Rolf and I, each holding an end of the rope, allowed my sister to reach the actual top first. As we were firmly anchored, there was little or no danger; otherwise, without a rope, it would have been anything but safe, since between us and the very highest point there was a well-marked crack in the snow, a warning sufficient to make us careful. It was just 5 p.m. when my sister stepped on the top of this peerless white dome, and completed the first ascent by a lady of the second highest mountain in Scandinavia, 8376 feet above sea-level. [10]

Although thoroughly Alpine in character, the view from Glitretind is not so fine as that from its loftier neighbour Galdhöpiggen, whose snow-white crest rose proudly out of the large glaciers of the Ymes Fjeld, just across the narrow vale. Still, it was very grand, and well worth the slight toil necessary for its attainment.

On the way down, we got some enjoyable glissades, and reached Spiterstul in four hours and twenty minutes. Here we found that an extra room had been added to the sæter since my previous visit. A little boy named Alphæus made himself most useful, and lighted us, during our cooking operations and preparations for a night's sojourn, with a pine torch. I slept in a "pocket Ashantee hammock" for the first time, and found it to be an excellent substitute for a bed.

The day after our ascent of Glitretind we got off at 9.15, again a late hour, intending to reach Skogadalsböen that evening. Our pace was slow as our packs were heavy, but mine grew lighter with every meal, and as I carried the food, my motto was, "Early meals and often." Shortly before reaching Kirken, we had to cross the river Visa, and were obliged to throw in masses of rock to make it at all feasible. In the seventies and earlier the fording of rivers in Jotunheim was the principal danger to be encountered, and though with much practice I became more or less of an adept, I was on three occasions nearly carried away. In one case I was quite alone on the south side of Lake Gjendin and tried to cross a glacier stream, barely knee deep, on my way home from an unsuccessful reindeer stalk, my hunter having returned in a boat. The stream was not above twenty yards wide, yet I was over an hour in crossing it, and now and then had to use my rifle as a fourth leg, a long stick which I had cut being the third. Few fatal accidents have so far happened to tourists in Jotunheim, but in the year 1873 a young student lost his footing when attempting to cross the Breidlaupa (broad leap) – usually a little beck, which flows into Lake Bygdin – and was carried away over a little fos and drowned.

My sister and I much wished to climb the noble Kirke, but that inexorable slave-driver – time – would not allow us, and we plodded gaily along past the Leirvand and thence into Gravdal, the valley of graves, a peculiarly suitable name on account of its proximity to the church. Rolf showed us many of the ancient "grave" or reindeer pitfalls.

The most interesting feature about the fine walk down the valley is the sight of a singular square-topped mountain which suddenly bursts into view in a short side glen above a fine icefall. Mr. Hubert Smith, who travelled with his gipsies by this route, thought in the dim twilight that it was an ice-cliff of huge size.[11] It is, however, one of the many quaintly formed Smörstabtinder, and is now called Store Björn. It was first ascended by Herr Hall in 1885, though Mohn and I were only just beaten upon it by a snowstorm in 1876.

At 8.46 we arrived at Muradn sæter, which only possesses one hut or "sæl." From its high position, its great distance from the lowlands, and the absence of wood, Muradn is necessarily the reverse of a luxurious abode, so we were anxious to get on. The following conversation was held between the girl whom we found there and myself:

"How far is it to Skogadalsböen?"
"I do not know; perhaps half a mile (Norse), perhaps more."

"Which is the way?"
"Across the river, but you cannot get there to-night."

"Why?"
"Because the bridge was washed away last winter, and has not been restored."

Seeing horses grazing across the river: "Cannot we cross the river on a horse?"
"Not now, because the water is too high for anyone to wade over and fetch one."

"How is that?"
"The sun has been very hot all day, and has melted the ice and snow so very much."

"Well, we must go on to Vetti to-morrow, somehow."

Here Rolf chimed in. "The best way will be to go to Skjolden, and then to take the steamer to Aardal. I know most of the road."

"So do I. We will go as we said we would, down Utladal to Vetti and Aardal."

The girl : "Well! The river will be lower in the morning, and the boy can wade over for a horse to take you across; but you will have to stop the night here."

Though the accommodation was of course very meagre, the milk, fladbröd, and butter were excellent, and our hostess did all in her power to make us comfortable. She told us that a bear had killed one of her cows near the sæter only a fortnight earlier.

The scene outside the sæter in the early morning had a peculiar charm of its own. A few cows and a large flock of goats, summoned by the shrill call of the "budeier," had come to be milked and were very curious to know who we were and what business we had to come into the wilds. The goats, as is so often the case, were really very cheeky. Down the valley, right in front of us, were the Horungtinder, and some of them, tipped with golden sunlight, projected their strange forms through the encircling clouds of the early morning and contrasted grandly with the snow-flecked hillsides, the rapid river, and the green sæter pastures. A biting wind came down the valley from the many glaciers, and we were glad to get some steaming coffee.

In due time the horse came; the poor boy had however been obliged to go some distance up the valley, and to wade up to his middle in the icy waters in order to get to the horse. After taking leave of the good-natured girl we left the sæter at 7.20, and soon reached the river. Rolf first crossed over with our luggage, and whilst he did so we had time to look about us.

The Utla here was a good deal widened by an island in the middle, just below where the ford was made. The total width was about sixty yards, but in order to land easily, a course had to be taken a good way down the stream between the island and the farther bank. Rolf soon came back. Then my sister and I were to have a try. The horse had neither saddle nor bridle, but simply a halter. I rode in front, and my sister clung fast to me behind. About half-way across we had to make a turn, and there got amongst some horrible-looking boulders. The horse bumped up and down, and from side to side, and a look into the icy water was sufficient to make one shiver. At last we got over, and climbed up the opposite bank. Then I took the horse and brought the boy across, and he in turn returned for Rolf. The horse had thus to cross the river eight times. The boy proposed to accompany us to Skogadalsböen, so as to help us across the river there. We were only too glad of this; indeed, without the horse we should have had great difficulty in fording so rapid a stream as the Skogadöla.

There is now a fairly well-defined track between Skogadal and Fleskedal over the heights of Friken; but in 1875 this was not the case, and we made the great mistake of keeping too low down, and so became entangled amongst dwarf birch and willow and ferns growing with rank luxuriance amongst the remains of ancient stone avalanches, now moss-covered. For several hours we toiled along the brink of the southern wall of Utladal, the wildest cañon in Norway. Recent traces of a bear added to the interest.

The view of the Horungtinder, just across the gorge, once seen in fine weather can never be forgotten. On this occasion clouds robbed us of much of its charm, but still allowed us to see bit by bit the whole of the range. In fact I was able for the first time to study Skagastölstind, and chose then the route which the following year led to the summit. At 5 p.m. we reached the top of the Vettisfos, having been seven hours on the way from Skogadal when we ought only to have been about three. We stopped, a long time looking down the awful cliffs into the foaming Utla, 1300 feet below us, then walked down the almost interminable zig-zags of the path to Vetti, where a feast of eggs, strawberries and cream, and good coffee, with a promise of nice clean beds, and the luxuries of washing-basins and a wooden floor, naturally put us in a happy frame of mind.

After supper, by twilight, we went to see the Vettisfos from below. By this light the roaring river, close to the path falling from the almost perpendicular cliffs on each side, the white foam in the gloomy darkness and the fos 1100 feet above us combined to give us a deeper realisation of the enormous scale upon which Nature presents her beauties in this profound defile than could ever be obtained in the sunshine of a summer's day.

Next day we went to Aardal, and here our Jotunheim expedition practically ended. Thanks to the good weather it had been most enjoyable throughout. Had we had heavy rain on the third day it would have been a difficult matter to find pleasure in the adventure on the slopes of Friken. All however went well, and we felt sorry to part from our trusty, friend Rolf, who had done everything in his power to make our journey one of real enjoyment.

The story of this successful adventure led many ladies of various nationalities to don walking costumes and hob-nailed boots, and to seek pleasure and to gain health and strength in Nature's rich storehouse, the high fjeld of Jotunheim.

Chapter 6: The Mountains Of Lake Bygdin, Uranaastind And Others

"Montagnes de qui l'audace
Va porter jusques aux cieux
Un front d'éternelle glace,
Soutien du séjour des Dieux:
Dessous vos têtes chenues
Je cueille au dessus des nues
Toutes les fleurs du Printems,
A mes pieds, contre la terre,
J'entens gronder le tonnere,
Et tomber mille torrens."
            DUC DE CAMBRAY.

"A certain degree of reverence for fair scenery is found in all our great writers without exception."
            RUSKIN.

During the long winter months of 1875 and 1876 my friend Emanuel Mohn [12] and I had a voluminous correspondence, in which we laid the framework of a summer campaign in the wilds of Norway. Our programme was certainly ambitious, and included the ascent of many a fine untrodden peak and the crossing of several unknown glacier passes.

As an outcome of this, I was heartily welcomed at the quay at Christiania on July 8th by my future "fjeld kammerat." Never have I had a pleasanter crossing over the uneasy and irritating North Sea, and never did I hear more astonishing yarns than were told in the smoke-room of the Wilson Liner which had just brought us over. M. Du Chaillu had a wonderful fund of anecdote, and was usually able to cap those told by other adventurers. The smoke-room on board ship, when the weather allows of it, certainly encourages story-telling, perhaps in two senses, and many a jolly hour have I passed hearing of adventures which have happened to men in all quarters of the world.

Mohn and I approached the Jotunfjelde by way of Valders and Östre Slidre, a pretty route little known to English tourists. It was by this that the two actual discoverers of Jotunheim, Professor Keilhau and his friend, K. Boeck, entered the magic circle in 1820.

As we left the sun-warmed valley, the higher we got the fresher was the air, and one by one the bright Alpine plants welcomed us home to the mountains. Four days after leaving Christiania we reached the south-eastern gate of Jotunheim, Raufjord, a sheltered creek at the eastern end of Lake Bygdin.

Here is the so-called Raufjord Hotel – a cosy log hut, 24 feet by 20, with two rooms and four or five beds – a place I am very fond of. It belonged, when I first knew it, and I believe does still, to Knut Lykken, a well-known reindeer hunter and mountain guide, whose services we had engaged for two or three weeks.

As Knut had gone down to his farm to mend his boots, and would not be back for a couple of days, we agreed to do a little climbing without him. We selected Kalvaahögda, a fine massive mountain, for our first walk. With two lusty rowers our boat sped quickly across the creek and entered the stormy Bygdin. In two hours we reached Hestvolden, a wretched "fælæger," [13] where we found its two occupants hard at work smoking on a bed of hay. After a pleasant chat, we hied to the fells and soon reached a little glacier. A storm came on, but as we could almost see blue sky through it, we hurried upwards, and twenty-five minutes later we shook ourselves dry in sparkling sunshine on warm rocks, whilst a sea of mist obliterated all sight of the world below, save when through a rift we could see the deep-blue Bygdin. We had a wonderful view of the Thorfinstinder, and saw that none of the three peaks were to be trifled with. We planned one route up the little hanging glacier on the east side, from which a steep gully leads up to a gap between two of these pretty aiguilles – a tempting route which, strange to say, has not yet been taken, though I have often suggested it to climbing friends.

From the ridge of Kalvaahögda we had what Mohn rightly called a wonderful "overraskelse," or surprise – a view through thick clouds of the wild seracs of the Leirungsbræ. A stone dropped from the edge of this cliff took close upon ten seconds, before it struck the ice 1500 feet below us. Perpendicular precipices of so great a height as this do not exist in the Alps. In Norway they are not uncommon, and are very impressive. We were denied a view of the crags of Knutshultind just across the grim Leirungsdal; but I saw them the following year from near the same place when reindeer-stalking. Kalvaahögda, which had several times been ascended, is 7160 feet in height, or 3730 feet above the lake, and though its ascent from Lake Bygdin is very easy, it is quite certain that there is first-rate climbing, including glacier, couloir, and rock work. Mohn's sketch of a portion of this mountain, which he called "Leirungs- kampen," in *Nor. Tur. For. Aarborg* for 1872, p. 32, shows this.

On our return to the lake we had great difficulty in launching our boat, and finally we had to leave one of our rowers, who followed along the shore and was taken in later on after many a vain attempt.

We had a ball in the evening. True, the orchestra consisted solely of a Jew's harp and a boy whistling; but there was energy in it, there was life, fire, and enthusiasm, and the boys in turn danced with the one belle in the "spring-dands" with a vigour which did them infinite credit. I was not personally initiated into the mysteries of this dance until a year later, when I joined in this and other dances one Sunday evening at Nystuen. In Norway, Sunday begins at 6 o'clock on Saturday evening and ends at 6 on the Sunday evening. In the "spring-dands," the couples walk round the room hand in hand until, at the dictation of the music, the girls whirl quickly round and round several times under one of their own and their partner's arms; first they turn to the right, then to the left, then they take a trot or two round the room; the whirling comes on again as before, and lastly a polka brings it to a conclusion. When a good many are dancing it looks very pretty. The "Halling," an acrobatic dance only performed by males in some places, is very popular. Amongst other eccentricities in the dance is that of kicking down a hat suspended some distance above the dancer's head, followed by a back somersault. Not many years ago this dance was still known in our own village in Yorkshire.

Knut came in during our festivities, a wiry little man with merry twinkling eyes, and a great look of the sportsman about him. He had a venerable pair of leather breeches which I fancy he had inherited from a remote ancestor, a thick homespun wadmel coat and waistcoat with many buttons, a woollen scarf, thick warm stockings and shirt, a long oilskin macintosh, and a soft hat and warm woollen gloves. He had never seen an ice-axe before, and was much struck with the neatness and handiness of those we had brought, as well as with the Alpine rope.

During several days we had bad weather and high winds at Raufjord, which made boating on Bygdin too dangerous to attempt, though the surface of the neighbouring Strömvand was barely ruffed. One day I climbed Bitihorn, a deservedly famous "belvidere"; but, for the most part, time hung rather heavily on our hands. It was a lemming year, and we saw thousands of these pugnacious little rodents, also scores of the hawks, snowy owls, and eagles, which always follow in their train.

One evening the clouds rolled away from the Thorfinstinder, and we determined to be off early the next morning. Soon after we went to bed, to our consternation three batches of tourists came trooping in, and sleep for the next two or three hours was out of the question. Food had to be cooked and eaten, clothes to be dried, pipes to be smoked, and confusion reigned supreme. However, they were right jolly fellows, and it was a pleasure to meet them.

Next morning, though the wind was high, I pointed to our wished-for goal then cloud free, and said that the weather was perfect, and after a time I persuaded Mohn that it was so too. With half a dozen Norse tourists we were rowed across the Raufjord and on to the big lake, where however, as it was much too rough for a boat to live, we were forced to land. We walked along the treeless north shore at a great pace as far as Nybod, where at the actual base of the Thorfinstinder are a "fælæger" and a sportsman's private log hut.

From here the mountain looks very grand, and menacing as well. No other mountain range from the shores of Bygdin can compare with it. The poet, O. Vinje, once stayed eight days at Nybod merely to admire its crags and pinnacles. Above the lake, for some 1700 feet, are steep grass slopes, with a few crags to break the monotony. Then come 2000 feet of screes, and above that wild time-furrowed crags of the Sgurr-nan-Gillean type much exaggerated, which are crowned by dark pinnacles connected with each other by narrow curtains of rock. Three main gullies or ghylls have been chiselled by Nature in the face. In some places they are too steep for snow to lie in them, but where there was snow, it showed traces of many a cannonade from the fantastic peaks above. The real top is invisible from Nybod, and but for Knut we should not have known which high crag possessed it. It is, however, that in the centre which the Fækarer term "Bruden" (the bride), whilst the rival peaks on each side are called the "Brudefölge" or the Wedding Procession. (Many a jagged ridge in Norway rejoices in the latter name.) In the case of the Thorfinstinder the wedding presents appear to be very numerous, as each of the many attendants bears some precious gift, such as a pendant or jewelled casket, in the shape of the countless little snow-spangled minarets and spurs which form the crest of this beautiful mountain.

The Fækarer naturally enough said that the mountain was inaccessible. Knut thought there was a remote chance of success, and said that the only way would be to storm the actual face of the mountain by one of the gullies. By two of these we could trace a probable route to within a couple of hundred feet of the top ridge. Beyond this, there were most unpromising smooth walls with a *cheval de frise* at the top. With the help of Mohn's excellent little telescope, and after a long study, we concluded that the middle gully offered the best chances of success.

We went quickly up and over the green slopes and lower crags, where a pair of noble eagles soared round and round over our heads, just like lapwings at home, until we had passed their eyrie. [14] Then came the screes, and we had another short study of the problem in front of us. Knut declared that the right-hand ghyll was the best, and he was probably right. I prospected the centre gully some little way and found no stoppage, but as the danger from falling stones was very likely greater than in the other case, I soon rejoined the others.

Below the gully, large and smooth slabs of rock rose out of the screes without a foothold for many feet, but under Knut's careful guidance we managed to make a traverse over a slab just below the mouth of the gully 1890 feet above the lake. The view of the many minarets, small and great, literally over our heads, was very wild, but little stones which came pattering down the gully dictated caution. The day was hot, and we were under the direct influence of the sun which would unlock many small stones, frozen fast during the previous night.

The ghyll throughout was very steep, and at first offered us no choice of routes. We were in a trough, and must keep there. Now and then snow came as a relief to the rotten rocks at the bottom, but here and there it was so thin that each of us occasionally broke through and almost disappeared. We used the rope very early; Knut led, I came next, and then Mohn. After issuing from a very narrow portion of the ghyll we came to an irregular basin with horrid rocks on every side. Above smooth, rounded slabs of rock were some large snow patches; over these rose a fearful jagged-topped wall several hundred feet in height, and beyond, we knew, must be the summit, not far away.

Knut, who was a capital cragsman, was much puzzled, and well he might be, as there was little encouragement to be gained. On the right there was certainly a pretence at a gully, but the looseness of the rocks and probability of an avalanche made me object very much to it; besides this it might after all probably only lead to a minor peak, from which it might be impossible to gain the "brud" herself.

As an alternative I proposed a route to the left over a snow patch on some smooth and slippery but firm rocks to a little chimney, apparently leading behind a buttress and on to the wall itself.

We untied the rope, and Knut and I went to prospect – he to the right, I to the left. After a time, Knut shouted out that his way would go, but that it was unsafe. Meanwhile I had crossed the snow patch, and with the aid of my axe had climbed a smooth boss of rock and had crept along a broad safe ledge where overhanging rocks prevented me from walking, and had discovered that the small chimney was most hopeful. I shouted out my discovery and descended to the top of the boss of rock and, when firmly anchored, I lowered my spare rope to Mohn, who soon came up. Then I sent it down to Knut, but the reindeer-hunter's pride would not permit him to use a rope on a place where a foreigner had preceded him without one, and he nimbly scrambled up "disdainful of danger," if any existed.

Mohn told me afterwards that when Knut saw me climbing up the boss he said, "Han er gal, Engelsmanden," and "Han draeper sig, Engelsmanden," ("The Englishman is mad," and "He will kill himself").

After crossing the crawling ledge, we reached the little chimney or "kamin," where we had some interesting zigzagging, and no danger, and all at once we found ourselves on the narrow frost-riven arête. Then we turned a little to the east, made our way over an easy snow-slope several acres in extent, but which from Kalvahögda appeared as a mere white dot, to some lichen-crowned rocks. On these we could walk without using our hands – then a novelty to us – and we all three stepped together upon the highest slab where never man before had trod, and the bride was won.

This was Mohn's first maiden peak, and his enthusiasm was unbounded. Never before or since have I seen any man in such raptures with the beauty of Nature. It was delightful to hear the eloquence of a man who in the valleys was rather reserved than otherwise. The words "glimmren udsigt" ("glorious view") were probably the most commonplace which he made use of.

Only those who knew Mohn amongst his native mountains can realise even in a small degree what these mighty works of God meant to him. Never was their grandeur, never was their exquisite beauty on a still summer's evening more appreciated, and never will they be more appreciated by any son of Norway than they were by Mohn. His friendship, now that he has gone to his long rest, I look back upon as one of the great privileges of my life and shall always cherish the memory of his companionship as a most treasured possession.

We had been exactly three hours from Nybod. The height of Thorfinstind is 7046 English feet above sea-level, and 3616 feet above Bygdin. The view comprises the grandest peaks of wild Jotunheim. In addition to rock, ice, and snow, blue lakes and green pastures form a peaceful variety.

Knutshultind, which Knut had ascended the previous year with Herr Heftye, rose as a mighty pyramid above an ice-clad tarn in Svartdal, just north of us. Amongst numberless interesting sections of the view, the Smörstabtinder claimed our attention, and four of them seen end-on looked like the sharp spikes of some colossal railing whose posts were hidden from view by an intervening ridge. Stölsnaastind and the Falkenæbbe together formed an exquisite and well-defined crescent, with the concave side uppermost, which was strangely beautiful. For half an hour the Horungtinder were obscured. Then slowly the clouds crept down the mountain sides, and the peaks themselves stood like dark islets out of a stormy sea, a beautiful sight twenty-five miles away.

Galdebergstind, then unascended, so plainly beckoned us to climb its ice-bound ridge that we determined to take it on our way to Eidsbod the following day.

We went someway on the north-western arête to see what other routes were practicable, but saw little to encourage us to attempt to descend either by way of the hanging glacier on the Thorfinsdal side or towards Langedal. Still, I believe both of these ways are feasible. After the usual cairn was erected we started down and found that great care was necessary, and that the little cairns which we had placed on the ascent in order to mark the route were most useful. In an hour and three quarters we reached the screes below the gully, and were greeted by the pair of eagles at exactly the same place where they had left us on the ascent. A long glissade helped us gaily along to Nybod, which we reached in two and a half hours from the summit. A bathe in the lake increased our appetite, which was barely satisfied with a meal of fladbröd and butter and chocolate boiled in milk.

Knut slept with the fækarer in their mud hut. Mohn and I shivered in that of wood, as I have done once since then.

We turned out early the next morning. The beautiful bride above us was enfolded in her bridal veil; my aneroid had fallen two-tenths during the night, and our prospects were not very bright. Still, Nybod without blankets and bedding did not tempt us to prolong our stay, though it is an admirable centre for many grand expeditions, so we trudged off over a bleak moorland where we crossed a river by a snow-bridge, and saw reindeer spoor in all directions.

Knut seemed to be able to read by a glance at the footprints, how many deer there were, their age, the number of does and calves, and other details. In the soft ground from which the snow had recently melted he pricked the footprints of foxes, and here and there of a glutton, the reindeer's foe. Later in the day we found the mangled remains of a reindeer which had most probably been run down by a glutton, whose spoor Knut pointed out to us. These gluttons are really horrible vermin of a large size which do not scruple to kill sheep and goats. I was told of one case where a flock of twenty-five sheep jumped over a cliff and were killed, in order to escape from the dreadful fangs of one of these beasts which was chasing them.

When mounting the easy glacier which leads up to the snow crest of Galdebergstind, Knut stopped suddenly, and pointing through the mist whispered: "See! there is a herd of reindeer at the edge of the snow close to those big rocks." "Where?" said Mohn and I. "Up there. They are going behind the rocks; there are about twenty of them." "Yes, there they are."

"Halloa! They're flying away." So they did, the "ryper" or ptarmigan which they were in reality and only a few yards distant. The "rocks" too, were only small stones on the snow. The good-tempered old hunter stood the chaff which we rained upon him very well, and in due time brought us to the end of a long, wedge-shaped ridge which he declared, and which we afterwards proved to be, the top of the Galdebergstind. At the end and on each side was a horrible precipice many hundred feet deep.

After putting up our cairn Knut amused himself by heaving over masses of rock and watching them disappear in the abyss of clouds, and hearing them crash on ice or rocks below. A snowstorm swept over us whilst we waited in vain for a view. Oxedalshullet, a grand cirque just below, which I have thoroughly explored when reindeer-stalking, must look very weird from this point of view. Still, though the height of the mountain is only one hundred feet less than that of Thorfinstind, I do not think that the view from it can be nearly so grand.

We hurried down; and when taking a sitting glissade I looked with envy upon Knut's leather breeches, and made up my mind there and then that I would get a pair for mountaineering – a resolution still unfulfilled; and, strange to say, I have done very well without them. At seven o'clock we reached Eidsbod, a wooden hut at the head of Lake Bygdin and on the "eid" or isthmus between that lake and Tyin. These lakes are both the same height above sea-level, 3625 feet, and are only separated by a low moorland barely two miles across.

The hut, which takes the place of a wretched and almost invisible "fælæger" was built by three mountain enthusiasts, Professor E. Sars, the poet Vinje, and H. Thjome, and though I have spent many nights there, and have been glad of its shelter, I cannot help expressing a doubt if there be a more draughty or a colder site in all Scandinavia. For many years it has been used as a mountain inn, and has been run by Ole Rödsheim.

We had intended to begin our mountain campaign at Eidsbod. Two English friends were to have come, but as they were unable to do so, we had engaged Knut's services. Before I heard that my friends could not join us, I received a letter from Mohn from which I quote as follows:

"Should you and your friends come up there some days before me, you can spend the time by climbing Koldedalstind, which has not been ascended since 1820, or Stölsnaastind on which no human foot has ever been; but before my arrival you must not climb Uranaastind or Skagastölstind, for on these peaks I must be with you; neither must you tell any one that we think of climbing Uranaastind, lest some other should take it from us. Before the beginning of July it is of no use going into Jotunheim, because before July 1st no folk will have come to the tourist huts at Tyin or Bygdin; and before the middle of July it is useless to attack Skagastölstind, because there will be no folk at the sæters of Muradn, Skogadalsböen, Vormelid, or Guridal, which are the only places where we can get food and shelter; and the rivers up there, the Utla and Skogadola which it is necessary to wade, are in such flood in June and even in the beginning of July, that it is extremely difficult, and in some years impossible, to cross them before the middle of July. These minutiae make wanderings in these high-lying and wild tracks almost an impossibility in the month of June...

Concerning the length of days, we have in the whole of July and far into August still such long and light days that, in good weather, darkness does not come on before ten o'clock, so that it will not hinder us much, and we must have some time for rest and sleep."

"We begin by climbing Uranaastind, a stately and noble mountain, a true aristocrat, which is probably over 7000 feet in height, and has never yet been climbed... Next we climb the eastern Styggedalstind... If we see from it that there is any possibility of reaching Store Skagastölstind from the Maradalsbræ, we must go from Vormelid up Maradal and over the glacier, though I doubt if we can come up from that side... If it appears to be unclimbable by that route, we must go *from Vormelid over Ronaldsnaasi down into Midt Maradal, and try to storm the peak over the glacier which lies in between the peaks south. If it is impracticable also from that side (though I believe if it be climbed at all, it will be that way), we must try it from the west,* from the Skagastölsbræ. Failing there also, we must try it in the middle of the angle on the Styggedalsbræ, and if it is impossible also from that side, we can with a clear conscience declare its impracticability... Before we give in, we will try it to the uttermost."

For a bye-day we walked to the tourist but of Tvindehougen on Lake Tyin, only three miles away, from which there is a lovely view of the Koldedal peaks. Gudbrand, the "opsynmand," or man in charge – a tall, well-built man – was in high glee because he had recently sold to an Englishman an old powder-horn on which a horse and other figures were carved. The horn originally had "Anno 1669" well marked upon it. Gudbrand, sly dog, got a burning-glass, burned out the figure 9, and then put the figure 1 at the left hand, which made the date of the horn to be 1166. We take it for granted that the powder used in the reign of King Henry II was smokeless. We bought a large and heavy tin of preserved meat from Gudbrand, which I engaged to carry over Uranaastind, our next mountain.

We left Eidsbod in the early frosty morning at the same time as Herr Dietsrichson, the editor of the *Nor. Tur. For. Aarbog.* His last words were, "Take care not to break your..." The final word was suggested by holding his neck with both hands. When we saw him step into the leaky boat which was to convey him over the deep waters of Bygdin, we felt surer than before that the mountain paths were the best, and probably the safest.

Our route took us over Langeskavle – the long snow-heaps – a hummocky hill containing too many ups and downs, which after a time developed into a broad ridge between the Uranaasbræ to the left and the Melkedalsbræ on, the right. The latter terminates in a wild tarn, the renowned Melkedalsvand, on which little icebergs may usually be seen floating. One arm of the Uranaasbræ does the same, but I question whether any other tourist besides myself has seen it. I only popped on it quite suddenly when stalking.

The Uranaastind rises precipitously from the snows of the large Uranaasbræ, and when we first saw it was wreathed with light cloud drapery. At noon we put on the rope. Knut led, Mohn came next, and I, heavily laden mortal, came last, bearing the meat-tin from which we expected so much. As usual, we had seen plenty of fresh reindeer tracks, and after going a short way on the snow we saw a small herd just under the opposite crags. They looked like mere specks, but with Mohn's glass Knut made them out to be one doe, six young bucks, and one doe calf. Knut longed for his rifle and August 1st the opening day, and said he could easily have stalked them – a statement which we did not believe. They soon detected us, and cantered off to the ridge which we had left.

We steered for a gap north of the peak, and had an hour's snow trudge, during which a slight snowstorm passed over us. The crevasses were not very troublesome, though they afforded us some interest. A bergschrund, very wide and glittering with icicles, had, as is so often the case, one weak place in its armour, and we got over by making a big jump, and soon reached the skar, 2918 feet above Bygdin. Here we left our knapsacks and turned south. The last 500 or 600 feet were steep, and consisted of loose blocks of gabbro, which were covered on the windward side with little hard-frozen snowy plumes like countless sprigs of Deutzia. Snow plumes can often be seen in the Alps in changeable weather; but to see them in perfection one must go where there is a damper climate, such as in Cumberland, the Western Highlands of Scotland, Norway, or I suppose the west coast of New Zealand, or probably better still, on the mountains of Tierra Del Fuego. The most beautiful which I ever saw were one day in April years ago on Sca Fell Pike, where the north or windward side of every rock and stone was fringed with horizontal feathers of ice, many of which were fully eighteen inches long, and all were gilded by bright sunshine. They are doubtless formed by a sharp frost freezing a wild driving mist.

The ridge, broad at first, narrowed to a mere knife-edge of loose stones which demanded steady going. If a stone were loosened, it was a question whether it would fall on to the glacier, or down the dark western cliffs. The top is a flat ridge about one hundred feet long. The highest point was then probably about the centre. Professor E. Sars had a great wish to make the first ascent of this peak, but was unable to accompany us as he had intended doing owing to rheumatism and professional duties, so I proposed to Mohn that we should leave the actual top still untrodden, so that Sars might still make it his own. As Mohn thought it unnecessary to do so, we stepped on to the top together.

On this narrow and crumbling ridge Mohn proved himself to be a fearless and sure-footed mountaineer, and was quite as much at his ease on the top of this treacherous mountain-wall as he would have been behind the battlements of a Norman tower.

Uranaastind is 7035 feet above sea-level, and it affords one of the best views in Jotunheim. To the west, just beyond the grim cañon of Utladal, may be seen the grandest side of the Horungtinder, and far beyond them the wavy and subtle lines of the Justedalsbræ. North and east are a fine array of storm-battered peaks and weird aiguilles. South and south-east are Lakes Tyin and Bygdin, which look their very best from this vantage-point.

This view, however, was then denied to us, though we sat shivering in a cold wind waiting for the clouds to blow away for a good hour. Then we hurried down, and I climbed alone a little peak beyond the col whilst the others waited there for me. I never went so fast in my life, and I had a rich reward, as, when close to the top, the clouds lifted, and I had probably the finest view I had seen up to that time. The peak, which Mohn named after his English companion, is only 390 feet lower than Uranaastind. The latter looked grand from here, rising proudly on the one side out of a pure white snowfield, and on the other with horrid black cliffs out of a tarn still blacker, save where a tiny iceberg floated on its surface. Tyin, sunlit, blue, and beautiful, could be seen for many miles. But no more now. A hastily built cairn, and off I went, and soon glissaded close to the top of the broad pass connecting the Uranaasbræ and the Skogadalsbræ which may safely be termed the Uranaasbræ skar. The top of the Skogadalsbræ was pretty steep, and there were some wide and deep crevasses. The snow too was soft, and when we came to the flatter portion below, it was horribly slushy. My meat-tin was very heavy, and I often thought of letting it roll quietly out of sight, until I remembered that sæters were to afford us board and lodging for some days to come, and that for hard mountain-work we required muscular tissue, which surely ought to issue from the tin.

The glacier terminates much as the Mer de Glace now does, on the top of some high and smoothly polished crags. Before we reached these we had to cut many steps down the glacier snout. Knut then cleverly picked out a feasible but irritating way down on the right bank. A flat walk of three miles, and a very difficult crossing of the Skogadöla and at 6.30 we reached the stone-built sæter huts of Skogadalsböen. Mohn bathed in the river. I was much too tired, and sat down admiring the birch-trees, which give the name Skogadal – the woody valley – to this place, having seen no trees near at hand since entering Jotunheim.

After the inevitable milking was ended my meat-tin was opened, and it gave us an excellent meal. The sæter sæl – one of two – was the reverse of luxurious. It had three rooms the first for milking and cooking, the second for living and sleeping in, and the third for embryo and completed cheeses. It was built of stone and had mud floors, and as it had no chimney the smoke oozed out through a dry wall, the doorway, and a small hole in the roof. In addition to the usual girls, who were most hospitable, three men were there. As Mohn, Knut, and I had to occupy a bed which was small for two, sleep was out of the question. Nowadays, as I have often proved, tourists can spend many days in great comfort at the tourist hut at Skogadalsböen, a hut which is to all intents and purposes practically an inn, admirably kept by two girls and a man or two, under the direction of Herr Sulheim.

Our expedition had been a great success, and all who see the lovely pyramid of Uranaastind for the first time from a boat on Tyin will agree that we did well not to leave it for others. The pass had probably been crossed by reindeer hunters before us.

Chapter 7: The Gjertvastind And Vormelid

"And long the way appears, which seem'd so short
To the less practised eye of sanguine youth;
And high the mountain-tops, in cloudy air,
The mountain-tops where is the throne of Truth. "
            MATTHEW ARNOLD

The day after our ascent of Uranaastind was to be Mohn's benefit; we were to climb, if possible, the Gjertvastind, the ascent of which Mohn had set his heart upon more than that of any other peak in Jotunheim, and it was agreed that, in case success met our efforts, Mohn should have the honour of first stepping upon the highest point, whilst a similar favour was to fall to my lot if we climbed Skagastölstind. Each was pledged to help the other to the utmost to gain the prize in view. The tinned meat which had been carried from Tvindehougen formed the *piece de resistance* at breakfast; indeed, we should have been badly off without it. Though up at six we did not get under weigh before eight o'clock, and delays were the order of the day. After going a mile or two, a telescope was missed, and a return to the sæter was necessary.

Half an hour's walk brought us to a bridge over the Utla, which we crossed. It was a novelty to us. Then came the Gjertvas stream, which was very high and difficult to ford. The day was fine, but the tops were mostly cloud-capped. Gleams of golden sunshine striking mossy slopes of spotless verdure, the red rocks at the mouth of Raudal (the red valley), and greyish-blue cliffs, combined with foam and cloud, showed exquisite colouring which recalled the Western Highlands of Scotland.

At nine o'clock we reached the ruins of the abandoned sæter Gjertvasböen, the actual base of the mountain. Mohn planned the route, and a very good one it was, almost due west over a naasi called Klövbaklien. The old Amtskart shows a large glacier upon this, which apparently flowed east. This does not exist, but there is a little one which drains south and throws its terminal sérac down upon the Maradalsbræ. We soon reached a belt of snow, then steep but good rocks, which brought us to the little glacier I have just mentioned. Here we got our first sight of the summit far ahead through a break in the clouds, and very fine it looked, an irregular cone. Our naasi gradually narrowed, became steeper, and had apparently four snow belts including the little glacier.

A line of crags rose straight out of this glacier, apparently inaccessible; but on the right, near the head of the glacier, they were lower and possessed a promising snow gully. We made for this, and after cutting up some hard-frozen snow we reached it and had some good fun, as it was steep and narrow, and afforded an opportunity for Knut to try his prentice hand at step-cutting.

As we ascended the interest increased, as it always ought to do when ascending any properly constructed and well-behaved mountain. The ridge grew narrower, in one place almost sensationally so, and the blue crevasses of the great Maradalsbræ could be seen through occasional cloud-rifts at least 1000 feet below the sheer wall on which we stood. Across this glacier two weird monoliths, the Maradalstinder, rose also straight out of the ice; one of these some years later afforded a good climb to Dr. Claude Wilson and other friends [15], whilst the other, now named Jomfrue, gave an equally good climb to a French climber and Herr Sulheim. [16] We sat down, and whilst Mohn smoked I sketched until in a moment all the view had vanished. Have we been dreaming? No; a narrow lane of light reveals a portion of a glacier, and soon all is gloom again; but it is cold, and a shiver suggests an advance. We erect little cairns here and there to guide us on our return, and have many interesting rocks to climb, then we come to a peerless and steep crest of snow reposing upon a narrow rock ridge. There is no cornice here, and the snow-crest is guarded on each hand from a fall of destruction by rows of firm rocky teeth on the verge of the cliffs.

At 2.15 Mohn had the satisfaction of being the first man to stand on the summit of his well-beloved mountain. Though we had often seen the Gjertvastind in profile, and knew that there was a great precipice in place of a western ridge, we were hardly prepared for the reality. Within a few yards of the summit a little rock platform runs out into space, and a stone simply dropped, not thrown, over the edge, touches nothing for the long period of nine and a half seconds, when it strikes the ice some distance from the base of the cliff. We heaved many rocks over the edge and timed their flight very carefully, by sight not by ear. The actual calculations for a fall of 9½ seconds gives 1440 feet, but to avoid exaggeration we will say that this slightly overhanging precipice is 1400 feet in height. Where is there such another? Possibly on Glitretind, but even if it be still higher, it is not so sensational, as it cannot be seen in profile against the sky. Can Lauterbrunnen, the Grandes Jorasses, the Zinal Rothhorn, or the Petite Aiguille du Dru rival this? Perhaps not in the same line, but in other respects. Ah! I love the Alps almost as much as I love Norway. "Comparisons are..."

At first a sea of tempestuous clouds dashed against the crags and whirled through the gap just below us, covering us with cloud foam, and the stones which we threw over the edge disappeared from sight long before we heard the crash. Fancy the horrors of a nightmare in which a dive is being made into such a sea! Horrible! Fortunately, mountaineers never seem to visit the scenes of their adventures in dreamland, and it is well that this is the case, otherwise members of the Alpine Club would be unpleasant bedfellows.

Seen from the south-east, even as far as from Lake Tyin, Gjertvastind, or the eastern Styggedalstind, as it was called when we climbed it and for many a long year afterwards, has the appearance of a half cone cut down from the apex to the base. The piece – the small half, by the way – which has been cut away, seems to have been carried bodily to the extreme west of the Horungtinder, where it now exists as a very fine mountain which bears the name of Austabottind, but it has lost height in the transit. After a long wait, a dismal ghost clad in white appeared through the clouds beyond the precipice and vanished in a moment, only to reappear shortly afterwards. This was Store, or the great, Styggedalstind, a grand peak which has persistently defied me. Bit by bit we saw the whole of the Maradalsbræ, the finest glacier in the chain, and the noble mountains which overlook it, but the siren Skagastölstind never once withdrew her veil.

At 3.45 we started off again, and when some little way down I suggested as a variety that we should descend to the great Gjertvasbræ by a steep tongue of glacier which comes up close to the arête. Knut, who was in a most boisterous humour, said he was ready for anything, but Mohn, the wisest of the three, pointed out that we had plenty of work before us with Skagastölstind the following day, since much to our chagrin, Knut declared that he could only spare one more day to be with us. So prudent counsels wisely prevailed, as the suggested sporting route would have entailed much step-cutting, and we returned by the way we had come and had many most enjoyable glissades. At 5.35 we regained civilisation in the form of our knapsacks and soon were greeted by graceful birch and alders, most of which were down-beaten by winter snows.

A walk of two or three miles through lovely sylvan scenery in the trough of Utladal brought us to Vormelid at seven, well pleased with our day's work.

Two pretty rosy-cheeked girls called Live and Oliva welcomed us to Sulheim's sæter. These girls came from the parish of Lom, a guarantee that their habits were clean and tidy, and our porridge, coffee, and milk were served to us in most fanciable crockery on a beautifully clean-washed table. The principal room was light and airy, and only needed a boarded floor to be luxurious. There was one bed which was set apart for Mohn and myself, whilst Knut and the girls went to the other hut. In addition to the usual sæter furniture were a gun or two, and a little cannon which was occasionally used to scare the bears. Some horns were also used for the same purpose as well as to call the cattle. Bears always have been and probably always will be a source of great annoyance at Vormelid, and many are the adventures which have befallen the old dwellers there.

During the seven years, from 1869 to 1876, in which Sulheim had held one of the sæters of Vormelid, no stranger had visited this verdant amphitheatre but ourselves, and for several years after I was the only visitor, and I think I am probably right in saying that, until our arrival, the only persons who had been to this fascinating place were Mr. James Backhouse and his son, who made a most adventurous botanical tour in the year 1851, when Mr. Backhouse, junr., made a remarkable painting of the Horungtinder range from the Suletind during the total eclipse of the sun. They were fortunate enough to meet a bear near Vormelid, which piece of good-luck has never fallen to my lot, though I have often just missed seeing one.

After as good a meal as the sæter produce, supplemented with Liebig and chocolate, could afford, Mohn with a pipe in his mouth, and a Greek play in his hand looked as happy as a bumble-bee in a foxglove. He had climbed the peak on which, above all others, he had set his affections, and I could not help a feeling somewhat akin to jealousy. Was my peak also to be conquered as Mohn's and Sars's had been? The weather, though fine, was undoubtedly treacherous, and all depended upon the next day, as Knut, on whose sturdy legs, well-knit muscles, and vigorous lungs I so much depended, was obliged to leave for home two days hence, and it was perhaps now or never. Is it to be wondered at that I hammered away at the old maxim, "Early to bed and early to rise," to little purpose unfortunately? My companions were too comfortable. We had made four new ascents in five days. Why hurry? Yet another birch log on the fire, another pipe, and – confound it all – another dram, and "late to bed."

Chapter 8: The Conquest Of Skagastölstind

"When time, who steals our years away,
Shall steal our pleasures too,
The memory of the past will stay
And half our joys renew."
　　　　THOMAS MOORE.

Whether it was the result of the hardness and narrowness of the bed, the thoughts of joyful conquest, or of ignominious defeat which alternately crossed my brain, or a guilty conscience, I cannot pretend to say, but when I unrolled myself from my Scotch plaid, and crept from under the sheepskin coverlet at three o'clock, on the morning – ever memorable to me – of Friday, July 21st, 1876, I did not feel that early rising was exceptionally virtuous. How could I do so, when I heard the musical voices of the bright-eyed Live and Oliva calling their cattle to come and give their rich store of morning milk? No, I felt that though Mohn had won his laurels, mine depended on the day before us, and I longed to be up and doing, and to get the most I could out of Knut on this his last day with us, as we had every reason to believe that the ascent of Skagastölstind would prove to be very severe. Vormelid is only about 1600 feet above the fjord at Aardal, and as Skagastölstind is 7874 feet, there was a considerable ascent to be made, in addition to the crossing of a high spur, before the actual base of the mountain could be reached.

Early rising, when mountaineering, is not of such prime importance, in the almost nightless days of July in Norway, as it is in the Alps in the same month; still, when we waved an adieu to our hostesses, we could not help feeling that seven o'clock was at least two hours later than it ought to have been. However, as may be inferred from the heading of this chapter, "All's well that ends well" is an axiom that may rightly be associated with this day.

Though the barometer had risen during the night, the weather was unpromising, and all the neighbouring heights were enshrouded with dense clouds. Knut said, "You cannot climb anything to-day," to which I replied, "Possibly not; but we must go and do our best, and for anything we know, the whole of the higher Horungtinder may even now be quite clear above the clouds."

I have often started for a high mountain from out of the mists of a low valley and have had a glorious day both in Norway and in the Alps. Low-lying clouds alone should never prevent climbers from starting. Some of the most enjoyable days I have ever spent amongst the eternal hills have been when in the early morning, if not during the whole day, the tops have been screened off from the view of those in the valleys. Twenty-four years ago my guides and I had a grand day on the Weisshorn, and revelled in golden sunshine, whilst the whole Visp valley was full of clouds, and when we got down to Randa we heard that a violent thunder-storm had been raging off and on most of the day, and the signs of recent heavy rain were unmistakable. Though just above the thunder-cloud, we had neither seen the lightning nor heard the thunder. On another occasion, five separate parties started from the Riffelberg about 2 a.m., for five different expeditions, and all were successful; that in which I was a member climbed Castor and Pollux. Meanwhile, the numerous mountaineers at Zermatt got up, looked out, and seeing nothing but heavy clouds, went to bed again, and were fearfully jealous when they heard that we had all been successful.

As Knut was evidently tired, owing to hard work and a succession of bad nights, I engaged to carry both my own rope and one of his, as well as most of the food. A steep, zigzagging cattle path led us easily alongside a fine cataract, the Maradalsfos, into the Maradal, a short valley so far as vegetation is concerned, which is headed by the Maradalsbræ. This is the finest glacier in the range of the Horungtinder, and several grand mountains rise out of its cold ice, one being the Gjertvastind, on whose snowy crest we had been the previous day.

At the top of the fos, which is 1295 feet in height, just above the birch-tree limit, and where the dwarf willows begin to grow, we called a halt, nominally to admire the view, but in reality because our limbs and lungs demanded it. Truly it was a fair picture to look upon, the peaceful sæter with cattle and goats browsing around it in greenest of pastures; the foaming river Utla below, here a tempestuous rapid, there a deep pool; then, beyond the river, crag piled upon crag, terrace upon terrace, where until some rude avalanche shall suddenly come and sweep them away, grow the sombre pines and graceful silvery birches, which blend in most harmonious colours with the purest emerald of the mosses, and the rocks of greyish blue and brown. Other crags, as black as darkest winter's night, formed a strong contrast to the snows, the gauze-like cloud veils, and the milk-white cataracts. Of sunshine there was little, and up the valley, where we were to go, clouds reigned supreme, and left much for our lively imaginations to picture.

A short rest sufficed, and Mohn led us up the valley. Amongst the rocks we found many large plants of *Angelica archangelica*, each of which had its top recently eaten off by a bear, whose footprints were plainly visible where the ground was soft. Since then I have often been to Vormelid, and have invariably seen fresh traces of Herr Bamsen.

A short distance from the glacier we turned to the left, to cross the buttress of Rolandsnaasi, then we descended 314 feet into a valley, which was there and then dubbed the Skoddedal – cloud-valley – where we could not see twenty yards in front of us. The ground was new to us all, and the maps were faulty, so we erected many diminutive cairns to guide us on our return. The weather was decidedly unpromising, we could see nothing, and nearly ran our heads against the base of that grim obelisk, the eastern Maradalstind.

Mohn and I had often noticed that, after being enveloped in thick mist for nearly a whole day, the higher Horungtinder frequently shone out with double beauty late in the afternoon or evening, and we told Knut that such would be the case to-day, though I fear we thought otherwise.

On nearing the top of a second ridge, 3276 feet above Vormelid, we found that the higher we got, the lighter were the clouds, so I ran forward to the highest point, and saw a most glorious sight.

Across the cloud-filled Midt Maradal were the serrated ridges of the Midt Maradals and the Dyrhougs-tinder, which form a colossal and nearly perpendicular wall between 2000 and 3000 feet in height. The contrast which the top of this black wall showed to the white clouds below was wonderful. I shouted to Mohn and Knut to hurry up, and when they arrived they shared my delight.

Soon after their arrival we saw the trough of Midt Maradal, 1500 feet below us. At the lower end of this valley there is excellent grazing land, usually a mine of wealth in Norway. However in this case the herbage is left to the bears, which are in the main herbivorous and not carnivorous animals, and to an occasional reindeer buck which has crossed the Skagastölsbræ at the risk of losing his life in the bergschrund on the north side of the pass. Certain it is that in the year 1877 Anfind Vetti, the owner of this valley, who had seen it thousands of times across the Utla gorge, not half a mile off as the crow flies from his sæter near the top of the Vettis fos, had at that time never been in this romantic valley, and asked me to guide him into it.

Clouds again swept up the valley and for a few minutes blotted out the whole of the view. Then a grand and inaccessible-looking peak, a continuation of our ridge, appeared.

"Is that Skagastölstind?" we all exclaimed. We could only see the top, and the clouds lent it such additional grandeur that we had no proper conception of its height, nor of its relative position. It disappeared from our view as quickly as it had come, and all was gloom again once more.

After a minute or two, a truly noble aiguille appeared, a never-to-be-forgotten sight. Further doubt was impossible. This was Skagastölstind and the former peak, Mohn rightly said, was only one of the Maradalstinder. Another peak then appeared between the two, and for a while each seemed to be floating in clouds. The marvellous panoramic changes caused by the drifting of the cloud curtains are far beyond my descriptive powers. Suffice it to say that we gazed in wonder and bewilderment until the guardian clouds were dissipated, and in a few moments all was clear.

Our excitement and anxiety were intense, as may be easily imagined. No thought of fatigue now. No memory of the meagre fare, the hard beds, and the short snatches of fitful sleep, with which we had perforce been contented during the last ten days. No. Our task lay unfettered before us, and without a word being spoken we began scrambling at noonday down the rugged crags into Midt Maradal.

A walk of a mile or so over horrible debris brought us at one o'clock to the flattened snout of Midt Maradalsbræ, at the actual base of our mountain, and 4396 feet from the top. Here we lunched in the glowing sunshine, and carefully reconnoitred the proposed route. The guiding was all left to me, as Skagastölstind was considered to be my special mountain, though of course I consulted the others.

The grandeur of Midt Maradal is in great measure due to the fact that the lowest pass across the range of the Horungtinder happens to be close to the highest mountain, and entirely cuts it off from its near western neighbours, and this mountain is only connected with the peaks on the eastern side of the pass by a narrow ridge 518 feet below the summit. Hence, too, Skagastölstind possesses a delightful isolation. It rises majestically some 3000 feet above the head of the pass, and out of two fine glaciers, the Midt Maradalsbre and the Skagastölsbræ on the north side. There is also a much steeper and wilder glacier descending like a cataract of ice from the heights of the eastern range. This glacier skirts the south-eastern walls of Skagastölstind and Norse mountaineers with the generosity of their race have honoured me by associating it with my name. At the time of which I write, this glacier ended abruptly at the top of a line of crags 60 or 70 feet in height, over which the terminal seracs fell, and formed the nucleus of a minute secondary glacier below. The stream which drained the glacier made a waterfall into the snow, and added variety to the wild scene. Since then the icy foot has been withdrawn a little way up the mountain, though some other neighbouring glaciers undoubtedly have advanced, and still maintain their forward position. It was this rugged glacier that my sister and I had seen in the distance the previous year, and had considered to be the natural highway to the summit.

I proposed that we should cross the fan of the lower glacier, that we should climb up a little gully between two bosses of rock, which would lead us on to the right bank of our wished for icy highway, and so gain the glacier itself. In fact, it was our only chance thus late in the day, though a few years later the route now almost universally followed was discovered entirely by rocks from the Midt Maradalskar – also called Bandet, the band – on the south-west.

On looking upwards, we saw a narrow belt of dark rocks at the head of the glacier which separates it from a steep snow slope above. Here we apprehended difficulty, and Knut said, "De kan ikke komme frem der, sneen er alt for brat." (You cannot get forward there, the snow is much too steep.) I replied that it was the only way where there was even the ghost of a chance, and that we must try it. Mohn loyally supported me, as he and I, having both seen the mountain from the north, thought that there was no possibility of climbing it on that side, whilst Knut, who had never been near it before, was inclined to think "our best as bad." The snow-slope leads up at a very steep angle to a gap or skar, rather more than 500 feet from the top, and though from the base we could not see whether it continued farther up the mountain, as it was hidden by a projecting crag, we rather expected a chimney or a friendly ridge to lead from the skar to the summit. The south-eastern face rises almost perpendicularly out of the glacier, so nothing could be done there.

We had no difficulty in crossing the fan of the lower glacier, and soon got up the gully, and on to a spur which separates the two glaciers. Here great caution was required, as the rocks were smooth and steep. We presently reached a snow-patch which we had to cross – where we saw before us footsteps! Crusoe's surprise at finding footprints in the sand could not have much exceeded ours. Horrid thought! "Have we been forestalled?" "Is some unknown party of mountaineers now on the top?" "Surely not; we must have heard if other climbers were in this wild region." A close inspection revealed the fact that they were the fresh tracks of a bear. What Bruin could have been doing up there, out of the way of all vegetation, we could not divine but there were his traces, quite recent too. Perhaps he too was on a tour of exploration, or possibly we had frightened him the previous day, when we threw stones down the overhanging precipice of the Gjertvastind. He had proceeded in the direction we were taking, and when we reached the glacier a few minutes later, we found his tracks again, and followed them to our advantage, through an intricate maze of crevasses, until they turned off towards the lower crags of Centraltind.

I have very often seen spoor of a bear on Norse glaciers, and on two occasions have followed them as we did here, and feel quite certain that Bruin understands the hidden dangers of the snow-fields almost as well as we do ourselves. Probably a bear is a better glacier-guide for human beings to follow than a chamois. It is certain that, though I have never been led wrong by a bear, I have on one occasion got into great difficulties by following a chamois, when descending from the Aiguille du Plan.[17]

We had some interesting step-cutting through some seracs where a jutting crag contracted the glacier. After this, we turned a little to the left quite under Skagastölstind, which towered proudly 3000 feet above us. Hardly any debris seemed to have fallen from this awful precipice on to the glacier; a good sign for us, which suggested firm rocks above, whilst on the other hand an avalanche thundered down to the far side of the glacier from the ridge above it, and echo answered echo again and again.

Near the top of the glacier, there about 500 yards wide, a large crevasse stretched nearly across. Where we first reached it about the middle of the glacier, it looked like a ravenous, open jawed monster, awfully deep and ready to swallow a whole Alpine Club. As there were no snow-bridges here, we followed it to the western side where the friction of the rocks had broken down the snowy wall and had partially choked up the crevasse. Here we made sure of crossing. In the best place, however, there was a wall of névé, 12 feet high, above the snow in the crevasse. My companions anchored themselves safely and paid out my rope while I climbed down into the hollow. Twice I cut my way up the wall, but though I cut a dozen large steps, I could not get over on the top, as the snow, at that late hour of the day, was too soft for my ice-axe to hold in, and twice I came down again to the soft snow in my fruitless endeavours. The second time, my feet passed through and revealed uncanny depths and a blue haze which was not reassuring. If the snow had been strong enough to hold a second man safely, we could have got up the wall, as I could have stood on his shoulders and have hacked away a sloping staircase to the platform above. I tried once more, and though I failed, I all but succeeded. For some time, Knut had been calling out "Til hoire" (To the right). Now, I replied, "Ja, nu maa vi gaa til hoire." We retraced our steps and, to our great joy, found a substantial bridge close to the eastern side.

The glacier became steeper, but we soon reached the black belt of rock, where from below we expected to find considerable difficulty or possibly defeat. Fortunately the bergschrund at the head of the glacier and at the foot of the rocks was choked up with a snow avalanche, which gave us a ready-made road on to the rocks.

Though we were still 1114 feet below the summit, Mohn said he felt tired and needed rest. Both of my companions on principle wore boots which were quite innocent of nails or spikes, and in consequence they had found the steep portion of the glacier to be very trying, and they both acknowledged that their theories were wrong, and that Alpine nails were excellent and prevented many a fall.

As it was nearly 5 p.m., and the great tug of war was yet to come on, I said that we could not afford time for a rest, so I untied myself and soon reached the steep snow-slope at the top of the belt of rock. This snow-slope was nearly 600 feet high. As it was partially frozen it required very great care, and an ice-axe was a *sine qua non*. I rather feared the descent of this part, as being in the shade the snow crust was then hardening, the angle was severe, and a fall was not to be thought of. Where the rocks were feasible I preferred them, and left the snow until the rocks were too steep to climb.

An hour after leaving my friends I reached the top of the skar, and then took a look around. On the north or opposite side to that which I had ascended, instead of a friendly glacier or couloir close at hand, there was a grim precipice, and at its base was a glacier, the Skagastölsbræ, the sister to the Midt Maradalsbræ, which projected its icy foot into a mountain tarn, on the placid surface of which many quaint little icebergs were floating. Above the tarn and glacier rose the black precipices of the northern Dyrhougstinder, a grand wall.

Looking towards the true Skagastölstind, 518 feet above the skar, I felt that I was beaten after all, and my dream at an end, as it is difficult to imagine any mountain presenting a more impracticable appearance than is shown at first sight by this peak from the skar. The skar consists of a narrow and flat ridge, perhaps 100 yards in length, of which one end abuts against a huge oblong tower of gabbro, the great peak itself. On the right is the precipice above the tarn, and on the left the base of the tower springs from the glacier which we had ascended nearly perpendicularly and almost entirely without ledges. There seemed to be no proper arête to connect the peak with the skar, and merely a narrow face, mostly consisting of smoothly polished and almost vertical slabs of rock. The first 150 or 200 feet appeared to be the worst, and I thought that if those could be surmounted, the top might be won, but really I did not then think there was the slightest possibility of doing it. Of course there was no snow couloir, as the rocks were much too steep to allow snow to accumulate there in any quantity.

Behind me, and rising some 300 feet at a comparatively gentle angle from the other end of the ridge, was another peak now called Vesle, or the little, Skagastölstind. As this seemed to be relatively easy to ascend, and thinking that it was better than none, I set off to climb it before my companions arrived. When I had gone a short way I looked down and saw the others rounding a rock just below the skar, so I hurried down and joined them.

"What do you think of it, Mohn?"
"Well, I suppose that we can now say it is perfectly impossible."

"We have not yet proved it to be so; we must not give it up without a try. Will you come?"
"No."

"Knut, will you?"
"No, I shall not risk my life there."

"I will at least try, though I do not think I can manage it."

Fortunately I was perfectly fresh, and of course had an excellent stimulant in the uncertainty of my enterprise and the delights of entering still further into the unknown; and besides this, it is rarely safe to say that a mountain wall which you have never studied in profile, but have face to face with you, is unclimbable.

I recommended the others to climb the lesser peak – then unascended. Mohn said philosophically "Aut Caesar, aut nihil." Then I left them and passed under a snow cornice which overhung the northern precipice like a wave arrested when about to break on a shingly beach, and I soon reached the rock wall. Now! farewell to snow, that great aider of mountain ascents, and! – 500 feet of cold rock! I found a small buttress projecting from the face of the rock a little to the south of the skar. It formed a corner. Up there I must go, or nowhere else: of choice there was none; but still, when viewed closely it looked more hopeful than at the first glance. I soon found that the rocks were firm; the ledges, though so tiny, were secure. The strata of the rock inclined the right way, downward from the out-face towards the centre of the mountain. [18] Better than all, I was quite cool and in perfect training. Still, no trifling must be indulged in here.

After being hidden from my friends by the snow cornice, I came into view again, and every movement was eagerly watched by my well-wishers. Soon I got into difficulties in the comer, and, but for a ledge not so broad as my hand, from which I had to knock away the ice, I should thus early have been defeated, because without the aid of this foothold the mountain, on this side at least, would be inaccessible. My friends saw me at this place, and vainly tried to call me back, but with the help of my well-tried ice-axe I surmounted the difficulty. I avoid going into details about this and other places, though I made minute notes the following day because if I were to attempt to describe them I should undoubtedly be accused either of exaggeration or perhaps of foolhardiness by readers unaccustomed to alpine work, when at the same time I might be guilty of neither. Suffice it to say that what under the most favourable conditions must be a tough piece of work, was made more so by the films of ice with which every little ledge was veneered. Three times I was all but beaten, but this was my especial and much-longed-for mountain, and I scraped away the ice and bit by bit got higher and higher. In sight of the others I reached what from the skar we had judged to be the top. I raised a cheer, which was renewed below, when I found that there was a ridge – a knife-edged affair – perhaps sixty yards long, and that the highest point was evidently at the farther end. There are three peaklets, and a notch in the ridge which again almost stopped me. For the first time I had to trust to an overhanging and rather a loose rocky ledge. I tried it well, then hauled myself up to terra firma, and in a few strides, a little above half an hour after leaving my friends, I gained the unsullied crown of the peerless Skagastölstind, a rock table four feet by three, elevated five or six feet above the southern end of the ridge.

As to the view, which was perfectly free from clouds, it would be futile for me to attempt to describe it at length, except to say that on every hand, some of the wildest crags, aiguilles, and glaciers in "Gamle Norge" looked their very wildest. On one hand, our luncheon place, 4396 feet below, seemed to be only a stone's-throw off. On another, below an almost vertical precipice 3000 feet in height, was a portion of the glacier which we had ascended. On another, some 4000 feet down lay the mountain tarn with its icy flotilla, and above it the glacier and terrible cliffs I have before alluded to. Forests and green pastures here and there relieved the scene of most of its harsher characteristics, and in the distance the many beautiful domes and subtle curves of purest snow which together form the great Justedalsbræ showed for a distance of 45 miles from the Kamphammer pass to the snowy heights of Fjærland, a most lovely and harmonious horizon, a beauty which insensibly grows upon one year after year, and which is seldom appreciated when first seen.

The exquisite colouring for which Norway is so deservedly famous appeared in all its richness and variety; but in such a place, alone, out of sight of every living creature, one of the greatest desires of my heart granted to me, it will be easily understood, when I say that a feeling of silent worship and reverence was more suitable than the jotting down of memoranda in a note-book. The scene was too overwhelming for notes. I longed to have my trusty friend Mohn by my side, and his absence was a bitter disappointment to me. Had he been with me his enthusiasm would have been boundless.

After a drink of cold tea, a bite of goat's milk cheese, a crust of rye bread, and a few prunes, I set to work to build a cairn, but as the rocks were so marvellously sound, I could find very few stones, so only made one two or three feet high. I put a pocket-handkerchief under one of the stones, which was afterwards seen in the distance through a telescope. By my aneroid I made the height to be 6200 feet above Vormelid.

At 6.53, after pocketing a few little stones and some reindeer moss, I left the top in warm and golden sunshine, and after traversing the top ridge, turned into cold shade on the ice-clad rocks of the north-eastern face. The descent to the skar was certainly difficult, and being alone, the difficulties probably appealed to me more forcibly than they would if I had had company. [19]

The steep snow-slope was now hard frozen, and the greatest care was necessary, but I passed it very well and was soon over the belt of rocks and on the glacier, where a few glissades materially helped me. I was very thankful to join my friends near the top of the glacier at 7.45, when they most heartily congratulated me. It was bitterly cold, and our warm gloves were a necessity.

At 9 o'clock we reached our former luncheon place, and I shall never forget Mohn's kindness in sharing with me his last bit of cheese and bread, as mine had been finished long before. A simple gift indeed, but nevertheless an act of self-denial, appreciable only by those who know the real value of a crust when nothing else is to be had.

We found the 1500 feet which we had to ascend on our return very fatiguing. I was the freshest, but probably success sustained my animal vigour. From the top of the great ridge – or naasi – which we reached in twilight at 11 p.m., we had a most sublime view of sharp peaks still rose-tinted by the setting sun, though Jupiter shone like a bright beacon apparently on the snow-crest of Stölsnaastind, a beautiful mountain above the Vetti's fos. The snow was crisp and hard and sparkled like diamonds.

In Maradal it became much darker, and each of us tripped up now and then over the junipers and dwarf birches, but we arrived at the sæter all right a little after 1 a.m., where we found the elder girl awaiting us. She soon got us a roaring fire of birch logs, made us coffee and Liebig, and did all in her power to make us comfortable. Then we slept the sleep of the weary until the sun was high in the heavens, and the cattle were gone away a couple of miles to graze.

Such was the first ascent of what is usually called the finest mountain in Norway. The illusion of its inaccessibility had been at last dispelled, most probably too at the first determined attack upon its grisly towers, and a solid fact took the place of an ancient fable.

Though the ascent has become a favourite amongst experienced mountaineers, it will never become what in the Alps is termed "a fashionable mountain" for tourists such as those whom one meets at Zermatt, and who are pulled and shoved up fine mountains by indifferent guides. The last bit is too bad for that. I for one would never have attempted alone rocks such as those upon any other mountain, but it was the particular one upon which I had centred my energies, and those 518 feet which I climbed in solitude, I always look back upon with a feeling of veneration. They formed an event in my life which can never be forgotten; and although I have climbed very many of the higher Norse mountains, yet the ascent of none has left such a vivid impression in my mind as this. We had set off in the misty morning with feelings of hope perhaps, certainly not of expectancy. The first portion had been all in clouds, and we were oppressed by doubts; the second was in brilliant sunshine. Success had been granted to me at all events and, better still, a safe return to us all.

The day following that on which Skagastölstind had been ascended, though the weather seemed to be quite settled and perfect for mountaineering, Mohn and I felt so great a longing for the joys of civilisation, that we determined to leave the fells for the fjords and to pay a visit for a few days to a friend of Mohn's and then to return to continue our mountain programme.

After drinking "skaal" together we parted with Knut at the Guridal bridge with mutual regret. Knut, a lazy man by nature, had done very well for us, and though he did not carry an ounce of our baggage, we had worked him very hard during the week, which was all the time he could spare for us. In six days, five notable maiden ascents had been made, which is probably the most successful little campaign which has ever been waged in Jotunheim, and the hardy reindeer hunter was very proud to have taken a part in it.

Needless to say, we walked very leisurely over the Keiser pass; Mohn was fairly fresh, but I was dog-tired. At the head of Helgedal we had a grand view of the range of the Skagastölstinder above the Styggedalsbræ and much to my joy, we saw through Mohn's glass not only the little cairn which I had built on the top of the great peak, but also my handkerchief. At 10 p.m. we entered the cosy little inn at Fortun and received, as I have done on many another occasion, a most hearty welcome. How delightful it was to have, even at that late hour, a sumptuous meal nicely served, to be able to wash comfortably and to sleep between spotless white sheets, none can tell unless they know what "roughing it" means.

That night we slept the clock round and then had delicious pancakes to breakfast, and did not leave until after midday. The thermometer showed 82° F. in the shade; we sauntered slowly along to Eide, where we found Frue Sulheim, but not her gallant husband. Hearing that we came from Vormelid she said: "Have there been any bears there, and are all the cattle alive?"

To these questions we were able to give a more reassuring answer than would have been the case had it been a week later, as in the meantime a bear had visited Vormelid.

Ten days after the ascent of Skagastölstind, Mohn and I arrived late one evening at Rödsheim, where a goodly assemblage of Norse mountain enthusiasts, including several university professors, happened to be staying. They had heard many vague rumours of our adventures on the mountain. One report reached them that Mohn and Knut had reached the top and not the foreigner, and at this they were naturally much pleased. Then another told that the foreigner was the successful one, and great was their disappointment. Lastly, they heard that Knut was the only one who had reached the summit, and they were much relieved by thinking that a countryman at least had done the deed. When, however, we reached Rödsheim and the truth was told, I could see a shade of disappointment passing over their faces, which is not to be wondered at. [20] However, they toasted, congratulated, and made me complimentary speeches, to which I replied in the best Norse I could muster, and we passed a right jolly evening together. Amongst the company was Professor E. Sars, to whom I had the pleasure of giving a stone from the summit of Uranaastind, his favourite mountain.

Reports of our ascents soon got into the Christiania and Bergen papers, and pretty highly coloured they were too. My personal appearance was described, I rather think, after a German model, and it was evident that a keen interest in the sport of mountaineering had been awakened in the country at large.

As to the subsequent history of Skagastölstind, I will briefly relate it. In 1877, partly in consequence of the letters in the Christiania newspapers, Herr Harald Petersen, an artist, and a capital fellow to boot, tried the mountain from the north, but failed. Nothing daunted, he set off again in 1878 with two guides, one of whom was Knut Lykken, who led him up to Mohn's Skar and then forsook him, exactly at the place where I began my solitary climb in 1876. Petersen went on alone, and much to my gratification succeeded, and found my pocket-handkerchief, which had braved the storms a little more than two years, and sent it to me by post. Petersen thoroughly deserved his success, and, inasmuch as he had not been so well and loyally supported as I had been by Mohn on the upper glacier and steep snow-slope, I think that possibly more credit, if less honour, is due to him who made the second ascent than to the foreigner who was fortunate enough to win the first laurels. Petersen too had at that time very little mountain experience, and he was forsaken by Knut when he could not plead fatigue and loss of sleep, which on the first occasion, and then only, could be urged as a legitimate excuse for shirking his duty.

It was not, however, until the year 1894 that Skagastölstind appeared to attract the attention which it deserved. The two first ascents of this year were made by Englishmen, and in each case the guides were Knud Fortun and Ole Öiene. Then, on July 30th, the first lady's ascent of the mountain was made. The heroine, I am glad to say, was a Norse lady, Fröken T. Bertheau, who has since then made many notable ascents. The following day two parties climbed the mountain. In one of these was the second lady, also Norse, Fröken Fanny Paulsen. Next day, August 1st, a third lady made the ascent. This time I am delighted to think that the honours fell to an English girl, Miss Evelyn Spence Watson. By a strange coincidence the mountain, which had never before been attacked by the fair sex, was climbed on three consecutive days by a different lady.

However, as can be seen from the list of successful and unsuccessful attempts recorded by my friend, Herr Carl Hall, in the *Nor. Tor. Fur. Aarbog* for 1891-92, which I translate and partly quote below, it will be seen that Skagastölstind was only ascended eight times in sixteen years, although seven unsuccessful attempts are recorded during the same period.

1. 1876. July 21. Wm. Cecil Slingsby. [E. Mohn and the guide Knut Lykken went as far as Mohn's Skar.]
2. 1878. Harald Petersen. [Knut Lykken remained behind on Mohn's Skar, whilst Thomas Lystring was left farther down.]
3. 1886. Johannes Heftye with Jens Klingenberg and Peder Melheim.
4. 1882. The Danes, Alf. Lehmann and C. F. Weis-Ernst, and the Norseman J. N. Brun, with Peder Melheim and Niels Vetti.
5. 1885. Carl Hall with Thorgeir Sulheim and Matias Soggemoen.
6. 1888. F. H. Fox and H. Fox with T. Sulheim.
7. 1890. Hans Olsen Vigdal from Skjolden.
8. E. J. Woolley and Benj. Goodfellow with Johannes Vigdal.

Three of the ascents named above were completed by solitary climbers, a form of mountaineering which can hardly be too severely condemned, unless the conditions are wholly exceptional.

Detailed accounts of all the early ascents of Skagastölstind, with the exception of the third, which appeared separately, and of the sixth, are to be found in various numbers of the *Nor. Tur. For. Aarbog*. The only two in English are those of 1891-92 and 1897.

All mountaineers who have climbed in the Horungtinder will agree with me when I say that to Herr Carl Hall of Copenhagen we are deeply indebted for the lucid and descriptive accounts of the numerous maiden mountain ascents which he has made in the range, for the many careful records of ascents by all climbers, and perhaps, above all, for the excellent illustrations from his own photographs which have so often enriched the pages of the *Aarboger*, and have induced many an active young fellow during the last dozen years to leave the valleys and to glean health, strength, and pleasure amongst the eternal hills.

Chapter 9: The Ascent Of Stölsnaastind

"See, from afar, yon rock that mates the sky,
About whose feet such. heaps of rubbish lie;
Such indigested ruin."
        DRYDEN'S Virgil.

"He that knows not whither to go, is in no haste to move."
        DR. JOHNSON.

A few years ago, in company with two trusty friends, I ascended the Glärnisch, the most northerly snow mountain in Switzerland, and though the mountain had been ascended scores if not hundreds of times before, comparatively little was known of it by most members of the Alpine Club; hence, at the request of the editor, I wrote a short paper about it in the *Alpine Journal.*

"What on earth has this to do with the mountain whose name appears at the head of this chapter?" I can imagine some one saying. The answer is that I want to borrow the two first paragraphs.

"In each group of mountains in the Alps, Nature has provided one or more peaks, apparently for a most excellent purpose, namely that of affording for her lovers remarkable views from their summits. These peaks are the watch-towers of the Alps, and the views comprise peeps of the vales, the plains, the rivers, also of villages and peaceful homesteads as well as of the sterner scenes above the snow-line. It does not follow that these views are the finest that can be obtained; indeed they may not be half as glorious as the view of Mont Blanc from Le Jardin or from Le Grand Plateau, nor half as beautiful as dozens of views of the Faulhorn, Gorner Grat, and Monte Generoso type, but they certainly appeal to us mountaineers with a force not to be equalled by any which can be seen by merely walking on a footpath up to the top of a hill which is probably desecrated by a drinking-booth.

These peaks must of necessity have rock crests or snow crowns. They are placed, as the Aiguille de Trélatête and the Eiger, at the corners or ends of the main ranges, or of those lateral ranges which fortunately are so numerous in the Alps; or like the Dent d'Herens and the Todi they form centres from which several valleys radiate; or, as the Galenstock, they head some great valley; or, like Monte Leone, they stand as sentinels guarding some great gap in the main chain; or they tower, as Monte Viso does, head and shoulders above their neighbours. But in every case they invite, nay, they command mountaineers to touch their proud crests."

It is just the same in Norway. As to Stölsnaastind, its position is unrivalled. This beautiful mountain – the monarch of the Koldedal peaks – rises out of the forest plateau of Vettismark, it overshadows the Arctic tarns of Koldedal, and stands face to face with the Horungtinder on their grandest side across the deep, dark ghyll of Utladal.

Think but for a moment from how many places the Stölsnaastind is visible, and forms a principal feature in the view, and doubt, if you can, at the glorious view from its summit, but marvel greatly why such an extremely tempting peak was not climbed ages ago.

From the top of the Keiser Pass, what looks finer than that obelisk of black rock, with the one white snowy belt running obliquely from the wavy glacier below almost to its summit? From the three Maradale, how sharp the peak! From Tvindehougen, what additional grandeur the towering peak gives to Keilhau's triumph – the Falkenæbbe! From the mountains of Bygdin, Thorfinstind and others, or from the skar above Oxdalshullet, see that sharp-pointed crescent, each end up-turned inquiringly to the heavens; that to the left hand is the Falcon's Beak, the other is – our friend. See the peak again, from the east, from any commanding height you like, and still admire. Go into the recesses of Morka-Koldedal, and shudder at its precipices. But look not at the mountain from either Sulutind or Stugunöset, for from there alone it is robbed of its grandeur by the intervening Gjeldedalstinder.

I had often cast longing glances at Stölsnaastind, and had partially studied its ascent, and eventually fixed on July 28th, 1877, as the day on which the ascent should be attempted if the weather were favourable.

With this end in view I wrote from home to ask Knut Lykken to join me at Vetti on July 27th, and kept the appointment myself.

"Is Knut Lykken here?"
"No; I expect he is getting ready for reindeer-stalking."

"I asked him to meet me here and to climb Stölsnaastind with me. Anfind, you are a strong, active man; will you climb with me?"
"I don't know. I should like to; but I'll ask my wife."

After a good deal of confabulation, the wife gave an unwilling consent. The fact was, that the ascent of Skagastölstind the previous year had endowed me with a wholly undeserved reputation for recklessness amongst the natives, who did not then appreciate, as they do now, the fact that mountain-climbing is a great and a most legitimate sport. Anfind, who knew me well, was ready enough to go, and in fact he had a great desire to climb the peak which he had so often admired. Herr Reusch, the well-known geologist, was at Vetti, and though he said he was not a mountaineer, he consented to go part of the way with us.

Adieu to friends who set off early to walk to Aardal, and at 6 a.m. we faced the lung-proving zigzags above Vetti, and at 6.55 we gazed down into the black abyss where the silvery water-thread from the stream above forms the peerless Vettisfos. A glittering spray of kaleidoscopic beauty was blown by the morning breeze, and watered the bright Alpine plants which carpeted the ground.

We pass the sæter or stöl, and make our way through the forest to the mountain buttress or naasi beyond, as the direct route to the peak, or tind, above – the Stöls-naasi-tind. Recent footprints of a bear we take as a matter of course. The Horungtinder are cloud-wreathed, but the day is early. "Gloomy now, but bright later on." So we say.

The walk was easy. Soon we forsook vegetation and trod the herbless gabbro. Mist and rain came on, and we sheltered under Reusch's umbrella and the lee of a rock. Then snow came, but it soon blew away.

We crossed a portion of the Fleskenaasbræ then heeled over to our right to a very steep, unpromising glacier. This ended, so far as we could see, on the brink of a high Koldedal precipice, which I knew from below.

My two comrades, each of whom said he was not used to glaciers, stepped fearlessly on the steep snow, and I saw almost at a glance that I had two men with me who, however little they professed, had plenty of pluck.

Thinking we were too low down, we took to the rocks above. My hat blew away on the snow, and gave me an exciting chase. Still involved in a thick clammy mist, we followed the rocks north-east, and soon reached a high glacier, flat at the top, but sloping off, apparently sharply, at the edge on each side. Here we used the rope for the first time, and at Anfind's wish I led. We could not see above thirty or forty yards in front of us, so of course saw no peak. The maps at that time were very faulty, and I steered solely from memory. On our right, towards Koldedal, there was a snow cornice, to which we gave a wide berth, and in doing so altered our course a little. In the gloom we saw rocks ahead, which we thought we recognised as some crags above Fleskenaasdal. We turned again and steered, as we thought in the mist, in the same direction as that we had pursued when we first stepped on the glacier. All at once I saw footsteps close to us, parallel to our course. They were ours, and though the snowy plateau was narrow we had performed a circuit, and were returning. Out came our compasses, and our course was reversed. Anfind and I could hardly believe it at first, as steering there seemed to be such an easy matter. However, there we were, blindly making rings on the snow.

No one, whose experience on the mountains is limited to fine weather, can imagine how very easy it is within a very circumscribed limit to get completely heeled round as we were on this occasion. The fault, if fault there were, was mine, and I frankly acknowledge that it is not the only time when I have led a party wrong in a fog. Some years ago I guided a large party of eight or nine friends, including three ladies, from Borrowdale to the Pillar Rock. After climbing the rock it was agreed that we should ascend the Pillar Mountain, and then cross Kirk Fell and Great Gable to the Sty Head Pass on our way back to Rosthwaite. We easily followed a rock rib to the summit of the mountain in a heavy snowstorm, and set off immediately for Black Sail, east, not being able to see above half a dozen yards in front of us. In due time we came down to a pass, and a rift in the clouds revealed the fact that we were in Windy Gap, west from the Pillar. A few months later I told old Will Ritson of Wasdale Head of this mistake, very shamefacedly I must own. All the old veteran said was: "Why! that's nowt. Ah can bang that mesell. Ah mind yance we'd been hunting ower t' Ennerdale fells, and hed kilt a geart dog fox on t' Pillar Fell; he was running for t' bield under Esh Crag, and Rattler just gripped him afoor he gat intil t' whoal. Weel, ah mind t'mist corn doon, and we could see nowt, and wander't rowed and rowed, and laal Tom Nicholson of Branthwaite says, 'It's nea use graping aboot like this, let's mak doon teua Black Seal,' and afoor we could see owt to ken t' road by, we fund oursels in Windy Gap. Yan can easy git wrong on t' fells." However, if care be taken, a party of three roped together, and about twenty-five feet apart, ought not to get very far astray on the level, as the last man can notice if the leader makes any deviation from a straight course, and can at once correct the mistake. I believe that every man walking in the dark on the flat goes unconsciously and persistently to one particular side. In my own case I believe that my tendency is to go to the right hand, and I know one man who invariably turns to the left in similar circumstances.

Then we steered due east, and came to a row of lofty turrets of rock, perpendicular to the northern glacier. We soon reached the highest point, and found a mighty precipice in front of us. "Where are we? Who knows?" None of us. "We are on a tind, but will swear it is not the one we wish for. Where is it?" Anfind points eastwards, saying, "Somewhere there." So do I. We look eagerly for any break in the clouds, and take our second breakfast. A breath of wind touches our faces, the cloud-curtain begins to agitate; it is torn in two, and we see below us a wavy-lined, ice-clad skar, a sea of phantasy, and in it the hull of a storm-struck wreck whose masts are cloud-hidden. A moment only and it is gone. Then, a few seconds later, far, far above the wreck, a small black cross of rock appears, and seems to be looking down upon us. There is no doubt now, there is our goal. Twice, and twice only, we saw this beacon, and only for a few seconds each time during an hour's watching. During this time, however, we saw bit by bit perhaps the whole peak.

I looked eagerly for the snow-belt which, when seen from the Keiser Pass, is such a striking characteristic of Stölsnaastind and which I had imagined would give the solution of the ascent; but though I still believe that this peak can be ascended from the north, and by means of the snow-belt, I then found it to be much steeper than the distant view had led me to suppose; and when, after asking Anfind's opinion as to the mode of ascent, he proposed to try it from the Koldedal glacier, I fully concurred with him.

At 12.45, after a slight snow-shower, we all agreed to attack the mountain, and, if possible, to take it by storm. No thought of turning back was now entertained by Reusch. No, indeed. He had tasted the joys of mountain-climbing in spite of unfavourable weather, and had we needed urging forward, he was ready to use the spur.

We soon reached the Koldedal glacier, and after crossing a few narrow but deep crevasses, we stepped on the rocks on the south side, 892 feet below the summit. Here I asked Anfind to lead, as he would probably have to act as guide in the future, and after a little demur he did so.

We followed ledges, to all appearances systematically arranged to aid in the ascent, on which we placed many *varder* (cairns) to guide us on our return. We could see far up the mountain, but not to the top. Anfind led us well, and brought us on to the narrow eastern arête. Here we turned west, and our climb began to be more arduous, but at the same time more interesting. All who have climbed in Jotunheim know what good rock gabbro is for the purpose, and how well it holds the nails of an alpine boot. Here it was grand. The strong south-west wind added a little spice of danger, the precipice on our right was quite in unison with our undertaking, and a heavy snowstorm when near the top gave variety to our adventure.

Up and still up we went; wilder and wilder grew the storm, denser and yet more dense the clouds, but eager and ever more eager became our zeal for the work.

"Ah! here is the top in front of us. We shall soon see if human foot has ever trod the ground before us. Let us step together, hand in hand on to the top; it is big enough." We do so, and at two o'clock three snow-whitened mortals tread the summit of Stölsnaastind.

Anfind is almost wild with delight, and talks of the number of ladies who he is sure will make the ascent with him when it is known to be so interesting and free from danger. "Wait a bit, old boy, till we get to your sæter. We have still to return by the glacier."

For a moment, the great Gjertvastind with its terrific overhanging precipice stood out clearly from the clouds; so did the long, straight and narrow ridge of Uranaastind, as well as the top of the neighbouring Falke Næbbe; but beyond these, though we felt we were on an almost unrivalled standpoint, we saw no other peak.

A stone man was soon erected, and we fixed on it Anfind's red pocket handkerchief, as a rival of mine of white which was still flying on the top of Skagastölstind, away across Utladal.

We waited patiently a long cold hour for the views which did not appear, and our geologist had ample opportunity to indulge in the innocent pastime of stone-breaking. At three o'clock we began to retrace our steps, and but for our *varder* would have had some difficulty in finding the way. As it was we had none. In thirty-two minutes we reached the glacier, and then turned down north towards Fleskedal. The crevasses were wide, deep, and gloriously blue. We had one snow-bridge to cross, none of the strongest, then a short, steep ice-slope to descend, where I had to make good steps with my ice-axe. Just beyond this we had a jump over a deep schrund, and a view into a fairy blue ice-grotto spanned by a wild snow-arch with many a pendent ice jewel, one of the most interesting crevasses I have ever seen. Reusch was charmed with it, and so were we all.

Near the bottom of the glacier, Anfind advised us to cross the right lateral moraine so as to avoid an ice-fall. This we did, and it brought us to a long snow-slope of some 35°, where we had an excellent glissade which saved much time. In spite of the fact of the long days in Norway, the snow rarely gets in the soft condition which one finds in the Alps in the afternoon. In the case of Norway the rays lose much of their power by shining obliquely on the snowfields; consequently, good glissades, which are not so often obtainable in Switzerland as we should like them to be, are very common in our northern playground.

In two and a half hours of pretty hard going from the summit we entered the Fleskedals sæter, where Anfind's daughters regaled us with wholesome sæter produce, but would hardly credit our tale.

Though a good many men, and a few ladies too, have since climbed Stölsnaastind, the ascent has not yet become a fashionable one, as I expected it would; and for some reason or other comparatively few tourists visit Aardal and the Vettisfos, in fact very few more than was the case twenty-five years ago.

It is perhaps not fair to judge of a view which I have not properly seen, but at the same time I feel I am right in saying that I know of no other peak in Jotunheim whose ascent is of such general interest, lacks actual danger, and gives such a glorious view.

I have often suggested to mountaineers who have applied to me for suggestions about new climbs that a most interesting ascent of Stölsnaastind could be made from out of the wintry Morka-Koldedal; but so far I believe that no one has taken my advice.

Happy thought! Go and do it myself.

Figure 1: William Cecil Slingsby

Figure 2: Falketind today - the Falcon's Beak

Figure 3: The Passage of Morka-Koldedal

Figure 4: Kyrka

Figure 5: Uranostind

— Skagastolstind —

from Vesle Skagastólstind

Figure 6: Skagastolstind

Store Skagastölstind

Original fotografi av
Daniel Enersen

Figure 7: Skagastolstind

Figure 8: The Hurrangane (called Horungtinder by Slingsby)

Figure 9: Above Bodalsaeter - the Bodalsbreen

Descent of Kjændalsbræ

Figure 10: Descent of Kjaendalsbrae

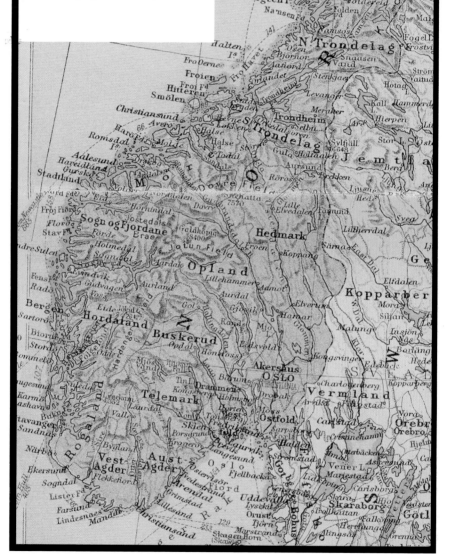

Slingsby's Norway

Southern Norway, at the time of Slingsby's last visit, in 1921.

Chapter 10: Round The Horungtinder In Winter

*"Fine weather for them as is vel wrapped up, as the Polar bear said
ven he was practising his skating."*
Pickwick Papers.

Round. Why round and not over, across, among, in fact anything but the word –
round – which does not suggest adventure? I'll tell you why it was round.

Two summer tours in the Alps had kept me from my first love – Norway. The
fates decreed that a projected tour in the summer of 1880 could not be realised.
Why not accept Sulheim's invitation to join him in another bear-hunting
expedition?

I reached Skjolden at the end of October, and was soon ensconced in Sulheim's
pretty house at Eide and welcomed with thorough Norse hospitality. Vormelid,
outlandish as it is, was to be the base of operations. A day was occupied in
making preparations, in which the greatest care was necessary, for be it
remembered that an empty sæter in winter does not mean *römmegröd* in the
evening round a fire ready prepared by a smiling girl. No indeed. All our food,
warm – that is heavy – clothing, rifles, and what not besides, soon added up to a
heavy weight which we pared down judiciously. Halvar Halvarsen was engaged
as a porter, and Sulheim's horse was to carry our things as far as Helgedal.

Though at Christiania at this time there was warm weather, in Sogn it was far
otherwise. Winter had already set in. The lakes and rivers were hard frozen, and
the crags in Fortunsdal, fringed as they were with huge icicles, played a fitting
prelude to the icy wonders in store for us.

Next day we were up betimes, and at 7.50 started off for our adventures. The
horse, the same which three years earlier had carried us over the Utla when in
flood, had a hard time of it up the Fortun's *galder*, and still worse up to Optun,
where the road was to all intents and purposes a frozen waterfall. Cutting steps
for a horse with an ice-axe was a novelty to me, but our gallant steed quite
understood it, and trod in the steps like an old mountaineer. The two inches of
snow in the lowlands were succeeded by well-nigh two feet as we neared
Turtegrö, and our pace slackened in proportion. At Berge we had borrowed *ski*,
and many were the falls I had before I learned how to use them. The route we

had intended to take was over the Skagastölsbræ into Midt Maradal, and thence by way of Rolandstigen – the bear path – to Vormelid. About twelve hours we thought ought to clear it; but now in deep loose snow, and with our heavy burdens, it was not to be thought of.

Skagastölstind, plastered over with snow or encased in ice, we could see was then impracticable. Near Helgedal sæter the horse broke through the crust of a frozen morass and stuck completely fast: we took off his load and dug him out with our axes – a tiring business – then we gave him half an hour's rest at the sæter and took him on with us. We left the sæter at two o'clock, with no hopes of reaching Vormelid that night, and but faint hopes of Guridal. Seldom did path seem longer than this, and never was distance more deceptive. The depth of the snow was anything between two and six feet, and was too soft for using *ski*.

At four o'clock the last rays of the sun shone on Skagastölstind's glittering crown, and for a half-hour we were partly compensated for our toil by some of the most exquisite sky colouring I have ever seen. Ahead, over the Keiser Pass, was a deep, dark star-spangled blue, which graduated imperceptibly on either hand and in the zenith, through all shades, to the lightest azure, and then through green to gold and carmine over the wavy line of the Justedalsbræ.

The slopes under Fanaraaken were horribly tiring, and recalled the almost interminable snows of Mont Blanc and Monte Rosa. The path was visible, though in deep snow. Our horse went first, and partly paved the way for us. At 5.10, when twilight was fast deepening into the sombre shades of night, and we were still a long way from the top of the pass, we decided to leave our luggage there and to beat a retreat to Helgedal sæter.

The horse was our guide, as it alone could keep to the track in the darkness; and in fact if ever we tried to cut a corner on the zigzags, we were sure to roll head over heels in the snow. Dog-tired we struggled into the sæter one by one between eight and nine o'clock, and passed a night of shivers, with the thermometer at 3° F. below zero outside, and precious little better inside, the only furniture being one chair. There was something very uncanny about the chair, as both of my companions solemnly asserted that on several occasions during the night it moved half-way across the room, backwards and forwards, and made a great noise. Meanwhile I was asleep.

Next morning at 7.30, after Sulheim had bound his legs with hay bands, we parted from our gallant steed and driver, and marched quickly over the now well-trodden path. At 9.45 we gained our baggage, and our toils were renewed. Sulheim and I with *ski* fared better than the overweighted Halvar, who with his *faettersko* (moccasins) sunk up to his middle at every step on the plateau below the tarn. We crossed this instead of following the usual track, as there was less snow there. On the steeps above we had to carry our baggage by instalments, as it was impossible to take it all at once.

At last, at 1.50, the top of the Keiser Pass, 4920 feet, was reached. Yes, think of six hours from the sæter, you who now enjoy the luxuries of Turtegrö, and saunter quietly to the top of this pretty pass in summer's sunshine. Very good going too, was ours. You must not however expect to see such glorious views as we did, or you will be disappointed. Each one of us, used to mountain views as he was, was perfectly enchanted with the peep into Jotunheim. No one who has only seen Stölsnaastind in summer can have even the faintest conception of its majestic form and surroundings in winter, when all the dull brown ridges are transformed into shimmering snow-fields which seem to make the grand pyramid stand out in the blue vault of heaven to all appearances 12,000 feet in height, and a very Matterhorn in form. The sun gilded its proud crest and also the summit of Uranaastind, the Melkedalstind, and many another fine mountain, whilst their lower precipices looked by contrast colder and more terrible than ever.

It must not be supposed that all was white, for such a condition would indeed be monotony. No. Those dark precipices, which each Jotunheim peak possesses on one or more sides, can never hold snow, they can only be peppered as it were, and their swarthy sides do but enhance the purity of the eternal snows above. I wish that each one of my readers could at least once in his life see such a scene as this, for even if he saw no other this one would be enough to awaken in him a love of mountain scenery which could only end at his death. But this may not be.

The cold did not allow us to linger over our well-earned lunch, and even during the few minutes we spent there, a change as of a kaleidoscope came over the scene as the bright gold vanished from the mountain-tops, and dark shadows crept stealthily up the grim Utladal, warning us to hasten, and proclaiming at the same time that winter in all its grandeur reigned supreme.

My *ski* gave me many a fall but plenty of fun, and we sped quickly down the snow slopes to Guridal. Here we left most of our baggage and our *ski*, and determined to reach Vormelid that night at any price. Now, as Sulheim's associations with Vormelid were bright, warm, and sunny he was bitterly disappointed to find that the snow was as deep in the Utladal gorge as on the high *fjeld*, and that it was weary plodding through the pinewoods. A bright *Aurora borealis* was our only light, and we were thankful to have it. Many a time we rolled head over heels in the snow, and but for Sulheim's excellent guiding qualities we should have failed to reach our haven of rest. At 9.10 we stumbled, tumbled, and rolled into Vormelid, tired out and with no rosy-cheeked *pige* (girl) to welcome us and to minister to our wants. No, alas!

Whilst the others were kindling a fire I undertook to fetch water. Where was it gone to? The usual trough was dry, but far below the snow I heard a gurgling. After many vain attempts I made a well with my ice-axe; but before I could bring a pail from the hut close by, the water was hard frozen and had to be broken again. Fatigue was soon forgotten before a repast of soup, corned beef, and other good things. When broken window-panes were stopped up, a snow-drift removed from the floor, the hay on the bed turned and fresh logs thrown on the fire, we went to bed. As it was too narrow for us all to lie the same way, Halvar lay dovetailed with his head at our feet, and we all had to lie more or less edgewise; but tired men soon sleep.

In the morning we put our castle in order and received a welcome visitor in the form of a beautiful Titmouse (*Parus major*) which hopped about everywhere picking up crumbs and fat, and this visitor remained with us most of the time we spent at Vormelid. A pair of Water-ouzels hopped about outside, but could not be coaxed to come in, though they must have been very hungry. Sulheim and I then set off to seek for "Herr Bamsen" (bear) down the valley. We often crossed the Utla, which instead of being a large, muddy, and furious glacier river, was now a peaceful frozen stream of purest blue water. After hours of hard scrambling to and fro we found ourselves near the top of Kirkestigen, where twice before I had scared away a bear. Now our wish will be realised. Ah! vain hope, not a trace could we find. We descended by a very difficult snow couloir, and were glad of our axes, and a little depressed in spirits we reached Vormelid at nightfall.

Profiting by experience, as my knees had been cold the first night, I adorned myself for bed as follows, with three pairs of stockings, two pairs of very warm nether garments, trousers and woollen leggings, and then put my feet into the arms of my coat and buttoned it up, over my knees; next I had two jerseys, a very thick *Islandströie* (Iceland jersey), two shirts, a waistcoat, an overcoat with a hood for my head, a knitted cap over my ears, and warm gloves. I spread my plaid over all three of us. Then! What then? – Sleep.

Next day we were to search some caves under Friken. All tourists who have walked over the track between Vetti and Skogadalsböen know what an awful precipice there is above the Utla on that side, and that it must be difficult to ascend or descend in summer. Such is indeed the case. Fancy then what it must be in winter, the snow knee-deep over icy debris, the trees bowed down with their snowy burden, so low and so thick too that extraordinary contortions have to be performed to get through, over or under them with rifle and ice-axe in hand.

We crossed the river just below the crag on which the sæter is perched. The snow had blown off the ice, and we could see through this glassy covering to the bottom of the river, perhaps twenty-five feet deep. About 1000 feet above the Utla we reached a steep bare slope which had been cleared of trees by an ancient avalanche. Crowning this slope, which gradually increases in steepness, is a lofty cliff, at the base of which is a ledge and the cave Troldhullet, which can be seen from Vormelid. Here we were to meet Herr Bamsen, not exactly by appointment, but because we had made up our minds to meet him there. Sulheim had seen him near there in the summer, and had found traces of him in the cave. Surely he could not disappoint us this time?

Many of my readers know what it is to climb a long snowslope of 40° or 45°, and that care is needed when the snow is in good order. Here the snow was soft, much of it had to be kicked away, and the angle was certainly over 45°; in fact it was as steep as the top of the grand snow-gullies one meets with on the north face of Ben Nevis in the early spring. We were carrying rifles too, and were on the tiptoe of expectancy, and who could say whether Bruin was awaiting us securely entrenched above, and sleeping with the proverbial one eye open? At first Sulheim leads and hacks out steps carefully in the snow, and as we approach the top the angle becomes very steep. Then I come abreast of him, and hardly daring to draw a breath, we press noiselessly upward with our rifles in front and triggers at full cock. Only two feet more and we can look over. The top is like a wave of snow ready to break upon us, and horribly steep. Step by step we take together by instinct. We each scoop out a large last step with an ice-axe, then carefully get into it stooping, and after a hasty glance at our rifles and at each other, we raise ourselves slowly and look over the top. Is he there? If he be, he's gone "i hi" (hibernated), and has been asleep some time, as the mouth of the cave is guarded by a seeming portcullis of icicles. We carefully look, and see at the entrance the bones of Sulheim's best calf, but Bamsen is away. Shall I say that we were much disappointed? Yes. Shall I also say that the disappointment was tempered by a feeling of relief that our shaggy friend had not pounced upon us, as he easily could have done, either on the narrow ledge or on the snow-slope, where he would have had nearly all his own way? Yes, a thousand times yes. When we had time to look around we found many rowan berries and angelica growing quite near and untouched. Evidently our friend had retired elsewhere soon after his feast of veal, or such vegetable dainties would not have remained undisturbed.

The view from the cave was magnificent. The birch-trees, oddly enough, were still in full and golden leaf in spite of winter, and formed a lovely contrast to the ice, snow, and dark crags around. The sæter huts of Vormelid appeared like two rocks far, far below us.

We decided to hunt for spoor up in Uradal. For nearly an hour we had some interesting and difficult climbing along the narrow ledge, where there was mostly a sharp ridge of hard snow glazed with ice from the drip of the icicle-fringed cliffs. In several places the icicles completely barred the way and had to be knocked down. The ledge wound at first gently and then steeply upwards. By dint of climbing, creeping, and holding on, we managed to get along, but were very glad to reach the little plateau by the bridge over the Uradöla.

In Uradal – the valley of debris – a heavy snowstorm came on, and we wished ourselves back at Vormelid. As I did not relish the notion of descending by the way we had come, I proposed another but longer route. Sulheim would not hear of it; the Viking's blood was up, so I merely thought "in for a penny, in for a pound," and agreed to follow him. We soon reached our *"pons asinorum"* or rather *"pons ursae,"* and with care got well over it. On the way down we saw several thousand little chirping reddish birds, presumably Lesser red-polls.

A strong wind had drifted the snow most alarmingly about the sæter, and there seemed to be every probability that we should be imprisoned there indefinitely. In the evening Halvar set to work to make snow-shoes, and I gave one of my many lessons in English to Sulheim, while the wilder the night wind howled the more we piled up birch logs on the fire and determined to be jolly, and we succeeded too.

Sunday was a day of much-needed rest. In fact the weather would hardly have allowed of anything else. Like a luxurious mortal I had breakfast in bed, chicken, coffee, and toast. Sulheim had never seen bread toasted before, and was much pleased when I gave him some the first day. I wore a pair of træsko – sabots – all day. When not engaged in cooking, we sang and read. Dinner was a great success. Water was difficult to get out of the snow-drifts, and water-fetching was one of my duties.

As there were no traces of Bruin about Vormelid, there was no object in staying longer than necessary. What next? The Keiser Pass again? No, no – the mere thought of it was enough to make us shudder. Sulheim and I understood one another's thoughts on the subject. Each loved adventure. What could we do better than to try to reach Vetti by way of the Vetti's gjæl, and complete our explorations of this marvellous cañon? As the crow flies the distance is insignificant, not above seven English miles, and the ice on the river might make easy what in summer is no doubt impracticable.

Next day, November 1st, three heavily laden mortals bade adieu to Vormelid at 8.30, and very soon each plunged up to the neck in snow. What matter? "Fram." Sulheim, as a Viking of ancient days, insisted on leading. Soon, on the river, we got along cheerily over the snow. Then came a rapid, beautifully frozen and clear of snow. What a pretty embattled tower of blue ice right across the river! Ice-axes helped us down, and again we went quickly along. A Dipper, Fosse konge – or king of the waterfall – as he is often called, kept flying and stopping just in front of us, and reminded me of scenes at home.

In little more than an hour we came near the most contracted part of Utladal at the foot of Kirkestigen, where I had been both with Mohn and also with Sulheim. Here the huge rock Kirketaarn, over a shoulder of which the waters from Midt Maradal tumble a little over a thousand feet into a shoreless pool of the Utla, are confronted with a rocky buttress which is backed by the most, uncompromising cliffs on the eastern side.

When we reached the buttress, the river no longer offered a safe passage, as an unfrozen rapid cut off our icy highway effectually. How could we reasonably expect it to be otherwise, as nowhere else have I ever seen debris of such colossal proportions, a very Karnac of nature's ruins? The Alps can show nothing like it. Indeed they can do very well without. If the reader can imagine himself wandering amongst chaotic heaps of rock, from the size of a piano to a large sæter-hut piled up a couple of hundred feet in height, and all covered, first with thick moss and then with two feet of snow, he can form only a faint idea of the work which lay before us. Our rifles were a great nuisance. In one place we had to climb over a rock about a hundred feet high, a very awkward place too. It was cruel work, but we felt that we must not grumble. We lunched in the middle of the river under the lee of a monster rock, and reconnoitred the buttress across.

Our lunch ended, we crossed the river, a difficult matter, and our real work began. We put our baggage under a rock, and Sulheim, who still insisted on taking the lead, was then bound fast with the rope, and during the space of forty minutes did some of the most brilliant climbing I have ever seen. The first difficulty was in climbing over an overhanging rock only about fifteen feet above where I stood. Very little, is it not? Don't say so till you see it. The slope below me was about 55°, and it was one of those indescribable places where it was impossible to give a helping hand to the man above. As to a shoulder? Why, it was out of the question, as the climbing had to be done in zigzag. The slope was too steep to hold deep snow. Still, where we had to climb it must be all cleared off, as we below found to our cost; then ice appeared, and it too had to be demolished. After twenty minutes the first rope's-length was consumed [21], a small platform was reached, and I can truly say that even with the aid of this rope, and with a by no means limited experience, I felt delighted when I had crossed that true *mauvais pas*, where a ledge in the rock half an inch wide was considered to be capital foothold.

With all this cold work my hands were getting frost-bitten, and I shall never forget our leader rubbing life into them with his own great warm hands. The baggage was hauled up, and then came Halvar in his fættersko, and how he came up in this extraordinary foot-gear I could never tell. We then had about forty feet more in the same style, except that here and there was a little vegetation below the snow. This length was up a straight gully, where I was able to give Sulheim a knee and then a shoulder as steps, after which he got safe anchorage and piloted me up. This process was repeated two or three times until finally Sulheim reached a birch-tree to which we lashed the rope and then drew up the baggage and Halvar. Though this gully was easier than the first pitch, it was difficult climbing and had a minimum of foothold. It had taken us fifty minutes of real hard work to climb a height of not more than seventy feet to the birch-tree, which gives a faint idea of the difficulties. My companions went grandly and never hesitated a moment, and I felt that with two such men so staunch and true, I could safely trust myself on the Weisshorn or Dent Blanche.

After ten minutes more of most enjoyable climbing along a narrow ledge and up a gully, where little trees helped us, at one o'clock we stood in a small gap at the top of the buttress. We were satisfied with our progress and deemed Vetti to be almost within our grasp, because ahead down the valley I recognised a pulpit-like rock on which I had stood on three different occasions, and which I knew to be *vis à vis* to the Vetti's fos.

We afterwards learnt, when Vormelid was a gaard and not a sæter as now, a man once went down the river in winter, climbed up to the gap from the back, then down to our friendly birch-tree, to which he affixed a long rope, by means of which the little pass was often used to fetch "næver" [22] and grass down. A few years ago I led a party of climbers up to Ossian's cave in Glencoe in deep snow, and was struck with the resemblance that climb, which under the best conditions is by no means easy, bore, when ice-bound, to the more difficult buttress in Utladal.

Over our gap we entered what bear-hunters call Baglien, a large horseshoe basin, backed by huge cliffs on all sides save the south, up which the summer sun must shine most powerfully, hence the enormous trees we met with, elms and birches of a size I have seen nowhere else in Norway. Many birches still showed scars inflicted on them by the "næver" cutters of old. I pointed out the scars to Sulheim as a proof that the Vetti folk were wont to come there. Tall fronds of *Osmunda regalis* cropped up above the snow, and wild raspberries, with their crystallised fruit still hanging on, grew everywhere. Huge trunks of noble elms lay where they had fallen a century ago, and between them was scarcely two feet of snow, which made it hard work to walk.

The Midt Maradalsfos, a grand fall close at hand and sparkling in the sunshine, was a gigantic pilaster of ice over a thousand feet high from the frozen pool of the Utla to the rock edge above. Close to this Mohn and I had experienced great difficulty in crossing the river in 1876. The ice masses piled up in the ravine just below Kirketaarn and at the foot of the fos were marvellously beautiful in colour and form.

I was the only one who knew anything whatever of the valley below, and my knowledge was limited to sundry views of it from the top of the cliffs, 1400 to 1500 feet above the river on both sides, generally in bad weather.

"Halloo! Here are footmarks; we're all right, and shall be in Vetti before dark."
"But where on earth do they lead to?"
"Ah! see, Herr Bamsen at last; those steps are his. Hang it! they're a day or two old, though."

We followed the spoor some little time, but it led upwards, and as we dared not spare any more time, we left the tracks. The beautiful and fertile slopes of well-sheltered Baglien soon changed to horrible screes, and we did not like to descend to the river some three hundred feet below us, where there was easy going, as we saw a place ahead where we should be obliged to keep up. Hour after hour sped by as we struggled on across spurs and gullies, the difficulties increasing as our strength and power to overcome them decreased. I pitied Halvar very much as he was carrying a cruelly heavy load, but I could not help him as I myself was overweighted. Though the pulpit rock seemed to get no nearer, a huge crag ahead of us looked more and more impracticable every minute. Except in one place this crag, which rose straight out of the river, was quite clear of snow and hence impassable; this one place seemed to be a narrow ledge about half-way up, and then, so far as we could tell in the deepening twilight, bare rock seemed to intervene and cut the path short. There was no hope of getting along on the river nor yet on the other side, where for a distance of about four miles the precipices are quite mural in character and from 1100 to 2000 feet in height.

Matters began to look serious, the debris got worse, and monster elm-trees, crossed over each other, lay on the ground like spilikins where they had fallen ages ago. The interstices were filled with snow, and falls were common. The time was 4.30, and it seemed an act of unpardonable foolhardiness to attempt a second difficult climb, in the dark too, and one where there was but faint hope of success. We were also coming to a part of the gorge from whence it would be nearly impossible to take refuge in the high-level or Friken route. Nothing seemed left to us but to find out a good camping-place, to stop the night there, and to take to the high level in the morning while we could get to it.

Far above us was a long line of lofty crags rising out of the screes. Surely here we could find a hole? We climbed up a slippery gully where Halvar once came down neck and crop and much alarmed us. However, like a good mountaineer he remembered his axe and soon brought himself to an anchor.

At 5.30, in pitch darkness, we climbed up a snow slope much like the one below Troldhullet, and by sheer good luck we discovered by match-light a most palatial residence, the drainage and ventilation of which would have satisfied the most exacting of sanitary inspectors. The cave was a long broad opening in the rock, going about 15 feet back and about 8 feet high in front, perfectly dry and well sheltered by projecting crags. A bright fire was soon ablaze, as fuel was abundant. We were all nearly worn out, but still Sulheim, always ready, went to prospect a gully by candle-light for the morrow, found it hopeless, and then tried another which he reported as hopeful. "Now for some tea."

"Where's the kettle?" said Sulheim.
"Here it is," I replied, holding up a small round meat-tin.
Sulheim pointed to a large unopened six-pound tin of Chicago beef. He soon cut it in two, took out the meat from one end, and said: "This is the kettle."

"Will you have snow for water?" asked Halvar.
"No, we won't," replied Sulheim and I together, each breaking off an icicle; "here's something better."

In a few minutes water was boiling. The icicles were most useful, because when the water threatened to boil over, the tip of an icicle was just dipped in and it cooled at once.

Knowing that we should be imprisoned for at least twelve hours we determined to keep up a roaring fire and to make a festive night of it. Lucky we were to have such ponderous baggage. Let the cold do its worst, we were prepared for it. When three hours had quickly sped away we resolved to prepare a grand midnight dinner. I was chief cook. As kettle number one was getting superannuated we requisitioned number two – the other end of the meat-tin.

Our menu comprised all the dainties of the season – in Utladal.

Soup	Julienne.
Fish	Sardines.
Entrées	Devilled chicken and tongue.
Joints	Chicago corned beef.
Dessert	Crystallised raspberries– chocolate.

After dinner we had tea, coffee, toasted bread, and fladbröd.

The bright fire made the icicles above melt now and then, but we easily avoided the drip. Candles illuminated our palace, and we read a good deal. I was reading *The Last Days of Pompeii*, and found it exciting enough. We sang songs and scraps of songs innumerable and hymns, both Norse and English. Sulheim had taken a great fancy to "Home, Sweet Home," some days earlier, and I had sung it about six times through every evening. Now, as may well be imagined, we had a double dose, and our hero learned the words and the tune very thoroughly, as many of my friends can testify.

Poor Halvar, the only smoker amongst us, had exhausted his supply of tobacco. Seeing my tea, he thought it looked smokeable, tried it, and pronounced it to be excellent. As it kept well lit and made smoke, what more could be desired? We formed a suitable subject for an artist, and I much wished for the power to put upon paper so picturesque a scene. Halvar had a most incongruous get-up with rough homespun clothes, cloth leggings tied round with string, huge yellow cowskin shoes with a lining of straw, and a skin cap over his ears. Sulheim had a red Sogn *toplue* – woollen nightcap – which looked delightfully warm. I had my Iceland jersey, hooded plaided coat, and Alpine knitted cap. The rifles, ice-axes, and rope all conspired to give a brigandish appearance to the place, whilst the icicles gave it the appearance of a Yorkshire limestone stalactite cavern.

All things must come to an end; so did this night. In fact our twelve hours sped away quickly and pleasantly, and luckily there had only been 22 degrees of frost. After a breakfast in the dark we got under weigh about 6 a.m., and set off in twilight to scale the crags above us. Our difficulties began directly, and for three and a half hours the rope and axes were indispensable. Whilst the birch-trees, that grew wherever there were crevices large enough for their roots, were often a horrible nuisance, still oftener did they render rocks practicable, which otherwise could not have been tackled at all.

The baggage had generally to be hauled up by two of us, whilst the third tied it fast below. The mountain-side consisted of a series of low perpendicular crags, connected with each other by steep scene-slopes, where ling, juniper, and birches grew. The mean gradient could not have been less than 55 degrees, and I shall never forget the grand climbing of my companions. Had we anticipated such difficulties, we should either have tried to force a passage across the river-bed or rather farther up the valley. As it was, we expected each obstacle to be the last, but no! one crag surmounted, another appeared.

Once we much feared for our rifles. By help of convenient birch-trees Sulheim had climbed a crag about twenty feet above us. We were at its foot, standing on next to nothing, and holding our treasures to prevent them rolling a couple of thousand feet below. The whole rock was hung with beautiful icicles, and the top part of the crag overhung, and so did the icicles. We knocked away all the dangerous ice within our reach, but the big fellows near the top we could not manage, and our rifles must be hauled up over them. The first went up grandly, but the second sent down an ice-spear which only just missed Halvar's head. Then we sent up a knapsack, which knocked down a shower of ice. After this I went up by the tree route to help to haul up Halvar's nondescript load and the remaining knapsack. There was little to stand on, and only a rotten tree to hold to. This sort of work was repeated again and again, and about 9.30 we stood amongst the pine-trees on less vicious ground, where we coiled up the rope and shouldered our burdens, overjoyed with our victory and with the grand view of the Horungtinder, standing up proudly in the clear blue sky and looking double the height they do in summer.

We found fresh bear spoor, but as it led down a gully we had not the pluck to follow it.

The tramp to Vettismarken sæter which we reached at 1.20 through deep snow, was the most arduous physical exertion I had ever endured, and though the previous year with a friend and two Swiss guides I had crossed Mont Blanc in one day of twenty-two hours from Courmayeur to Chamouni by the old Aiguille Grise route, and had carried a knapsack much of the time, that day was an easy one physically speaking compared with this tramp in Norway.

We went to the top of the Vetti's fos and enjoyed for a few stolen minutes the marvellous view, and then hurried on to find the top of the zigzag path before dark. Though I had often been on this weird path in summer, it is certain that, but for finding some old footmarks in the snow, we should have been benighted within sight of Vetti; as it was, it was difficult to keep to the path when rightly started.

At 5.30 we were heartily welcomed by friends at the old house at Vetti, as the first persons who had ever paid them a visit in winter.

The bear, whose tracks we had seen, had been at Vetti a few days before, and had been followed by two hunters, as far as the time allowed them to go, to a place above Baglien.

As to the passage of Utladal itself, it appears that some fifty years ago Jorgen Vetti and a brother went the whole way to Vormelid and back in one day about Christmas on the river, which was all hard frozen and free from snow. This is the only known passage. Bear-hunters have, however, now and then gone up the gorge as far as Baglien, and thus have crossed the rock which turned us aside, but that was when there was no snow. As far as this rock either side of the river is fairly easy, but rough, from Vetti. I hope some day to complete my exploration, which now only requires about an English mile.

Next morning young Nils Vetti, armed with crampons, went with us to see the Vetti's fos from below, and as Sulheim and I are the only tourists who have seen this grand waterfall in winter, a few words about it may not be amiss.

The jet-black semicircular cliff, over one corner of which the river takes its headlong leap of a thousand feet into space, is now well known to many tourists. Many too have peered over that highest place just opposite the fos, where a stone, simply dropped out of the hand, passes through more than 1100 feet before it touches the rock. Let them now picture, if they can, a colossal pilaster of ice from the bottom of the fos to the top. This has millions of ice jewels hanging in festoons from it, from the size of a finger of ice to grand fluted stalactites one hundred and fifty feet long, and each fluting is fringed with lovely ice embroidery. The colouring is every shade of blue to purest pearly-white like the colours visible in a large crevasse. To the left of the fall a series of gilded icicles nearly one hundred feet in height hang from the lip of rock, the result of peaty water which has trickled over the edge and then frozen. At the bottom of the fall there is a small glacier formed from frozen spray. A little water is still falling over the top, but the bulk of it falls in fine snowflakes around us. The whole scene is grand beyond description.

In summer the Vetti's fos is essentially a beautiful fall, as nearly all the elements of natural beauty are to be seen in its surroundings, and I am not sure whether, taking all in all, it is not the most beautiful fall in Norway. No doubt the best time for most people to see it is in the early summer when the snows on the uplands are melting fast, but let those who love Nature in her wildest moods pay a visit to this and to other grand waterfalls in the winter, and I can assure them that they will not be disappointed.

All chance of bear-hunting from Vetti for some time to come was dissipated by another heavy snowstorm. Indeed the cute beast would most likely have gone "i hi," as hibernation would certainly be preferable to starvation.

To Aardal then was the only possible move. The ghyll, grand as it is in summer, was now magnificent. Each black crag had its festoons of icicles, each rapid its towers of ice. The Afdal's fos, of course, was frozen solid and very beautiful. Still nothing could equal the sublimity of the Vetti's fos or the weird grandeur of Baglistigen which we had left behind.

A storm prevented us getting over the Aardals vand, which lake was still ice-free, though oddly enough the bays in the Lysterfjord were frozen, so we spent a lively evening and a restful night with Ole Hestetun at Farnæs where we met with one of the guides who had been with "Coutts" up Skagastölstind, and who gave us a very lucid and amusing account of the expedition.

Ole's excess of hospitality caused us to miss by ten minutes a steamer at Aardal, which in turn made me miss the fortnightly boat from Bergen to Hull.

We went by slow stages to Skjólden and arrived only just in time to prevent a search party being sent after us on account of the intense cold and snowstorms. Letters from England which had been on the boat that we missed, required my return home as early as possible, otherwise we should have gone again to the mountains, as rain had fallen, succeeded by hard frost which had consolidated the snow.

I then undertook a very cold journey over a partly frozen fjord and a long sledge drive over the Fille Fjeld to Hallingdal, in a howling snowstorm, when the horses had icicles a foot in length hanging from their nostrils, and the postman and I barely escaped bad frost-bites. In Hallingdal I had superb weather, and at Christiania the frost was several degrees below zero. On the North Sea I came in for the end of a terrible storm, and saw several derelict fishing-smacks out at sea, and many wrecks at the mouth of the Humber, a very sad sight.

This is a plain unvarnished account of an expedition of failures, but yet one of much pleasure and of genuine adventure, which bequeathed to each of us a legacy of health, strength, and most pleasant memories.

I cannot speak too highly of my two companions. Sulheim's climbing was really superb, and would have elicited praise from an Anderegg, an Almer, or an Andermatten, if such heroes of the Alps could have seen him at work. As for Halvar the brave, the patient, the strong. Well! he was absolutely the best porter I have ever had. He was always willing, obliging, and cheerful even on the most trying occasions. I never saw any man in my life work harder, or carry a heavy load upon such arduous and difficult climbing, yet no murmur ever escaped his lips, and he was always ready for an adventure. Sulheim and he together formed the best Norse climbing combination I have ever seen, but though I have had many a good climb since with Sulheim, I have never had the good fortune to have Halvar as well. Halvar was asked to form one of Nansen's party in the expedition across Greenland, but – to my mind foolishly – he refused.

Though I can hardly recommend anyone to follow our footsteps literally, I can do so to a certain extent. Say, for example, take a run on *ski* over Lake Tyin and through Morka-Koldedal to Vetti in fine weather in January or February when the snow is in good order, and see undreamt-of mountain views where each peak with its lengthened shadows looks at least double its usual height, twice as difficult to climb, and three times more beautiful than in July – then thank me for the suggestion. Sleeping at Tvindehougen and at Vetti, this would be a most enjoyable three days' expedition, which could be done easily in the short days if the snow were hard.

Chapter 11: Tunsbergdal To Loendal And Mountaineering From Gjendebod

"Mean thralls alone will to their mother-soil be chained unwilling; I will wander free, free as the mountain winds."
Frithiof 's Saga, translated by Rev. W. L. BLACKLEY.

"The glacier's cold and restless mass
Moves onward day by day."
BYRON.

On Sunday, August 14, 1881, Johannes Vigdal, a promising guide joined me at Skjolden and, as he expressed his willingness to follow my lead wherever I chose to go, I felt sure that a good time was in store for us. This was fully realised, and the campaign which we were entering upon proved to be one of the best I have ever had.

We took a boat to Röneid. The first hour we conversed in English, but it was hard work and did not pay, so we changed to Norse and continued it to the end. After a drive of about a Norse mile we left the main valley, turning up the narrow Leirdal, and after fifty minutes' walk we reached the Leirgaard.

A lad rowed us over the icy waters of a lake, and we ascertained that at the bottom of Tværdal there was a sæter, not shown on the map, and that we should find folk there. Tunsbergdal into which we had now entered proved to be mainly one huge bog covered with pathless brushwood, though there is good grazing here and there. The State usually keeps one or more entire horses here for the benefit of the farmers in Indre Sogn.

About 10 p.m. we got clear of the bush on a large terminal moraine, and saw towering above us and glittering in the starlight an escarpment of rugged ice, a noble termination to a noble glacier. Our destination was Tværdal, a tributary valley west, but the snout of the great glacier overlapped the mouth of it, and we could not at first see how to reach it in the dark. We made several futile attempts to climb the rocks near the ice, and just when we were getting disheartened we found a pathway up the glaciated rocks, and at 10.50 were welcomed by a most hospitable old woman to the luxuries of a good building with a boarded floor, which we who know what sæter life is like thoroughly appreciated.

Next morning we were up at three, and Vigdal wisely put some nails in his boots whilst our hostess prepared us some delicious coffee. At four we sallied out into the clear cold air, not knowing what would be our ultimate destination, but determined to explore the great unknown Tunsbergdalsbræ. After a descent of ten minutes we reached the ice just above its terminal ice-fall; but we should have done rather better if we had ascended about one hundred feet from the sæter to a ledge of rock from which the glacier can be easily gained.

We hacked our way upon the ice, but were obliged to leave it directly in order to turn some large crevasses. Soon we were jogging along at the rate of a good four and half miles an hour. The glacier much resembles the Aletsch glacier above the Märjelen See, and is fairly flat for some eight or nine miles. As it is almost straight, its beauty cannot compare with that of the serpentine Nygaardsbræ, nor with the Austerdalsbræ which has such a lovely sweep. The level and even surface of the Tunsbergdalsbrær causes it to be a singularly easy glacier to traverse.

On either side there are fine precipices, and on the west is a narrow cul-de-sac of rock fringed with ice. At 6.15 we enjoyed an alpine sunrise, the beauty of which cannot be realised until seen. While it is yet twilight, the sun suddenly touches the snowy crown of the highest peak with a soft rose colour, which insensibly spreads down the mountain, and as it does so the colour of the snow passes through the softest gradations and most delicate tints to pure glistening white at last. Each peak in order of height receives the gladdening rays, and whilst the stars fade one by one away, bright daylight takes the place of brilliant starlight, and warmth often replaces bitter cold.

The head of the glacier expands like a fan and is connected by steep rolling snow-fields, divided by ribs of rock, with the parent snows above. On the east side, just under some high cliffs, there were some tiny tarns of dark blue water which were held up by the glacier. We left the bare ice of the flat glacier and had a steep pull up rocks and snow, and at 8.25 we reached the top of the ridge, over which we could see the glaciers of Krondal. Here we built our cairn, had breakfast, and put on the rope.

At 9.10 we set off on the snow towards what was marked on the map as "Bræen's höieste Punkt, 6495 feet," apparently an hour's trudge. What wonder that we should bend our steps there and so probably score another maiden ascent?

At noon we felt that we were actually on the top, but it was about the most topless mountain I had ever been on. Used as I was to large expanses of snow, I was not prepared to see such a white Sahara as this. Excepting Lodals Kaupe, ten miles away, and some rocks north-west, there was nothing to be seen but undulating wastes of snow on every hand for many miles. All the neighbouring valleys had apparently vanished; and many snow-fields, far away beyond the Justedalsbræ proper, seemed on account of their extraordinary similarity in height and rounded forms to be really one huge snow waste. It was in some respects a most impressive view, and I am glad to have seen it. Nowhere else on the Justedalsbræ can you get the same idea of enormous space, and nowhere else are you so much impressed with the solemnity and solitude of the high mountains.

> *"Snows swell on snows amazing to the sky;*
> *And icy mountains high on mountains pil'd*
> *Seem to the shivering sailor from afar,*
> *Shapeless and white, an atmosphere of clouds."*

We prodded our axes as deep as we could in many places on this marvellous plateau, but could never touch the rock. Who can tell how deep these snows are here, 50 feet or 500? Even on the comparatively narrow ridge which forms the summit of Mont Blanc, where the wind can blow the snow over the steep slopes either into Italy or France, M. Jansen and his engineer, M. Eiffel, failed to reach a rock foundation for a proposed observatory. Here on the Justedalsbræ, if the north wind blows the snow a mile away from the top, a south wind may blow it back again the following day. It may be drifted about backwards and forwards, but there is no precipice near for it to be blown over, and in all probability the depth of snow is immense.

We steered towards the rocks north-west, and longed for ski. For perhaps two miles, not a crevasse was to be seen, and for one and a half hours we hardly descended at all.

All at once a snowy bay opened out before us, with a view of séracs, and rocks far down below. Just at first we did not know which valley lay before us, steering with a small compass on a waste of snow like this and with no landmarks whatever is not child's play.

It proved to be the Kjændalsbræ. Six years earlier my sister and I had climbed several hundred feet up this glacier from the foot. Naturally enough I had then examined the glacier critically, and thought that a pass could possibly be forced up it, if the seracs at the top could be avoided. At that time, however, there was very much snow on the glacier. After a little deliberation we decided to try the descent. In the morning we had had enough of the ordinary glacier work to give Vigdal confidence in his guide, and me in my pupil.

At 2.40 we reached the bare ice, about 3050 feet above the foot of the glacier as I afterwards proved. By zigzagging we got along merrily for nearly an hour, and then were driven to the rocks on Nonsnibba, just where the glacier became a magnificent ice-fall. At first we got along well and then came to steep glaciated rocks. We had some difficult places where a rope to help the first man down and an axe-head for the second were a *sine qua non*. We had turned the ice-fall, but now there was a bend in the glacier to the left, and we could not guess what there was ahead.

At 4.10 we came to a genuine West Justedal precipice, hundreds of feet without a ledge. What now? To the ice? Horrid thought! The precipice projected into the glacier, cutting it partially in two. Here we saw the glacier for the first time in profile, and I have rarely seen such weird, clean, and broken seracs. It was about two-thirds of the mean width of the Schwarz glacier, below the Schwarz Thor, but infinitely steeper and generally as much broken as the Glacier des Bossons. Here and there it was cut nearly in two by cliffs in its rocky bed, over which avalanches fell every few minutes. The whole was wedged in between two walls of rock, 1½ miles apart at the top, in true Norse fashion almost ledgeless, and only a quarter of a mile apart near the bottom.

Immediately in front of us were two narrow towers of ice which I can even now picture distinctly. They were 25 to 30 feet high and about 12 feet apart. The lower one was perched on the top of the cliff, and seemed ready to fall at any minute. Between these we must go or nowhere else. To the ice, or a night of shivering on the cold rocks. The distance between the towers was only about twenty yards, but surely that was far enough to run the gauntlet? After a moment's natural hesitation we got to work. We had to go a-straddle along a sharp ridge of ice and to climb up and down over many angular hummocks with the towers and huge icicles overhanging us. Once the rope got round a knob, and we spent an anxious time disentangling it. After some five minutes we emerged very thankfully from a place which possessed much of grim interest, though it was certainly dangerous.

Then we had to creep under an ice-table some 12 feet long, safe itself but with a crevasse underneath. Below us was a chaos of ice impossible to tackle, so we descended diagonally about 200 feet until we reached the trough of the glacier, when we went down some small avalanche debris for several hundred feet, and so got below the cliffs. Soon we had hundreds of steps to cut among the seracs, and had to leap and climb into and out of numberless crevasses. It was all hard blue ice, and we worked like trolds, each thoroughly trusting the other. Every trace of the fatigue which we had felt on the snow had long ago been driven away by the excitement. In a place like this two men can go twice as fast as a party of four. We fled to the rocks again, and by them scored some 500 feet more, when suddenly we were brought to a halt by another line of cliffs, higher than the previous ones. This was a dreadful disappointment, and again we were forced to seek the icy highway. Close to us was a hollow in the ice, a regular avalanche track, and in it a considerable stream of water which fell as a splendid cataract over the cliff visible from the valley below. Across this hollow was a second line of cliffs almost surrounded by glacier. In the face of this remarkable rock we saw a ledge running apparently diagonally down towards another avalanche lane below. Above the ledge there was an overhanging rock. Here we must try or nowhere else. Strangely enough there was no choice. Though there was what at first sight appeared to be an easy way leading into the centre of the glacier at the top of the rock, it was constantly being swept by avalanches.

The chances seemed against success, but there is nothing like trying. To the ledge then, but with much doubting. Vigdal was ready, and I was proud of his companionship. The stream paved with ice was difficult to cross, but we managed it and were soon under the ice of the overhanging rock. The ledge, a mere groove cut into the face of the rock, twelve feet deep, two feet wide and about twenty-five yards long, was no myth, and we crawled along it without difficulty and in perfect safety though a regular avalanche track was just a few feet above our heads and a frightful abyss was below us. Water and chips of ice, large and small, kept falling over us, but it merely added to the interest, and we were quite safe. At the end of the ledge, a jump of six feet on to the powdered ice in the avalanche lane, little as it seems, was no joke. Vigdal lowered me and held me unnecessarily fast while a stream of iced water trickled down my neck. Then I helped him down, and we glissaded down the lane. Near the bottom I got one foot fast in a tiny crevasse, and we had to dig it out with our axes. Needless to say we wasted no time over the process.

We had now turned our precipice, waterfall, and third ice fall. Surely now we were safe! We were on a long ice plateau the existence of which is quite unsuspected from below. Now we began to admire the grandeur of our surroundings, and to watch the avalanches fall in quick succession over crags which here and there broke up the eastern side of the glacier, the opposite side to that which we had descended. Kjændals Krone looked from here a grand mountain rising nearly 4000 feet, straight out of the ice, and, though such was not actually the case, it appeared to tower far above the snow-fields.

But night was coming on; we must hasten. Where we could do so we ran. We steeplechased over scores of crevasses and threaded our way through an intricate maze, when lo! an open-jawed beast of terrible dimensions, and quite unjumpable, closed that way to us, as it stretched from one side to the other. We retraced our steps nearly as far as the base of the cliff. When we were near it we saw a splendid ice avalanche topple over, which crashed down into the bed of a surface stream close to us, and about five feet deep. This soon filled, and with a rush, a roar and a flood the ice passed us and in a few minutes disappeared into a large crevasse. We stood, on the ice bank above and were quite safe.

We soon reached the rocks on the side, but they were difficult, and we passed the big crevasse, but again were stopped by a waterfall which fell from the crags above us and disappeared in a dark chasm under the glacier. Once again it was necessary to mount the ice. As every mountaineer knows it is often difficult to get on to a glacier from the side. In this case the best place was up a steep crystal wall thirteen feet high. Up this I cut coal-scuttle steps and handholds, starting from the head of Vigdal's axe in order to save time. I soon reached a narrow ridge of ice which I sat across and pulled Vigdal up. Then we had some straggle-legged locomotion, which later on gave work to the tailors. We went at a tremendous speed over places which in ordinary circumstances we should have felt inclined to shirk. I was reminded of a similar difficulty which I encountered once when I descended the Aletsch glacier quite alone from the Märjelen See to the Bel Alp. I jumped down on to a low ice-table, and then had no alternative but to go astride several sharp ridges which ran up and down at horrible angles.

After a time we gained good ice, and though we had to cut many a step, we got along quickly, and at 7.20, in dusk reached the bottom of this truly terrible glacier, and thankful enough we were to do so. After struggling through an alder copse and across many bogs, at 9.30 we reached a farm-house at Næsdal -a filthy place it is true, but rest for the weary for all that. The people received us most hospitably, though they thought we had come from the skies, and would not for a long time believe our tale.

I have had many a glacier adventure, but with the single exception of the ascent and descent of the ice-wall on the face of the Aiguille du Plan, where Mr. Mummery did all the work [23], the descent of the Kjændalsbræ will always be indelibly impressed in my memory as being the most formidable ice work I have ever shared in, and nothing could tempt Vigdal or myself to try it again. Where the great difficulties occurred there was no choice of routes. At a glance we could see that it was there or nowhere. The covered ledge was the most extraordinary outlet of escape I have ever seen in my life, and was the strangest solution to a difficult problem. Without it we should undoubtedly have been beaten and have been driven after a cold night over the mountain into the neighbouring Kvandal, where the descent is easy. I took copious notes the whole day, and I even jotted down the height of the ice towers when waiting for Vigdal. From where we put foot on the Tunsbergdalsbræ to where we left the ice, is, as the crow flies, a distance of eighteen miles, no little when we had to zigzag so much. Kjændal itself is only about 160 feet above sea-level, and the top of the glacier is 6495 feet. A descent of 6335 Norse feet was therefore made. On the eastern side of the glacier there is a continuous ice-fall of nearly 6000 feet.

Before the Justedalsbræ was as well known as it is now, I always advised those who came to me for information to go from the west to the east, because by doing so they would be less likely to become pounded on the top of an unclimbable wall on the east than on the west side. Preaching is one thing, practising another. By neglecting my own advice we met with the adventure on the Kjændalsbræ; I know that I ought to moralise on this expedition. I will however leave this really very simple duty to someone else and merely say that for many years I have, in season and out of season, preached the old sound mountaineering doctrines, such as, "Three persons form the smallest party which can with safety traverse the upper snows."

It is not so easy to believe now that three of the most popular tourist resorts in Norway to-day, Fjærland, Loen, and the Hjörundfjord, were up to a few years ago always associated in the minds of the few of us, who sought their inmost mountain recesses, with hunger and discomfort. Yet such was the case. Usually Fjærland was visited from Balholm, and Loen from Faleide or Olden, and, as to the Hjörundfjord one took one's luck and starved upon it.

In spite of this, what jolly days I have spent, and in what grand expeditions I have had the luck to share in each of these districts!

A little later, on the first day of September the same year, Vigdal and I set off from Gjendebod at 5.45 in the faint dawning light of day. The day bursts upon Gjendin with a keen frost and a bright blue sky. At 8.40, having passed over a little glacier, we reach the skar which forms a delightful portal at the head of that most interesting cirque, Simlehullet, overshadowed by a lovely pyramid, the Simletind. Down the glacier, not far fortunately, and into the gloomy Uladal, then, we turn sharp to the right over some horrible avalanche debris by the side of a noisy stream, and at 9.20 we reach a little glacier lying in the lap of the mountain we wish to ascend. A sharp ascent at a quick rate, for we are bitterly cold, brings us to a plateau of névé, when we know that victory awaits us. The apparently awful precipices which had rather frightened us a few days earlier have vanished, and the mountain reveals itself under its true colours for the first time. Steep it certainly is but is it not also surely a staircase? The western face can in fact be climbed almost anywhere, as in the case of the corresponding side of Knutshultind.

After forty minutes on the glacier, steep snow- and ice-clad rocks lead us to a gap on the southern ridge of our mountain, from which to my great surprise we find an easy snow-slope which connected the gap with the great Memurubræ, a slope which in 1874 seemed to me in the distance to be extremely steep.

Up and up we go, with never a halt, nor any wish to take one. The broad ridge narrows, but never becomes sensational. The interest as usual increases as we near the top, the air becomes more invigorating and the view more extended. One more point and we gain the summit of Heilstuguhö, 7690 Norse feet above sea-level, and the fourth highest mountain in Scandinavia.

We are wild with excitement though the victory has been so easily won. The day is perfect, and we remain for three-quarters of an hour enjoying to the full our measure of happiness, whilst the sunbeams pour upon us without stint their invigorating warmth, and but for cold feet we should linger much longer. The one drawback is the need to build the inevitable cairn, but how dreadfully disappointed we should feel had we found one already erected! The view is of course grand, but not so fine as from many other neighbouring peaks. The glaciers of the Ymes Fjeld, the Leirvand, and the eerie form of the

Smörstabtinder are the most interesting features, and we can see portions of both Lakes Gjendin and Bygdin. The northern ridge which connects the lesser Heilstuguhö with our peak much resembles the narrow and notched ridges so common in Söndmöre, and any party which cares to traverse it will much enjoy the sport which it will afford.

We had two plans for our return: the one to descend by the way we had come, then to climb the Simletind, and to descend from it to Simlehullet by the beautiful little couloir which almost bisects its eastern face – a sporting route, it is true; the other was to descend to the western Memurubræ, then to round the southern peak of the Heilstuguhö range, and to descend into Simlehullet by an old route of mine which I had once discovered when reindeer-stalking. Time, that inexorable master, sternly forbade the first route, so we took the second.

We were soon in the gap again, and quickly ran down to the big glacier, there as flat as a "pandekage." After a short but toilsome trudge in snow softened by the blazing sun, we looked again into that weird cirque which we had traversed in the early morning; and, as we had no rifle with us, we almost stumbled upon five reindeer, which for a few moments stared helplessly at us, as is their wont, and then galloped away over the glacier.

Vigdal and I felt our spirits to be in harmony with the weather, and, joy of joys, we had no horrid packs on our backs. We had time in hand, we felt the bliss of true freedom, and ran and glissaded down to Store Aadal for very joy of heart. Once there, we were both enchanted with the beauty of brightest blue gentians embedded in emerald green grass, where every plant seemed to be in bloom, and each individual flower, too, was wide open to catch the sunbeams.

> *"Like stars about our pathway*
> *They shine so pure and fair,*
> *Blooming in rich profusion,*
> *Greeting us everywhere."*

We had never been in Jotunheim in September before, and had no notion of the beauty of the flowers at this time. I was so overjoyed that, whilst Vigdal went on, I sat down on a rock for three-quarters of an hour; to have sat on the grass would have been almost a profanity, and to walk, which meant to step on the flowers, was really painful to me. The little darlings all seemed to be singing in chorus, "Welcome! Welcome! This is the time to come here; the snows have all gone, and we are come to brighten the earth."

Flowers are very companionable, and have often exerted a mysterious power over me. They have comforted and cheered me when tired, they have breathed hope and encouragement, and I love them dearly. I was once wandering alone upon Gjendetungen, which is, as many know, rather bleak and dreary. I was carrying a cruel load, and was rather down-hearted with having had poor sport for several days on the mountains. I saw a little dandelion – a plain old English dandelion. I put down my rifle and sack, sat down beside this homely little flower, and felt that I had found a friend which recalled a host of bright memories. Soon afterwards I found some lovely anemones, but they were no rivals of my dandelion.

We reached Gjendebod early. In the evening the lake looked most bewitching, and tempted me to fish. However, the beauty of the scene was so absorbing that I thought little of my rod and line, and only caught two trout. Long after the sun had left us the whole heavens were flooded with a transparent crimson light, which also overshadowed the mountains. It faded slowly, very slowly away, through purple, orange, and greenish blue, to the deep cold grey-blue of a frosty night.

I have seldom seen so beautiful an evening as this. The only ones which linger in my memory as rivalling in beauty this sunset on Lake Gjendin are two on the chain of Mont Blanc when bivouacking high up amongst the eternal snows, and one especially glorious night in Arctic Norway, where the colouring is even more beautiful than on the shores of Gjendin.

The morning after our ascent of Heilstuguhö, to our great surprise and bitter disappointment, was ushered in by light showers of rain, and veils of gauzy clouds lay folded round the Gjendin peaks. As the barometer was steady we still looked for fine weather. We were also due at Vormelid or Skjolden to join Herr Sulheim, and had engaged to climb the highest Styggedalstind as well as some other peaks with him, so we determined to move on at least as far as the Guridal sæter to glean tidings of him.

For some years I had resolved to ascend the Melkedalstind, a lovely horn-shaped peak as seen from Skogadalsböen, which often stood out clearly above the sea of clouds rising up from the humid Skogadal; and at such times, and they often occurred, an especial and distinctive grandeur was lent to this mountain which had impressed me very much. Clearly the Melkedalstind was the next mountain for us to tackle, as it could be taken on our way to Guridal. We took leave of the family at Knutshullet.

"Farvel Ragnhild. Farvel Marie. Mange tak for en behagelig ophold (delightful visit)."
"Farvel. Farvel. Lykke til reise." (Have a good time.)

A map and compass did us good service on Gjendetungen, because, though the rain had ceased we were enveloped in a thick mist, and steering on those wastes was difficult. There are many little streams which meander in and out and round about in a most perplexing manner. At first each seems to lead towards Raudal, until one finds after following it a few yards that its course is probably completely reversed. However by good luck and by utterly ignoring the streams, we reached in good time the round tarn which lies between Raudalstind and Snehö, which I recognised, as I had made a sketch from its shores four years before.

I called a halt and told Vigdal that here was an ideal place to have lunch. He shivered; I shivered too. There was a cutting wind and no shelter. We were not particularly hungry. Neither was there a view. Vigdal thought it strange that I ate my food so deliberately; and he kept looking down the Raudal, or rather into the mists which hovered over the tarn. I had once been over a low skar into Snehullet – the snow cirque – and that skar was close to us now. The Melkedalstind was up there too. Now Vigdal knew nothing of this. He thought we were merely crossing the fjeld to Guridal, and, as for other schemes, the idea was preposterous.

If only those wretched but happily uneasy clouds would take wings and fly away! I am certain that the patience which "raises hope and smiles away despair" is a virtue that mountaineering does much to foster and ripen. Indeed, an impatient man will never make a good mountaineer until he gets rid of his impatience. Bide your time, and you'll get your peak six times out of seven. True, it may not be to-day nor yet tomorrow, perhaps not even this year or next; but, if it is worth anything, it is worth waiting for. We now stood in some need of replenishing our stock of patience, but at last we were partially rewarded. The coy milk-maiden up beyond the skar just pulled her veil aside to have a peep at us – only for an instant though, as she drew it still more closely about her lovely face. But beauty is not intended to be hidden, and she peeped at us again and again.

"Now Vigdal, what do you say? Down the Raudal or up there?" The Solvorn warrior pointed upwards, as I knew he would. No persuasion was needed. No. He too had seen the milkmaid, and he was keen to woo her, and to win her too.

At 12.20 we left the tarn, turned west, and were soon in the clouds. We had some good climbing over ice-polished rocks, and quickly reached the little glacier under the peak itself. From previous observations I knew the south arête to be the most promising, but as we had our knapsacks with us, and might wish to cut off a corner when coming down, we agreed to ascend to the top of the glacier on the eastern face, and to try to ascend from there. After a short steep ascent on perfect snow, where there were no visible crevasses, we reached the top of this little glacier at 1.25. We could only see about 2000 feet up the mountain, as thin filmy clouds were chasing one another round and round the peak, but we had a reasonable hope that they would go away altogether by and by. For about 150 feet the way seemed clear, above that it looked bad. To go straight up we knew was impossible, as there was a perpendicular face of rock which we could see was an unsurmountable barrier. We however thought we could climb a spur of rock some 200 feet and then turn the barrier by making a traverse along a broad ledge to the left. This would bring us to what I looked upon as being the only really doubtful part of the mountain, a black rock on which the snow never rests. If we were to fail I felt that it would be there. It is at the head of a steep gully not far from the top of the mountain. The mountain was covered with recent hard-frozen snow, and as the face which we had before us had a north-east aspect and was out of reach of the sun's quickening rays, it was bristling with ice as well.

Leaving our knapsacks we armed for the fray, and were soon hard at work hand and foot. It was bitterly cold, and as our gloves were full of holes we had to beware of frostbites. At first it was easy, then difficulties seemed to cluster around us and we put on the rope. Snow and ice had to be scraped or hacked off each rock upon which we had to tread, and the mountain grew steeper and steeper. Our choice of possible routes became limited, and we thought seriously of relinquishing our attempt. We were tempted into a gully or chimney, half filled with ice, and for twenty or thirty feet we got on well. Then it became very bad indeed. I was leading, and often required a shove from Vigdal, and now and then a shoulder too, and gave him a hoist up in return. How we hated that gully! How I hate the memory of it still! Icicles, like the spears of some mountain fiend, seemed all to be pointing threateningly towards us, and we felt it to be an uncanny place and one to be left as soon as possible.

Easier said than done, as mountaineers well know, that of all places in the mountains a chimney is the worst to get out of when once committed to it. We only needed to ascend about fifty feet more in order to reach the broad ledge which we had seen from below, but how were those fifty feet to be passed? To get down by the way we had come we knew would be extremely difficult, perhaps even dangerous. It was surely worth a little struggle, especially as we knew that there was an easier route to descend by the south arête?

By a series of gymnastic wriggles, twists, and turns, much holding on by the knees and elbows, by sometimes ascending and at others descending, by work that seemed to call forth the whole of our muscles into play, during most exciting moments, when if we spoke at all it was only in monosyllables, we emerged from this horrible prison on to a broad ridge of rock again. This was not terra firma yet, but those icy spears no longer pointed at us, and we could move both to right and to left. It was delightful to have a choice of routes even if only for a few feet.

We had now about forty feet of very difficult rocks to climb. One place was peculiarly uninviting – a place which would have just suited my old friend Halvar Halvarsen. As he was not present, it behoved me to do the work, and fortunately, with a month's training, I felt conscious of the power of doing it, and this knowledge was a great help in itself; whilst the presence of a brave man below, firmly anchored and ever watchful of the rope, increased my power. The "mauvais pas" was a rock face about fifteen feet high where there were only two little ledges. With Vigdal's help I reached the first, which was only large enough to hold part of one foot. He gave me the head of his axe to stand upon, then I straightened myself and reached a narrow rounded ledge about five feet above the first hold. I slowly drew myself up to the second platform, a narrow rounded ledge about five feet above the lower one. Then a short traverse round a corner without handhold brought me into good ground on a broad firm ledge just within a rope's length of Vigdal. I was not more than a couple of minutes in climbing the bad place, but even Vigdal with a rope above him found that it was not easy. Fast-scudding clouds below us hid the precipice from our view, and enhanced the wildness of the scene.

We soon gained the broad ledge which we had seen from the glacier, and though not very easy to follow, it led us into better ground to the left hand, and we got on rapidly. Then came the black rock which I have already mentioned. We saw that we could climb it, and that it would be an interesting feature of the ascent if it were made direct from out of Snehullet. By standing on Vigdal's shoulders I reached a ledge which led round to the south-west and so on to the top, which we reached at 2.50, or in one hour and twenty-five minutes from the top of the glacier, during most of which time we had been engaged on extremely difficult work though we had climbed very quickly.

To our great joy, the clouds all blew away as we approached the summit, and disclosed a view the beauty and variety of which cannot be surpassed even in Jotunheim. Old friends, one and all, seemed to bid us welcome. Uranaastind looked like a monarch, and his glaciers immense. I longed for the presence of one who had made with me the first ascent of that mountain five years earlier. [24] His enthusiasm would have known no bounds had he been with us. Heilstuguhö looked as inaccessible as ever, though we had proved its ascent to be so easy the day before. The Smörstabtinder and their icy surroundings glittered in the sunlight. The – , but I must name no more mountains.

We fully appreciated our good fortune in having really perfect weather. The clouds had been dispelled as if by magic, and every peak was visible, though some of the higher valleys were flooded with a sea of mist. There was a gauzy haze too, which overspread the mountains and was just sufficient to soften and blend together into one grand harmony the varied tints, for which Norway is so justly famous, without obscuring a single peak.

There was plenty of room to run about and get warm on the top, and as much loose gabbro was lying about, we soon built our usual cairn. My aneroid showed 22.6 inches on the top, whilst at the head of the glacier it was 23.5 inches.

After a stay of half an hour we turned our backs regretfully upon this enchanted scene. We soon passed the awkward place near the summit by aid of rope and shoulders, and then we directed our course for some time towards Snehullet. But when the rocks became less steep we turned to the left, and so reached the glacier and soon afterwards our baggage, without encountering any especial mountaineering difficulty. Caution, patience, and rough scrambling, where hand came to the relief of foot at every turn and where one man now and then helped the other, brought us safely down.

We had a gentle descent down the northern glacier, and reached the trough of the Raudal (red valley) at 4.10. The Utla river, which is sometimes impassable, we waded over with ease, and reached Muradnsæter at 7.10, and Guridal at 8.15. Here we stopped the night, and if the truth be told, we wished ourselves back at Gjendin.

My boots, which I had used constantly during a month's mountain-climbing, were now in two senses "on their last legs"; each had lost its outer sole and each had holes in the uppers, and though I could easily go on snow, walking on stones gave me much trouble. In spite of this, the following day we went nearly to the top of the Gjertvasbræ, within half an hour of the summit of Styggedalstind, then unclimbed, and would most certainly have completed the ascent but for the fact that I had promised Sulheim to climb it with him in a few days' time – a great mistake, as it proved to be. We descended by the Styggedalsbræ, thus making a new glacier pass parallel to the Keiser, and I limped down to Fortun and drove to Sulheim's house at Eide where another pair of boots awaited me. To my chagrin, Sulheim could not return with me to gain the victory which had all but been within our grasp, and as Vigdal's time was up I was obliged to leave Styggedalstind alone and go elsewhere.

This grand mountain was first ascended by Herr Carl Hall and two guides a couple of years later, but though I have attempted its ascent twice since, once up the Maradalsbræ, bad luck has on both occasions attended me, and I have not yet been upon its summit.

To come back to the peak of the milky valley. I expressed the opinion years ago that this mountain is one of the most graceful in Norway. I have five sketches of it, taken from different standpoints, and each one shows that the milkmaid is beautiful. As the mountain stands close to the route between Skogadalsböen and Gjendin or Bygdin, it ought often to be ascended. So far this has not been the case, and I am surprised that this is so; but the time will come when the ascent of the Melkedalstind will be a very favourite expedition. It can be climbed either by the skar on the north, or by that on the south, from Melkedal or from Raudal.

The ascents which I have described are only a very small portion of the grand mountain expeditions which can be made from Gjendebod, and even at this late hour there is good new work awaiting the mountaineer possessed of the happy knack of discovering and picking up the unconsidered trifles which often turn out to be real prizes well worth winning.

Chapter 12: The First Lady's Ascent of Lodals Kaupe and the Mountains Of Loen

"The hill, though high, I covet to ascend,
The difficulty will not me offend."
Pilgrim's Progress.

"...an eminence...
The last that parleys with the setting sun."
WORDSWORTH.

The very name of Lodals Kaupe must recall, to my Norse readers at any rate, the names of four mountain warriors, of whom Norway will always feel justly proud. I mean Gottfried Bohr, Lieutenant Daae, Professor Keilhau, and C. Boeck, whose deeds of daring on this mountain are duly recorded in the *Nor. Tur. For. Aarbog* for 1874. These feats, enacted in 1820, may be favourably compared with any of a similar nature in the Alps at that date, and the writings of Bohr and Keilhau may be truly termed mountain classics. When it is considered how little was then known of glacial phenomena, their theories regarding the stratification of glacier ice, the formation of crevasses, sand cones, moraines, advance or retreat of glaciers, the daily rise and fall of the Justedal River, etc., are indeed excellent.

On Saturday morning, August 2nd, 1884, a party of six of us arrived at Olden. The weather was perfect. The Nordfjord had never looked more lovely than on the previous evening. The sight of the broad crest of Gjegnalund and its guardian snow-fields glittering in the rosy evening sunlight had increased our zeal and impatience to be on the snows. What wonder then that, though the ascent of the Kaupe did sound to be rather an ambitious expedition to be undertaken directly after our arrival from England, we should fix upon it as the goal of our ambition for the Monday!

At Faleide we met Dr. Spence Watson, who agreed to join us with his wife on the Kaupe; but, owing to the carelessness of our host at Olden in not despatching a message which we had promised to send to Faleide, they did not accompany us, which was a general disappointment.

Though sorely tempted, I will not linger over the beautiful scenery on the journey to our sleeping quarters at Bödal sæter on the Sunday afternoon, the row over the fjord, the walk through English park-like scenery, then the row over that most glorious of all lakes, Loenvand, nor will I describe our hospitable reception at Bödal farm.

Though we knew it was late when we walked up the stony path through the fragrant birch woods in Bödal, we often stopped to admire the view, for two reasons. The first, which we acknowledged, was because it was a very lovely view. The other reason, which possibly was not stated, arose from the fact that the path was steep. How often it happens that a most unpoetical, undemonstrative, and unobservant man will, when going up a steep hill, break out into a rhapsody and an apparently intense enthusiasm over the beauty of some very commonplace view which demands time for its gratification and time too for him to blow! Our party consisted of my wife,[25] my brother-in-law, Wm. Ecroyd, Dr. Tempest Anderson and myself, with Lars Janssen, an uncommonly handsome, well-built man, who ought to sit to some artist as a model for ancient Viking, and Jens Rustoen, the poet of the party, a tall and enthusiastic lover of the mountains.

It was no new ascent which we were about to attempt. No, the Lodals Kaupe, as well as Kviteggen and Slogen in Söndmöre, Galdhöpiggen and the Romsdalshorn were first climbed by an adventurous *bonder* who lived at the bases of these fine mountains in the period of mountaineering stagnation after Keilhau's time, before the reawakening of the sport of mountain-climbing in the late sixties and early seventies.

Bödal sæter, where we were to pass the night, consists of a good many different huts. Two of these had been cleaned out in anticipation of our visit, and the floors well sprinkled with sprays of juniper. The sæter occupies a sunny position, but the proximity of glaciers on each side of the valley makes it very cold.

The sæter girls were most obliging, and proud to act as hostesses to the first English lady who had visited them. They called us at three o'clock the next morning, and we felt that for once in a way an early start could be made. I soon woke up Lars and Jens, but the wretches went to sleep again and delayed us horribly, so that we did not get off till 5.30. A great pity.

At three, the mists were close down to the sæter, but here and there we saw blue sky through the rifts, and slowly the clouds rolled up the mountain sides and promised a fine day.

Over the bogs, where the *Drosera, Pinguicula, Comarum,* and *Cotton Grass* grow, and away to that long and heavy slab of granite which forms a bridge over the icy river. Then a mile or two on the level, and we reached the stream issuing from the blue caverns of the Sæterbræ. The river was high, the water was cold. As Lars and Jens had not had their morning tub, we felt no compunction in letting them doff their hosen and carry us over.

A sharp ascent brought us to the basin of the Brattebakbræ – the glacier of the steep hill – we crossed its river by a snow bridge and made our way on to a buttress which descends from the great snow-field on the south side of our valley. We now had our first full view of the Kaupe. There seemed to be three peaks, the Kaupe the most northern, then the Lille Kaupe, and a minor peak. These all rise with fierce precipices from the shores of the Kaupe vand, a lake then and usually frozen. On the north a snow-capped mountain wall also rises almost out of the lake, the whole forming a very uncanny and snowy amphitheatre.

From the head of the lake a long narrow and steep snow-belt led immediately under the basement cliffs of the Kaupe to a glacier which projects an icy tongue far up the mountain itself. This snow-belt naturally suggested itself as our highway, but as much step-cutting would probably be required, prudence dictated an easier course up our buttress to the snows and a trudge along the tops of the south walls of the amphitheatre, over the Lille Kaupe, and a traverse to the icy tongue.

The weather had steadily improved since our start. Sunbeams had chased the clouds away, and the peaks and snowfields were projected with clear and sharp outlines against a bright blue sky. During a short rest, however, a few ominous signs came stealthily to warn us of a change. First of all the wind gently whispered from the west. Then a feathery cloud hovered like a bird over the mountains of Olden. Another floated over Skaala, and far away in the west a fleet of cloudlets seemed to be sailing through the deep azure seas, and we began to fear that they meant to attack the Kaupe itself.

After a steep and tiring ascent in the hot sunshine, we reached the Justedalsbræ once more, and directly afterwards were robbed of our view east and south. We roped in two parties, and had nearly a mile of flat walking. Then steep and easy rocks proved a grateful change, and we were soon on the first of the three peaks. The top was flat and its edge was fringed with a splendid snow cornice through which we hurled rocks down the precipices.

The little Kaupe rises from the northern end of this peak, and is thought by Lieut. Lorange to be the one climbed in the year 1820 by Bohr, though this is a point which can never be settled. We crossed easily over the top, and then had a short descent on a narrow snow ridge to a gap under the Kaupe. On the right some jagged ice-pinnacles looked like dismal ghosts grinning through the gloom, and this scene was rendered still more ghostly by the frequent fall of avalanches. On our left now and then we could see the Kaupe vand. In front, but far above our heads, a dark square tower of rock appeared occasionally. This was the Kaupe, and this side has not yet been climbed.

Thanks to a sketch drawn on the buttress, our way was clear. We crossed the steep Kaupebræ to the foot of the tongue of snow which leads far up the western face of the mountain. The snow was unexpectedly good, but the weather was bad, and we seemed to be doomed to disappointment just at the last. A snow-storm came on, we held a brief consultation and unanimously agreed to make a trial.

After a struggle and flounder through snow crusts at the edge of the rocks, we took to the crags and faced south. A steep gully of loose snow-covered rocks led to a rock face of large and loose slabs of gneiss, which enforced caution upon us. After half an hour of interesting climbing, the cairn was reached, and the Kaupe was won.

Two o'clock, but thanks to the two hours lost in the morning at the sæter two hours too late. The fleet of cloudlets had indeed stormed the Kaupe, and they disputed with us for the victory. We had won the peak, but the cloudlets robbed us of the view, and we stood apparently on a rocky islet surrounded by a sea of cloud and mist, whose waves dashed against the black precipices and broke over our heads in a spray of sleet. Unlike the summit of most of the finest mountains in Norway, which are topped with gabbro, the whole rock pyramid of the Kaupe is built up of huge flakes or slabs of gneiss, which form, on the precipitous north face, a series of remarkable ledges, by means of which two other men and I made the ascent five years later.

After a hurried meal in the cold, we prepared to descend. As the rocks below were so loose, we took two parallel routes to the head of the tongue; Ecroyd, Anderson, and Jens went by the way we had ascended, whilst my wife, Lars, and I took a gully a little to the north. Our half hour's work was sufficiently interesting to make us forget for a while the cold wind, and the general instability of the rocks rendered care necessary though there was no actual danger.

After this, we sped along at a rapid rate, and in due time came to the mile of flat snow-field, the only place about which we felt any uneasiness. The mist limited our view to a radius of one hundred yards. We wished to keep above our former course so as to avail ourselves of some steep snow gullies down which we could glissade and so save time, and our footsteps were already blotted out by the wind and snow. Fortunately we knew the proper direction and so made use of a plan which is well worth knowing. We were still on two ropes. The first party set off and the other kept back until their comrades were nearly out of sight, when they followed. All now depended upon the leader of the second party, who had to take a sight along the line of the vanguard and to insist by calls of "to right" or "to left," as the case might be, that the view of the last man should block out the leader. This is an easy matter in the case of two parties eighty or a hundred yards apart, and it can be done, though less effectively, in one party of three or more persons by the last man. A gradual, or even a sudden turn may unconsciously be made in a mist, and the snow-fields of the Justedalsbræ would be a terrible place on which to go astray.

All went well, and much to our surprise we came upon a large cairn, which at first sight we mistook for a couple of bears. This cairn was doubtless erected in the good old times when men took as naturally to the snow passes between the east and west as their grandsons now do to their steamboats.

By running and glissading down the steep snow slopes we soon got to the zone of dwarf birch and willow, but the mist became thicker and the rain teemed down most viciously. Ecroyd said that we were too slow so ran off alone to secure his *römmegröd* before us, and Jens followed him. We two gained the valley a little below the Brattebakbræ and were much interested by the immense slabs of flat ice-polished rock, almost as white as snow, which paved the ground. We thought we would cross the main river which issues from the Kaupe vand, and thus make a shorter route to the sæter but a glance at its swollen waters and steep rocky bed showed that it was too dangerous an experiment to attempt, so we made for the other river draining the Brattebakbræ, but unfortunately a good way below the snow bridge which we had crossed in the morning. This river seemed almost as bad as the other, so we followed a cattle track down between two waterfalls and through a copse of dripping birch-trees growing out horizontally from the hillside. After this, we could defy water so far as its mere wetting properties were concerned.

Each river was yet uncrossed. I saw several places where cattle had gone through; but a quadruped has an immense advantage over a biped in fording a river. The former moves only one fourth of its legs at a time. The latter moves one half, unless he counts his stick as a third leg. At last I found a place just above where the two rivers meet which was feasible and carried my wife over, though I could not have managed it without a stick of some sort. At seven o'clock we reached the sæter and to our surprise were welcomed by Dr. Spence Watson, who was most kind and attentive in ministering to our wants. We were the first arrivals, the others came half an hour later.

Owing to the limited stock of our wardrobe, which in my case was rendered still more scanty by the burning of a stocking on the blazing logs, my wife and I, accompanied by Dr. Spence Watson, set off after a hasty meal for our headquarters at Olden, which we reached at three o'clock next morning. The remembrance of the two long boat rows in the cold night with wet clothes almost gives me a shiver now. In most countries, severe colds and rheumatism would have been the penalty, but in Norway, with most people, pure mountain air is a neverfailing specific.

Our choice of this day for the Kaupe was singularly unfortunate, as there were only two wet days during the six weeks we were in Norway. Soon after our ascent, we met Gabriel Rustöen, the father of Jens. He and a man from Indviken with another friend had made the first ascent of the Kaupe about the year 1844. Gabriel, who was an active and daring man in his youth, told us that ours was only the fourth ascent. Certainly no stranger had climbed it before us. Now the Kaupe is frequently ascended, and it is deservedly a favourite expedition. [26]

Every one who has been up the Olden valley in clear weather has admired the Melkevoldsbræ, and followed its course, almost unwittingly, through insensible gradations, from rolling snow-fields nearly 6000 feet above sea-level, down through to cataracts of ice, and lower still to the relentless ice-plough. This at times advances, rooting up the scant herbage and young trees that grow above the terminal moraines in the upper basin of the valley, and then retires once more, leaving a reign of peace behind it until another advance shall take place. Every one must also have noticed the large ice cavern, which for a generation has been seen on the western side of the glacier.

After a short expedition on the Brixdalsbræ, where we had rubbed off the rust from our ice-axes, a scene of marvellous beauty was presented to us as we rowed down the Olden's vand on a Saturday night in soft and silvery moonlight. The wavy snow-fields and glistening ice, intensely pure by contrast with the dark shadows under the steep mountains, were reflected upon the glassy surface of the lake. St. Cecilia's Krone towered above us, and glittering in the moonlight, her tiny glacier looked like a necklace of pearls hanging gracefully over her shoulders. The deathlike stillness, alone broken by the splash of the oars, seemed hardly of this world. Each one felt it to be a time for thinking, and not for talking, and each of us will treasure in our memories this scene as being one of the most impressive in the storehouse of Nature.

After our return from Lodals Kaupe, it is not surprising that an expedition up the Melkevoldsbræ and its unknown recesses in snowland should tempt Ecroyd and me to an exploration, and the only wonder is that no one had ever forestalled us. Lars, still thirsting for glory, and promised the use of my wife's ice-axe, hailed with delight the proposition that he should join us, and I believe would have been really glad to go without any payment whatsoever, had we wished to be niggardly, as he seemed to be very anxious to emulate the deeds of his ancestors, and to feel, as they undoubtedly did, at home on the snow-fields.

On Wednesday, August 6th, in perfect weather, we stole out of Olden in the morning twilight. At Rustöen we found Jens at work in the hay-field. We pointed to the glacier sparkling like diamonds in the sun, showed him a business-like axe, which we had brought for his use, and asked him if he would go up there *"for moros skyld"* (for pleasure)? "Ja, ja," he replied. What a contrast these West Justedal men are to many of the so-called guides in Jotunheim? Would they go up there *"for moros skyld,"* *"for penges skyld,"* (for money), or, "for any other *skyld"*? There are many exceptions I know very well, men who do not hesitate to follow the reindeer alone on the Smörstabbræ, the Memurubræ, the Leirungsbræ, and many another glacier. From geographical reasons alone, if for none other, the Justedal men ought to be the best ice men in Norway, and I dare say they are too. The rudiments of the science of ice-craft are in reality bred in them. If they wish to see their neighbours just over the mountain, they must either go over the glacier, or perhaps a hundred miles round.

An hour and a half's quick walking from Rustöen brought us to the foot of the glacier, which, like every stream of ice projected far down into any deep western valley from the Justedal snow-field, looked terribly steep and hacked up into most fantastic shapes by hands of Jötuls.

We had intended to climb up the rocks on the western side of the glacier as far as the big hole, and, after examining it, to cross over to the other side on what we took to be a small plateau, between the two ice-falls in the lower and most contracted part of the glacier; and we set off for that purpose. We soon saw that there was no shadow of a possibility of crossing the ice where we had intended, so we trudged away to the eastern rocks, which alone could offer us a passage. At first we climbed up the ice, but were soon driven off to the rocks, which were very easy; then difficulties arose, as the granite was polished like silver plate. We took to the ice again, but before long had to change once more.

After a climb of 300 or 400 feet we came to a most romantic place on the glacier. In a hollow, encased in an irregular chalice of ice crystal, there was a large and most bewitching pool of water perhaps 50 feet deep, through which every shade of blue – colours only revealed in their perfection to the mountaineer – was presented by the ice at various depths and in nooks and crannies of the pool. Above us, and reflected clearly in the water, tottering towers of ice which imagination peopled with innumerable gnomes, formed an impregnable barrier right across the glacier, and a fitting foreground to the snowy world far, far beyond. Just opposite to us, the fine mountain Middags Næbba projected its inaccessible precipices far into the glacier, whilst, on our side, steep rocky terraces led the eye far away to the eternal snows. Below, the pretty valley of Olden lay outspread before us, a gem of fertility smiling with golden cornfields, and the placid lake, hemmed in by towering snow and ice-capped fjelde.

What more inviting place for breakfast could be desired than by the edge of this crystal pool? And what more charming scene for fond memory to recall in the future?

The pool resembled those seen on large, flat ice-fields such as the Mer de Glace, the Aletsch glacier, the Gorner glacier, the Tunsbergdalsbræ. I wonder if it is possible that this lovely pool, and the big round hole just across the glacier as well, have originally been *moulins* on the flat part of the glacier basin, a few hundred feet above where they now are, and that, in process of travelling, they may have been turned over from a vertical to a horizontal position in their descent? If these two most singular looking cavities had been found at the top of the icefall, I should have certainly concluded that they were old *moulins*, as I have often come across ancient and disused ones in the Alps, but I fear that ice is of too plastic a nature to allow of them passing through the ice-fall without a general collapse. Still, there they are, and must remain for many a long day and the ice containing them has journeyed down from the plateau in some form or other. We saw several small *moulins* on this plateau later on.

After a hearty breakfast, over which we lingered long, at last we tore ourselves away from the loveliest little pool I have ever seen and took to the rocks again, but as close to the ice as we could get. We started with about sixty feet of very awkward rock; a tiny gully with smooth rectangular sides, one of which was vertical, was formed by two strata, of which one stratum had, in ages long gone by, been split off the other by the frost as far as the gully. This was the first of a series of rock faces and tiny gullies, varying but little in steepness by the difference in the angles of fracture of the upper strata. These gullies or corners were the only places where even a goat could climb up, as hardly anywhere on these ice-polished slabs was there such a thing as a nick or a crack to be found for hand or foot.

Lars led us here, and right well too; true, he often required a shove, or an axe-head to stand on, but we required a pull in turn. For many years Lars had been the man of Olden to undertake the rescue of any unfortunate crag-fast goat; in fact, he was the general volunteer for any adventurous work to be done either on land or water there, and on these smooth rocks, he felt quite at home. We three, I honestly confess, did not, having not yet quite mastered the mysteries of the art of clinging to smooth granite with the chest or elbows, and of wriggling upwards like caterpillars by drawing up the knees or thighs, and then in turn clinging by the latter and raising the former.

After, I will not say losing, where we were gaining knowledge and experience, but passing much time by this sort of work, we found ourselves far above the second ice-fall and its grim towers. The question then arose: Should we descend to the glacier plateau, and attempt a zigzag towards Middags Næbba, or should we join the glacier a little farther up, but where it was névé in place of ice? We soon decided on the latter. After an interesting climb alongside a waterfall, we came to some very steep snow shelving upwards from the glacier. We were then face to face with a fine mountain, which is visible from the Brixdal though not from Oldendal, and which is not honoured by a place on the *Amtskart*. I proposed that we should cross the upper basin of the glacier, and climb this, or another mountain from the back. Lars and Jens both demurred, said it was "*meget farlig*," (very dangerous) and that there were "*sprækker*" (crevasses). However, thanks to a most laudable rivalry which existed between these two men, and to their real love of adventure, their scruples were soon overcome, though it must have seemed to them opposed to all precedent to endeavour to force a way amongst the crevasses, when these might all be avoided by climbing the rocks up to the snow-field above, and then by following along its broad back. We were now nearly 5000 feet above the fjord. We set off at a run, as it was slightly down hill. Ten minutes brought us to some deep crevasses, well bridged over, then we began to ascend, and presently came to several wide transverse crevasses, which we avoided by zigzags and a bridge now and then. Once, Jens partially disappeared in a narrow crevasse, but like a sensible man he leaned forward, and came with his body on the snow. I was glad to see him fall in, for the sake of experience. After a time we came to a trough of névé on each side of which were huge crevasses. Our peak was guarded by a network of them, and from this side was invincible.

After an hour and a half since leaving the rock we got above all difficulties, and once more stood on the mighty undulating snow-field itself. There is, I am almost sure, no other place on the Justedalsbræ, and probably none in Europe, where the lines are so graceful and free from flaw as here in the trough above the Melkevoldsbræ.

Our object was to get to some point from which we could take a bird's-eye view into Stardalen and its two upper tributary valleys. After a trudge in good snow of about half an hour in a S.S.W. direction we saw some rocks ahead which we thought we could reach in fifteen minutes. When that time had elapsed, we seemed as far as ever from them. At last we reached the rocky islet at 3.50, and were rewarded for our pains by a lovely view, though we were not quite far enough to see the region of Sogn eastward.

Below us, wild glaciers and precipices carried the eye far away down to the sunless sæters of Fonsdal. Of Stardal itself, we could only see the tops of its cliffs. Far away westward, over the wintry Gjegnalund, the cliffs of Hornelen, blue with the distance, were unmistakable. Many a bright and sunny fjord, rocky island and green hillside, led away to the open sea; and two and three-quarter Norse miles away a beautiful peak rose majestically out of the snow, Lodals Kaupe. On seeing this Jens felt the inspiration of genius and wrote a few lines of poetry of a religious tendency, which were left in the cairn we built. As this little peak is not on the road to anywhere, and as there was no trace of heaped-up or overturned rocks, we assumed that we had made a new ascent. Lars dubbed it Onsdags Næbba (Wednesday Peak). We found the rocks to be almost covered with sun-loving alpine flowers.

We thought we deserved an hour's rest, so we took it, and literally basked in sunshine. Then we made our way towards the mountain which had tempted us earlier in the day, and reached its rocks after twenty-five minutes' quick walk, and soon were on a summit wholly composed of colossal blocks of detached rock. This hitherto unknown mountain is now well known on Oldendal by the name of the Lars Næbba. It is 5610 English feet high, and affords a splendid view of the great basin of the Melkevoldsbræ out of which it rises with grand precipices. After the usual stone-mason's work, we were quickly under weigh again on the west of Lars Næbba, intending to descend by the Olden Skar.

Lars had been very attentive to our guiding among the crevasses in the morning, and was a most willing pupil. In front of us was a network of them at the head of the western arm of the Melkevoldsbræ, which runs up between Middags Næbba and Lars Næbba. Our direct route lay across these, but they might have been turned by keeping higher up to the left. We pointed out the direction to Lars, and asked him to lead us. He very willingly took the reins in hand, and threaded his way cleverly amongst the crevasses.

After rounding this glacier basin, we came to the S.W. spur of Middags Næbba, which looked very pretty from here. Though it was six o'clock, we could not resist another appeal from Nature, so we unroped, and left our axes and knapsacks behind us. A climb of 455 feet up moss-covered rocks, where there was pleasant herbage, out of the way of goats, brought us on our third maiden summit. The whole valley, with the lake and also the fjord, lay outspread before us. Jens pointed with pride to a little brown speck beside the fjord. It was the home of his ancestors. The view was glorious, but time was relentless, and forced us unwillingly away.

A run and a climb soon brought us to our axes again, and to the glacier. From this place a long and hollow slope of snow, 1450 feet in vertical height; led down to the so-called path of Olden Skar. This slope was very steep, but there were no crevasses in it. It was the kind of place beloved by all true Alpine climbers when on a descent, and Ecroyd and I hailed it with delight. The snow was just right, soft enough for safety but hard enough for a glissade.

Lars went first, then Jens, and next Ecroyd, whilst I as head guide, was last. We started off merrily enough, then Jens began to flounder and roll over now and then, but we nevertheless scored several hundred feet in a few minutes. Towards the bottom rocks appeared, but through them, a narrow ribbon of snow seemed to lead down to a second wide snow-slope, and to the valley itself. Under the crags of Middags Næbba, but above the rocks I have named, a little fork of snow trended off to the right. It too seemed to promise a glissade beyond, and to a lower portion of the Olden Skar. Lars proposed this way for us to go; I had thought of the snow ribbon. In a weak moment I gave way, as Lars had steered so well up above. We had now to take a diagonal course and to descend very little for about 150 yards. We were going cautiously, with the rope taut, when, without warning, Lars fell on his back, starting off at a rapid rate, and was soon joined by Jens. Neither used his axe. Ecroyd and I instinctively dug our axes and feet well in the snow, and when we in turn were pulled off our feet, we turned on our faces, and dug in our elbows. By-and-by we brought the others to a standstill on the top of the rocks. If we had been without ice-axes, or going carelessly, the consequences would have been disastrous. As it was, however, it added considerably to the experience of Lars and Jens, who at the time were literally as helpless as horses poised in mid-air when being slung by a steamboat crane into a boat. If Lars had been directly below us when he fell, we could have stopped him at once. As it was, he was almost on the same level that we were, which was a very different case.

Though Lars wished to pursue the same course we had been doing, I peremptorily refused, and after a climb up and then across rounded bosses of glaciated rock, we came to a place where a wide jump would put us on the lower snow-slope. Seeing a grand and safe glissade before me, I slipped the rope over my head, made the jump, and had one of the quickest and best glissades I ever had in my life. The others, I fancy, thought I was bewitched or something of the sort; at any rate they gave me a few minutes' rest at the bottom.

As to the descent to the valley. A scramble through birch-trees growing horizontally out of a steep rocky face, and a tumble now and then into a juniper bush, or a slide down a wet mossy rock into a pool of water, then a half-run down rough screes, where all sorts of cunning traps trip one up, may give one a good lesson of patience, but for my part I had rather do without it. If the *Turist Forening* would pay more attention to this slope, a most interesting route over the Olden Skar would be within the capability of most pedestrians who visit Olden.

When we arrived at the first habitation, Ecroyd and I did full justice to the milk, whilst Lars and Jens disburdened themselves of much fine language about their exploits to their wondering friends.

After leaving Jens in the bosom of his family, and still pointing up at Middags Næbba, in due course we others reached Olden, well tired out, at 1 a.m.

If any one imagines that all the good new climbing about Olden is exhausted, he labours under a great delusion. Though most of the cream is skimmed off, there is yet a goodly amount left, before even the milk is arrived at; it too will last for many a long year yet. Lars and others recognised the fact that a climbing era was at hand, and each acknowledged the necessity of having nailed boots and ice-axes. In fact, Lars made himself an axe a few months later.

Chapter 13: A Four Days' Tramp From Fjærland With The Exploration Of The Austerdalsbræ

"And idle gleams will come and go,
But still the clouds remain;
The clouds themselves are children of the Sun."
TENNYSON

Nearly all who have visited the Sognefjord have been struck with the beauty of Balholm. Many have read the Frithjof Saga, the scene of which is laid here and on various other neighbouring promontories and bays. The tumulus of King Bale is also well known. Balholm is of special interest to me, as I look upon it as the gate to Fjærland and its mighty glaciers.

According to geologists the glaciers of to-day are but baby glaciers compared with those of old. A few miles east of Balholm the greatest depth of the Sognefjord has been sounded. This has the surprising depth of 660 fathoms, or 3960 feet. The adjacent mountains rise steeply out of the waters to a height of over 4000 feet. If the fjord were empty, the mountain walls would therefore be 8000 in height. Men who have studied glaciology in Greenland assert that this grim cañon has been cut out by the graving tools of ancient glaciers, and this belief is gaining ground. There are, however, many like myself who have for years looked upon glaciers as preservative rather than destructive agents, and though we cannot fail to admire the boldness of the glacier-plough theory on so stupendous a scale, we long to hear solutions of this great problem.

When I first knew Fjærland, a fortnightly steamboat was deemed to be a sufficient connection with the outer world, and even in the year 1889 the little house where Mikkel Mundal has his shop supplied ample accommodation for the few tourists who cared to stay for more than a day amongst the forest scenery in Sogn. Between the years 1889 and 1894 great changes took place, and, by the building of a large and beautiful hotel, it was proved that a supply may create a demand. During the fortnight which our family party spent at the Mundals Hotel in 1894, this well-managed house was mostly full, and has since then always been so during the holiday months.

By this period, several notable glacier expeditions had been undertaken; the principal one was made by Herr Annaeus Öyen with two guides in 1893. These three braves crossed the snow-fields from Suphelledal to Olden, a fatiguing tramp of twenty-six hours. The following year, Herr Öyen joined the unfortunate Wellmann Arctic expedition, and was left alone in Danes Island. The Fonsdalsskar, which had beaten us in 1889, had been crossed with ease, and Mikkel Mundal had at my suggestion crossed the glaciers at the head of Mundal, though he did not descend into Gröndal.

In the rough map which accompanied my paper in the Aarbog for 1890, are shown, so far as could then be ascertained, all the various passes, ancient and modern, which had been made over the Justedalsbræ. In 1894 I pointed out to Mikkel Mundal and to the bold climber, Herr Bing of Bergen, the one great blank on the map. I need hardly say that this blank was the Austerdalsbræ. When in 1890 I saw the printed proof of the map, I was quite startled by the insinuating manner in which this one untrodden glacier seemed to invite the exploration of mountaineers hungering for adventure. Ever since 1881, when Vigdal and I first traversed the long neighbouring Tunsbergdalsbræ, I had had the Austerdalsbræ in my mind. In 1889 three friends and I started from Stardal with the intention of descending by this glacier, but were defeated, and we had to content ourselves with a view from above of the grim northern walls and two of the three tributary glaciers which feed the sea of ice below.

Mikkel, whose enthusiasm is positively bewitching and infectious, seemed to be delighted when one day I asked him to join in a four days' expedition which was to include the exploration of the Austerdalsbræ.

On Friday, August 10, our party set off. It consisted of my nephew, Cyril Todd, Mikkel, and myself. Our first pass, a very ancient connecting link between Hveitestranden and Fjærland the Hveitestrandsskar or Skarbakken, is visible from the hotel, and seen from there is a most inviting one. It is through a deep V-shaped gap at the head of the Suphelledal.

We reached Ny Sæter after a delightful walk of eight and a half hours. The buxom girl who had given us so warm a welcome five years earlier was not there, but a younger sister was in charge, and when we asked for a night's lodging, she seemed to be rather overwhelmed by her responsibilities. However, Mikkel, who is a diplomatist, soon smoothed away her difficulties, and she and a girl from another hut made us a fire and soon boiled a kettle.

Amongst the provisions which Mikkel had not only provided for our four days' tramp, but had also carried, was a large tin of soup, on which our present hopes were built. On the morrow we were to explore new regions, still untrodden by mortal foot and unseen by mortal eye, the most mysterious recesses of the great ice world. For aught we knew we might meet with a belated griffin, a dragon such as one of those depicted in Scheuchzer's *Itinera Alpina* – even the two-tailed variety might prove an awkward adversary, if the time chosen for his attack should coincide with that of our crossing an awkward bergschrund or, worse still, a trold might bar our way. Prudence alone dictated the necessity for good feeding. The soup would inspire us with the necessary courage, and foster the growth of muscular tissue and vigour. Clearly enough, everything depended upon the soup. Mikkel deftly inserted the tin-opener into the crown of the tin. Then we heard a gasp, a sigh as of a troubled spirit, a ghostly murmur. What was it? Whence, and why did it come? We sat tight, held our breath, and looked round for our axes. But of what avail could an axe be against a spirit of Langedal? We tried to look and to feel brave, but were instead very hungry, and – oh! horrors! the groaning came out of the tin! Who could cope with a soup spirit? I for one could not.

Todd and I gazed anxiously into the tin, and then heard another, and almost a heart-broken sigh. This time there was no mistake: the sigh came from Mikkel. He poured out the liquid. It was olive-green, and we knew then that if we had to fight the dragons, it would have to be without the help of the soup. We managed to comfort Mikkel after a time; but he was much distressed about the tin. We had however plenty of other food.

Todd and I went to pass the night in another hut. We waged war nearly all the time, not against dragons, but *lopper*, which really appeared desirous of devouring us. The name *"loppe"* was introduced by Vikings of early days into the north of England, and the phrase, "as cobby as a lop," or, as active as a flea, is still heard in our dales.

Next morning, about two o'clock, we turned out to meet a cold icy wind, and in vain shook our clothes repeatedly to get rid of our enemies. While Mikkel and the girls prepared a rare good breakfast, Todd took a photograph in the half-light, which came out well. The mountains and distant glaciers were robed in light cloud-drapery; but we had every reason to expect a fine day for us to "climb the frozen Alps, and tread th' eternal snow."

After a flat three miles' walk, partly over the desert land which was formerly ice-clad, where bright *Silene, Cerastium,* and *Linaria* occasionally gladdened the eye, we reached the snout of the Austerdalsbræ at five o'clock. The river which drained this noble glacier issued from a fine ice cavern in a face of blue ice about eighty feet in height.

We could easily have skirted the south bank of the glacier for a long distance over some old avalanche snow. But we wanted a more sporting route, and wished to get on the north or convex bank, as we knew that better views would be afforded on that side, so we turned to the ice. We found a convenient ice rib and cut a staircase up it, and by the aid of Mummery spikes, which we all used and which saved much step-cutting, we crossed diagonally over to the left bank.

The glacier is a mile in width, about the same as its long-limbed neighbour the Tunsbergdalsbræ; but, whereas the latter consists of one straight river of ice nine miles in length without a single ice-fall, the Austerdalsbræ on the contrary, though only two-thirds the length, possesses a beautiful curve, by which the head of the glacier is entirely hidden from the foot. Thanks to this curve, the magnificent scenery, the exploration of which our party had begun in 1889, and which we were now to complete, was possible. It was still virtually a *terra incognita*, quite unknown to the map-makers.

After an hour's walk on the ice, we were forced by a maze of crevasses to some avalanche snow on the north side, where we made quick progress and easily gained the large plateau which heads the main glacier. The grandeur of the scenery increased as we advanced, and was revealed to us, bit by bit; unlike the case of the Tunsbergdalsbræ, where the upper snow-fields are seen from the foot of the glacier beyond a long vista of nine miles of ice.

The head of the Austerdalsbræ is a grand fan-shaped cirque or cul-de-sac. It is fed by three large tributaries, or three immense ice-falls, which drain the upper snows. The southern arm, which I named "Godt Haabsbræ," (Good Hope Glacier) drains the high snow basin into which we had contemplated making a descent in 1889. Fortunately for us, we did not attempt this. Early in the year its descent is no doubt feasible, but rarely so in August. Its lower ice-fall is probably 1200 feet in height. The middle tributary, or Mikkelsbræ, is an impassable ice cataract of 3000 feet in height. The northern arm is the wildest, and is much contracted near its base by the projection of the huge north-eastern wall, an almost vertical precipice over 300 feet in height, which rises without a shore straight out of the ice. This contraction causes the ice on the left bank to be curiously turned over like a gigantic wave just about to break. A remarkable feature of the cliff is, that there is on the face of it one broad ledge, and one only, which descends gently from the snow-field, and, after traversing the face of the cliff for about a quarter of a mile, runs into the rock itself and vanishes completely about 1500 feet above the large glacier below. It is just the sort of ledge down which a party of mountaineers might be tempted to follow from above. They would get on swimmingly at first, and then, almost without warning, their highroad would come to an end. In 1889 I saw a part of this ledge in the distance, made a sketch of it, and resolved to try to reach it from below. Vain thought!

We went very quietly so as not to awake any slumbering dragon. All to no purpose. No sooner had we set foot upon the ice plateau, than we heard a furious din near the top of the northern glacier. Clearly enough there was a dragon or frost giant up there. He was angry too; and though he did not spit fire out at us, he threw down hundreds of tons of ice in our direction, and roared out lustily as he did so. When we realised that he was chained fast and could not reach us, we laughed at him and derided him, as in days of old Ulysses did to Polyphemus. This increased the dragon's anger, and the avalanches became bigger and more numerous. We named the glacier Hymirsbræ. Long may the frost-giant rule supreme there.

For some time we had seen that the only probable way to reach the snow-field would be by climbing up the rock buttress south of the Mikkelsbræ, but we were by no means certain that it was feasible. We bent our steps towards it. The main glacier was extremely interesting. All the well-known glacial phenomena were well represented, such as glacier tables, all tilted more or less towards the south, sand cones, surface streams and moulins. [27] There were two medial moraines and some twenty-five well-defined dirt bands. All the moraines, both medial and lateral, are larger than those usually found on Norse glaciers; this is owing to the fact that there is a thick stratum of soft schistose rock near the base of all the crags at the head of the glacier, which is constantly adding to the supply.

Near the base of the buttress we came upon the usual hard-compressed avalanche snow. In this the crevasses were wide and deep, but we managed to pick out a zigzag lane towards one of the only two weak places which we could detect in the wall of the buttress. We found the usual bergschrund, and here, oddly enough, we put on the rope for the first time, as it was necessary to cross a long and narrow snow bridge over the dim blue depths of the icy chasm.

At 7.45 we set foot on the rocks. All was not joy here. They consisted of steep slabs of micaceous schist ready to slide down on the slightest provocation. Great care was needed; we scrambled or crawled upwards on all fours, and sent many an undainty morsel down to the greedy jaws of the crevasse below. As soon as we found a place where we could lie down safely, we had breakfast. A sitting posture was unsafe.

Just above us there was a long wall of rock, only twenty to thirty feet in height, but everywhere perpendicular or overhanging. Here and there it was seamed by cracks, which would have been easy and pleasant to climb if the rock had been gneiss or granite. As it was, we were puzzled to know how to overcome the difficulty. Of course we were determined not to be beaten on a first-rate expedition by a bit of a wall.

A shallow gully and mossy chimney some thirty feet in height was suggested, but in order to reach the foot of the chimney we should have been obliged to crawl across a very uninviting water slide. Mikkel pointed in the opposite direction to a dark corner and said he thought that he could climb up "somewhere about there." As our minds were wholly unbiased, Todd and I fell in with this scheme, though we had not the remotest idea what the attraction was. Mikkel possesses in a high degree the happy faculty of inspiring his companions with confidence in his powers, and on this occasion we followed him without question. A leader can always tell whether he possesses the confidence of those whom he leads, and when he feels that they have faith in his leading, his powers are undoubtedly increased and his judgment is clearer. If on the other hand, he hears suppressed or outspoken grumbling, or by other means feels that in some measure his companions do not fully trust his guidance, his powers are in a corresponding degree diminished and his judgment perverted. I have experienced both conditions on scores of expeditions, and I feel sure that all who have acted as leaders when mountaineering will agree with me in this conclusion.

We traversed the treacherous face very carefully for some 300 feet; it sloped down towards the bergschrund at an angle of about fifty degrees, and a slip was not to be thought of. We held on by feet, hands, knees, thighs, and elbows to loose slaty rocks, and to roots of *Saxifraga stellaria*, a rope-rooted *Sedum*, moss, dock-sorrel, and other water-loving plants which grew in rank profusion on the unstable bed at the base of the wall, and in process of time we came near the corner. Here we found an oblique crack about ten inches wide and six inches deep, which led apparently to a flat ledge about fifteen feet above the bottom of the wall. The ledge inclined gently upwards and ended in a hole through which we saw the blue sky. Above the ledge were towering and overhanging rocks clearly enough, but there were only about fifteen feet to climb.

Mikkel, whose working motto is *vi non verbis*, set off at once, merely saying "Hold firmly, please." "Yes," we replied, but I doubt if we could have held a twopenny bun. Our hero wedged himself in the crack, wriggled slowly and carefully upwards like a caterpillar, and reached the ledge without dislodging a single stone. He then planted himself firmly in a little cavern and told us to come on. Todd followed and joined him in the hole. Then the caterpillar crawled onwards and upwards through the little tunnel, and the work was done, as he was now standing on good honest gneiss. After this the camera, rucksacks, and I were hauled up. Mikkel was used to such places, we were not. I believe that one could qualify for such work by climbing for two hours a day for a month up some heap of disintegrated slates at a disused slate quarry, but I leave the experiment for the editor of a future text-book on mountaineering. The only place where I have met with such horrible loose rock as this was on the descent of the South Dent des Bouquetins, near Arolla, in 1887.

The buttress, carpeted with bright alpine flowers, sloped gently and pleasantly upwards. At 10.45 we reached the top, about 5800 feet above sea-level, and to our great surprise, we found a cairn of stones capped by a large lump of white quartz, and near it were some recent footsteps.

"Björnespor" – Bear's footprints – said Mikkel and I together. "Uncommonly like a man's," said Todd in his ignorance. "Ingen mand har været her" – No man has been here – observed the knowing ones. However, after following the track some 300 or 400 feet higher on a snow dome on the glacier above, we saw that they led to a hole in a snow-covered crevasse.

"Er björnen faldt i sprækken?" – Has the bear fallen into the crevasse? – I asked Mikkel.

"Nei langt fra, björnen vilde nok vide bedre. Det maa ha været en mand" – No indeed, the bear would know better than to do so. It must have been a man.

Todd's surmise was correct. A few days previously I had met Bing at Fjærland and had talked to him about the Austerdalsbræ and other choice corners of the Justedalsbræ. Partly in consequence he had crossed the Lunde Skar, and then with the help of Daniel Söknesand he had climbed, fortunately without any mishap, up to the snow-field by a savage gully and steep tongue of ice direct out of the head of the Lundedal, a feat which ought never to be repeated. Then they crossed the snows, and were benighted on the top of this buttress, which they found by sheer good luck, as it is the only one by which a descent could be made into Austerdal. They built the cairn a few hours before our arrival and descended the side of the buttress above the Godt Haabsbræ, while we ascended the end of it. They followed the right bank of the great glacier and we took the left. Consequently, though each party saw traces of the other, we did not meet until three days later. Thus it happened by a strange coincidence that Bing and Daniel share with our party the credit of exploring for the first time the fastnesses of the Austerdalsbræ, and I was glad to have the opportunity soon afterwards of congratulating the bold Bergen mountaineer on his success upon this and several other notable expeditions on which he acted as leader.

We plodded steadily ahead on snow in excellent condition, but soon entered into a thin mist, often the accompaniment of a northerly wind, so that we were unable to see more than the ghosts of three crags not marked on the maps, which I was anxious to locate and have photographed if possible. These crags, I fancy, only appear as rock faces on the south side, otherwise I should have noticed them in former years when traversing the snows north and west. It was all in vain; I could not even make as good a sketch of the ghosts as I did in 1889. An aggravating feature of the mist was that it was so light that we could see blue sky through it.

Our course, planned five years earlier, lay along the trough of a shallow snow valley which falls gently and almost imperceptibly from the watershed for about two miles towards the head of the Mikkelsbræ of which it is the feeder. There could hardly be a greater change than from the pure and almost spotless snow-field to the chaotic ice-fall beyond.

Mikkel led, and developed a by no means uncommon tendency to be always turning to the left hand. Being last on the rope, I could easily notice the slightest deviation from a straight course, and had to call out scores of times "Til hoire," to which Mikkel's cheery voice never failed to respond "Ja ja," and his course was altered, only to be foresaken again after a few yards.

After two hours' tramp the mist was thicker than ever, and I looked in vain for Onsdags Næbbe which I had twice ascended, and which ought to have been visible. We had crossed the watershed and were slowly descending. Though I felt almost certain that we had gone not quite far enough west, I ordered the course to be turned to north-west, so as to avoid any possibility of descending towards the Olden Skar. Of course we overdid it, and reached rocks at the head of the Brixdalsbræ, a terrible ice-fall, instead of the Melkevoldsbræ. We only proved ourselves to be wrong by descending a few hundred feet to a zone below the mists, where I recognised the glen of Brixdal far below. Eventually, we followed a route which a party of four of us had taken in 1884 on the right bank of the Melkevoldsbræ, and at seven o'clock, in cold, wetting rain, we reached the valley of Olden, and made our way to the Brixdals gaard, where we stopped the night very comfortably.

Our day of adventure was ended. A new and perhaps the mightiest and most picturesque of all the great passes over the Justedalsbræ was at last conquered, and we were very happy and contented in consequence. Though we had met with no great glacier difficulties, such will not always be the case. The high snow valley which we traversed so easily will sometimes be full of gaping crevasses.

We spent a jolly evening, and were naturally pleased with the world at large, and with ourselves in particular. It was Todd's first glacier pass, and the best expedition that Mikkel had ever made, and I believe that they had enjoyed themselves as much as I had done. That is saying a good deal.

Two of our projected four days' expedition had now passed. The third, fortunately short, we occupied very pleasantly in crossing the Olden Skar, a pass which will sometime become a favourite with pedestrians. We sauntered leisurely along, and took eight hours on the way to Aamot, though we could easily have walked it in five.

Old friends of mine gave us a hearty welcome. The son of Tolleif now owned the farm, and he and his bright and clever young wife had introduced several improvements into the house.

Whilst discussing plans for the morrow, a heavy shower of rain fell, and I began to doubt the wisdom of adhering to our original plan of traversing Fosheimsdal, so suggested to Mikkel, to whom the whole of the little campaign was new, that we should cross the Fonsdal Skar instead. But no, our warrior would have none of it. It had been done before, so did not smack of adventure and Mikkel was almost indignant at my proposal.

Our host consented to drive us next morning to Fosheim. We were up at three, but as the horse was away on the hills and had to be caught, fed, and shod, we did not leave till five o'clock. The drive of eleven English miles was lovely, and the views of mist-wreathed mountains, with a clear sky above, augured well for a fine day. We reached Fosheim in two hours. The fos, or waterfall, which gives its name to the farm, is pretty, but the only pretty feature of the valley above is its name. There are several sæters but what we remember the most are the bogs, the moltebær – cloud berries – and the hosts of pugnacious lemmings, which invariably challenged us by a shrill squeak whenever we passed within a couple of yards of them.

At the head of the valley we had a steep ascent of about 1000 feet to a little plateau, where, in a dark, sunless cirque, overshadowed by frowning precipices, we found a tarn on which many little icebergs were floating. There was something very uncanny about the place, and we felt glad that we had lunched before we came in sight of it. I proposed that we should cross over the top of a hump of a mountain named Björga, but the romantic Mikkel wisely suggested that it would be a much more beautiful walk along the top of the cliffs which bound the Kjösnæs fjord, and Lundedal on the north. We adopted this suggestion, with the result that we had one of the most interesting walks I have ever taken. Mile after mile we traversed the broad crest of those stupendous cliffs, and saw 4000 to 4500 feet below us the greenish blue waters of that weird arm of Lake Jolster into which we could almost have thrown a stone. The weather was perfect.

> *"A dreamy haze*
> *Played on the uplands, but the hills were clear*
> *In sunlight, and no cloud was on the sky."*

We encountered no difficulties, but passed over three mountain-tops, where we built small cairns. We descended one large snow-field which came down from Björga, and met in the middle of it a peripatetic lemming which was very wroth with us, when, for a moment, we stopped him on his solitary and snowy march.

Then we climbed a rocky hill which entirely disconnects the glaciers on Björga from the Justedalsbræ proper, and discovered that the most western limit of the latter is at a little gap just above, and due south of, the little Befringsdal. This western point is at the end of a narrow glacier arm which the great snow-field thrusts out over the head of Lundedal, and it was up this arm that Herr Bing and his plucky companion had climbed only three days before.

Our walk over the snow domes to the new path leading up to the Lunde Skar was straightforward enough, as no provoking mists were there to puzzle us, and about five o'clock we unroped. We were soon amongst the hurry-skurry and away-they-go tourists in the busy Böiumsdal below.

Our four days' expedition was now ended. Each had been most enjoyable. We had fulfilled my desire of thirteen years by exploring and traversing the Austerdalsbræ, and had connected Hveitestranden and Olden by means of a glacier pass. I had, however, previously proved such a connection to be feasible (*N.T.F.'s Aarbog for 1890*, p. 32). We had made a new pass from Fosheim to Fjærland and had discovered the true western limit of the Justedalsbræ. We were, in fact, well satisfied with the success we had attained, and for a few days took very kindly to the fisherman's gentle art.

Never was a leader better supported by his companions than I had been. Mikkel has an intense love of his native mountains, his enthusiasm is boundless, and he possesses the best qualities of the grand old Norse race. I considered it to be a privilege to act as leading guide to such a man. Though he left his shop, and the hotel which he manages with Herr Dale, at great personal inconvenience, he had not the least intention of accepting any remuneration whatever for his services, saying repeatedly that the pleasure which he had derived had amply repaid him, and it was with great difficulty that I ultimately persuaded him to accept anything whatever.

It was Todd's first campaign; he went as well as any man could have done, and I believe enjoyed himself thoroughly. In fact, my two companions spoiled me and did all the work, allowing me all the fun.

Farvel Mikkel, lev godt, Jeg haaber vi ofte skal reise sammen igjen.

Chapter 14: Three Days On The Skagastölstinder

"Who aimeth at the sky
Shoots higher much than he that means a tree."
GEORGE HERBERT

Perhaps the wisest course to pursue in the case of the heading of this chapter is, to say at once that the "three days" were not three consecutive days, as were the "Two days on an Ice-slope" in Mr. Carr's memorable paper. No indeed. They were merely three separate expeditions on some portions of the range of the Skagastölstinder.

There are five peaks in this range, four in a row, and one, the greatest, which has a basal axis almost at right angles to that of its companions, has in itself three peaklets which oddly enough stand parallel to the line of the four inferior peaks.

After some successful climbing elsewhere, a party consisting of Fröken Therese Bertheau (the first lady who ascended Skagastölstind), Howard Priestman, G.P. Baker, and myself, with our porter, Elias Monssen Hogrenning, managed to squeeze ourselves into Ole Berge's inn at Turtegrö in July 1900. The name Turtegrö signifies the place where "Turt" grows. Turt, a local name for the Mulgedium, is a tall handsome plant with blue flowers somewhat resembling Monkshood, though not nearly related botanically. The place has become a famous resort for mountaineers, as well as for those who through overwork or other causes need to inhale the pure breath of heaven. There are two rival inns, both are very comfortable, and both are kept by delightful men. I have stopped at both and like both.

What a jolly time we spent at Turtegrö! Is it heresy to say that the "off days" picnicking were as enjoyable as the days spent on the mountains? Perhaps it is, so I'll not say so. Think too of the evening dances, the games, the songs, the mountain lectures, and the recitations. How jolly everybody was, Norse, Swedish, and English! Ah! listen to the "sæter jente" at Skagastöl calling her cattle home to be milked. What mellow tones and lovely musical cadences she gets out of that little horn! Now it is midnight, and we want to start at 6 a.m. Just one more dance. How can one refuse when those who ask for it dance so well? I think of old sæter days, and come to the conclusion that if there were more poetry then, there is more food and fun now.

We climbed the Dyrhougstinder on a cloudy day and enjoyed a grand display of the "Spectre." This highly respectable ghost made strange antics above the Skagastöls tarn and glacier, now and then bathing in the cold waters. He was photographed, but I believe he is still an undeveloped ghost. We also reconnoitred the V gap in profile, with a view to the future. We had capital glissades, and though the weather was pretty bad, we enjoyed ourselves.

I think I shall not betray a state secret by saying that we delighted our host, Ole Berge, who is an excellent climber, by asking him to accompany us on the first suitable day on an ascent of Skagastölstind and the traverse of Vesle and Mellemste, or the-little-and-middlemost-Skagastölstinder.

At 5 a.m. on July 28th we sallied forth over the dew-laden and flower-dotted moorland, very gently, as befitting the beginning of a long day. In two hours we reached the Skagastölsbræ. The wild tarn into which this little glacier launches its icebergs was only partly frozen.

At 7.20 we reached the Skagastölshytte. This useful but consists of two rooms, and is solidly built of stones and cement. The roof was blown away several times, but now it is held down by plaited wires which are attached to iron stanchions fixed into the solid rock. A wooden hut, erected by Herr Sulheim at great expense, was blown down, and some of its timbers may still be seen embedded in the ice-walls of a large crevasse. The *Norske Turist Forening* subscribed 2000 kroner for the erection of the present building. The hut is situated at the top of the Skagastölsband or pass. The term "band" is an equivalent of the "hause" in the north of England, and is used where the gap between the mountains is relatively broad. If the gap on the other hand be narrow, the word "skar" is used. For the latter we have no equivalent in English, and the words "pass," "gap," or "neck" are not suitable, as is often the case, we generally draw upon the French for their word "col." I prefer the Norse word "skar," and use it. The view from the hut is superb. It is certainly in a draughty place, as those of us can testify who were there in a furious gale and hailstorm in the year 1889, before the hut was built.

In addition to Skagastölstind, which rises directly above the hut, there is choice of a dozen grand expeditions which may be made from here. Think of the Styggedalstind over Centraltind; of the wild pass over to the head of the

Maradalsbræ, made the reverse way by Herr Hall and never repeated; of that grand eastern ridge of the south Dyrhougstind made by Patchell's party; of the Midt Maradalstind climbs made by A.W. Andrews, A.H. Fox-Strangeways, and Ole Berge. Many more could I name, but it is better to go and see them than to hear of them, and best it is to go and do them.

The hut is well provided with blankets and cooking utensils, and is about 5800 feet above sea-level.

At eight o'clock we started for the climb of the western face, the so-called Heftye's route up Skagastölstind. For an hour we had interesting but easy scrambling up little gullies and over steep bosses of rock. One long steep slab of some 90 feet afforded a minimum of hand-holds, and I was glad when Ole lowered me a rope. At nine o'clock we allowed our photographers a quarter of an hour. The day was perfect and the rocks warm and quite dry. With new snow or ice on the slabs great care is necessary here.

After our halt we roped in two parties. The first consisted of Ole, Fröken Bertheau, and myself; the second of Priestman, Baker, and Hogrenning. For two-thirds of the height we go straight for the summit, which is soon seen after leaving the hut. In the centre of the noble tower which forms the top is a steep gully worthy of Cumberland. This was climbed in 1899, and afforded an excellent variety [28], but by taking it, the most sensational though perfectly safe portion of the climb is avoided. Ole was willing to go either way, but I told him that I wanted to see the well-known traverse and "Heftye's *rende*."

Ole led unerringly through a little portal in a rock curtain on to an irregular ledge. It goes down a few feet and is narrow here and there, but there is a sound rock on which to hitch the rope, and with ordinary care there is no danger. At the end it rises, and we come to another portal. Here we find a little platform, such a one as is welcomed on the Dent du Requin and many a grim Chamouni aiguille.

Now we have time to look about us. I have been on many a narrow ledge on the face of many a square-cut precipice such as that flat footpath on the Mer de Glace face of the Aiguille de Grepon, but never have I seen a precipice so absorbingly interesting as this. Look over the edge; don't be frightened, the others will hold you tight. See those seracs on the Slingsbybræ over 2000 feet straight below you. There is no lateral moraine there. No indeed. The rocks on this face of Skagastölstind are well-nigh imperishable. This huge perpendicular wall rises straight out of the ice, and there is nothing to carry the eye down till it sees the glacier. But let us go on. A few steps up and round a little buttress, but we are still on narrow ledges, almost like flies on a wall, and we arrive at "Heftye's *rende*." This steep chimney starts about eight feet above the ledge, and is undercut below. The first man steps from a convenient rock-stool on to the shoulders of one of the party, and easily reaches a tenpenny nail, which some sportsman has driven into a crack at the bottom of the chimney. This nail, like many of its brethren in the Alps, makes a good foot-hold. The chimney is now easily reached. It is narrow, and a long way from being perpendicular; still, the leader must be no bungler. He must know how to use back and knees, feet and elbows, and if he has had training in the ghylls of our Cumberland fells, so much the better. One man up, the rest soon follow.

We then traverse to the left, still on delightfully narrow ledges and firm rocks. Another steep little chimney, and at 10.48 I give Fröken Bertheau a hearty shake of the hand on the summit of Skagastölstind.

I will not catalogue the different points of interest which we saw in every direction, both far and near; but only remark that the snowy Folgefond, on the south side of the Hardanger fjord, was unmistakable, though 120 miles away.
<29>

It was a little over twenty-four years since I had the good luck to make the first ascent, and it was delightful to be now accompanied by Fröken Bertheau, who had made in the year 1894 the first lady's ascent. She is a born mountaineer, and loves her own native mountains as she ought to do, and by this I mean a great deal.

As we wished to cross the Vesle and Mellemste peaks, we only remained forty minutes on the top, but would have liked four times as much. We left at 11.28. I was now on old ground, and was anxious to see how well my recollection of the route, as far as we were to follow it, was correct or not. I was last on our rope, and was prepared to have my work well cut out for me on the descent.

Yes, the three peaklets I remembered perfectly, and also the way – down some 400 feet. "Ole, that is not the right way; you are going too much to the left." "No, I'm all right. See, here are some of the little cairns which you built yourself." "I went down here," pointing to a gully, "but let me see your way. You are the head guide. On you go." To my surprise he led down a series of steep shallow gullies and little buttresses, a perfectly straightforward way, where care was necessary on account of loose rocks, but where the climbing was interesting rather than difficult. We were all the time in sight of Turtegrö, and if we sent a stone down, it went on to the Skagastölsbræ, a novelty to me. Everything went well. It was a good climb, and resembled many a so-called difficult rock-peak in Switzerland, but the principal difficulties, which had originally faced me at the foot of the climb, were avoided altogether. We emerged on to Mohn's Skar from the north face, instead of from the east, as I had done.

Other surprises awaited me. Mohn's Skar now resembled a pier or sea-wall, with a steep battered wall on each side. On my first visit, the steep southern slope had much deeper snow than now, and a snow-wave was apparently breaking over the pier in the form of a large snow-cornice, and I had to go both under and over it, in order to begin my climb. A similar condition also prevailed in 1878 when Herr Petersen made his ascent. Now, on the other hand, the snow had shrunk, and no wave from it is likely to break over the pier for years to come. Whilst waiting for the second party, I had ample time to examine the mountain closely. I could see, away to the left, the exact place where I had begun my climb, and I am positive that the present route, one which every mountaineer would immediately choose for his highway to the top, did not exist in 1876, as, if it had done so, I could not have helped noticing it. [30] When I arrived all alone on Mohn's Skar on my first visit, I had plenty of time to examine the rocks carefully before Mohn and Knut came up, and I did so. I am certain that the ridge or pier abutted directly against a high wall of rock, and that no easy gateway then existed through or round the northern end of this wall. No, a large portion of this wall has been shattered and battered down by Nature's artillery, probably within a few years of my first visit, and it has, been carried away in the form of moraine by the Skagastölsbræ. Much of the wall still exists and will continue to exist for hundreds of years on the south side of the skar. My chimney will also remain.

Certain it is now, that within view of Turtegrö, an irregular line, where a choice of routes is even possible, leads upwards from the end of the pier. None of the few climbers who have made the ascent from Mohn's Skar since 1878, seem to have been much impressed with the first 100 feet, though they all speak of difficulties on the final ridge. That has always puzzled me, but it never will again. In my case, by far the worst, in every respect, was the first steep, glazed chimney on the south side of the pier end.

Another fact is also very noticeable, namely, that the upper glacier portion of my route is more difficult now than it used to be.

The warm sun had melted all the snow crystals from Skagastölstind, and hence we were all thirsty. To Vesle is now the cry; but a halt is to be called at the first trickle of water. This soon happens, and we enjoy our lunch on some warm slabs, in full view of the noble peak and its greatest precipice. After a pretty climb of some 350 feet, we arrive on Vesle's crown at 1.40.

I frankly confess that, until that moment, I had never fully realised what grand exploits, during many seasons, had been scored by Herr Carl Hall. His foot first trod the peak we were now on. He first traversed the grisly rock ridge to right and to left. Nay, more; he first climbed Mellemste Skagastölstind, that fine rock-pyramid to which we are now making our way. The Centraltind and Styggedalstind, and their jagged connecting ridge, which Sulheim and I talked of traversing twenty years ago, but didn't, claim Hall as their conqueror. Hall has twice climbed Styggedalstind, and by different routes. I have twice tried it, and have twice failed. Ah! think of those two grand passes, each from the Maradalsbræ. They are magnificent. Look westward, and still see Hall's conquests. His footprints are everywhere. No one conversant with the climbing history of the Horungtinder can stand on Vesle Skagastölstind without acknowledging that Carl Hall has laid his plans well, has worked patiently and persistently to execute them, and has met deservedly with great success.

After a half-hour of delightful ridge-climbing up and down, we arrive at the *pièce de résistance*, a smooth rock wall, thirty feet in height at the lowest place, which runs right across the narrow ridge. True, we are on the top of it, and can slide down a rope as Hall did, when he first completed the traverse. But he had to leave two men behind.

Patchell, Bowen, and Vigdal, coming the other way, turned the rocks on the east, and Ole, too, had descended by that way in 1899, and showed us an old rope hanging down a crack in the ridge. By this way we were to go, but a new rope was to be fixed up, and left there. This was soon done, and was tied to a jammed stone, which overhung the top of the gully. Ole went first, and we lowered him out. It was a horrid place, with a truly Norse precipice, a good 3000 feet below us, and we did not much like it, even with our two ropes. It rather resembles the top of Savage Gully, on the Pillar Rock, but has a narrow crack up one side of it.

When Patchell's party made this ascent, Vigdal was hoisted up by the others, and he jammed an axe fast in this crack, then Patchell climbed up, and eventually pulled himself up and over the jammed stone. It was as fine a piece of mountaineering as has been done in the Horungtinder; but, as is often the case when great deeds are done, the doer of it made light of it. [31] Few, if any, men would care to climb down without a rope above them. With one, of course, it is different. After sliding down and landing upon – well! nothing in particular, each of us in turn goes gingerly round a corner, and is told by Ole to "hold on," which he does most grimly. In thirty-five minutes all are down, and the ridge wandering begins again.

"Just look at Skag. What a grand view! Hang it all! I've fired off all my plates, and it's the best view in the Horungtinder. Why hasn't anybody taken it before?"

We all exhaust our stock of suitable adjectives, and, having done so, begin again.

"I'll come again. I must have this view." It certainly was glorious, and came upon us in the nature of a surprise. Skagastölstind stands up like a huge gable, and looks infinitely finer from here than from anywhere else that I have seen. It reminded me of the end view of the Grandes Jorasses which suddenly bursts upon one on the top of the Col Ferret when going from the Swiss side – a view the grandeur of which quite startled Horace Walker and myself when we crossed the pass a few years ago.

Up and down, round or over, on we go. Ole never hesitates a moment. Here, the ridge is only a few inches wide; there, it is as many feet. The rock is almost invariably firm and good, but now and then we find a loose slab, and when we do, we rarely resist the temptation to roll it down, down to the great glacier below. Sometimes three or four of us sit down and shove off the rock with our feet. What a thud, and then a clatter, clatter, for it has broken into a thousand pieces.

At 3.23 we reach the top of Mellemste, and having broken the back of our day's work, we determine to rest and enjoy ourselves. Dry rock means no snow and no water. Eventually, the resourceful Baker finds an icicle, or hard snow, I forget which, and in process of time we are each treated to a couple of spoonfuls of water. We stand in a row and wave handkerchiefs. At last, friends at Turtegrö see us, and their flag is raised and dipped in our honour.

There was one portion of the ridge of this range which had not yet been traversed, and one only. A link was needed to connect the two northern peaks with the Mellemste. It was the vicious-looking V-shaped gap in a depression of the ridge which we had reconnoitred in profile a few days earlier. The 'V' had a tilt over to one side, with the result that, though the northern side was steep, the southern side was all but perpendicular. The passage of this obstacle had been attempted more than once, and was pronounced to be impassable. What better recommendation could one wish for? None.

"Ole, come and let us look at the 'V' from the top." "All right, I'll bring this rope."

Leaving the others peacefully sleeping, and perhaps dreaming that they still had a lot of plates to expose, Ole and I start down the north ridge. I am lowered carefully over some nasty slabs and find that the top of the 'V' can be reached from above, though it is not quite a promenade. That is one point gained. To try to descend it at that late hour of the day with our large party is not to be thought of. We must try it from the north, and so meet the difficulties on the ascent.

"Wake up, you fellows, Dampen piber" (steamer whistle). We set off at 4.32, having been over an hour on the top. Until 6.10 we have magnificent climbing which reminds me, in respect of the intricacy of the route and of its general characteristics, more of the Petit Aiguille du Dru than of any other mountain with which I am acquainted, and great credit is due to Herr Hall and his Romsdal guide for discovering it. For another hour we keep on the ropes, and it is wise to do so, though the sensational parts of the climb, are past. Screes, horrible screes, large and small, succeed. Then a long glissade comes as a great relief.

At 9.30 we reach Turtegrö well pleased with the world at large and the inhabitants thereof.

Though we enjoyed perfect weather and bright warm sunshine on the two days when it was most essential for us to be so highly favoured – first, when crossing the Tyve Skar in Loen to the Nygaardsbræ in Justedal, and, secondly, on our ascent of the Skagastölstinder – the summer of 1900 will be remembered by mountaineers in Norway as being peculiarly treacherous, and the weather prophets were more often wrong than right. Snow fell the day after we climbed the big peaks, and we had no chance of paying a visit to the 'V' for several days, and even then it was with the faintest hopes of success.

It was the last day of July, and we did not start until 12.10 p.m. At three we reached the top of Nordre Skagastölstind, the peak first climbed in 1820 by the plucky scientists, Professors Keilhau and Boeck. Here we remained till 3.35, waiting in vain for the sun to get round. Then we crossed the Næbbe and all climbed some way down the 'V' and shivered in the cold wind. Our party was the same as on the last occasion, except that an active young journalist, Herr Eilert Sundt, had taken the place of Fröken Bertheau, who, to our great regret, was unable to accompany us.

The precipices on the east side of the gap were very savage and contained little hanging glaciers in their hollows, and though clammy clouds boiled furiously up and over all, we could see through occasional rifts that there was no chance of turning the 'V' on that side; and we knew that it could not be turned on the west except by a traverse low down to the usual route up Mellemste. We concluded that if the 'V' be climbed at all, it must be straight up.

A front view of a rock face, whether distant or near, reveals much, but much more is always hidden. From the front one can never properly gauge the mean angle of the rocks as a whole or in detail, and the difficulties almost invariably appear to be greater than they are in reality. A reconnaissance of a difficult rock face should be made in profile as well as in face, if possible. We had done this from the Dyrhougstinder and from the western slope below the 'V' to a certain extent, and we knew pretty well that the face to be climbed was but few degrees out of the perpendicular. We had in addition the mountaineers' tell-tale snow, of two days old, which lay in little streaks here and there on the face of the crag.

Priestman, Ole, and Hogrenning, or "the boy," as we called him, climbed a few feet above the bottom of the 'V' and found that the first serious difficulty could be overcome. Amongst us we picked out the salient features of the crag, which we judged to be about 250 feet in height. We sketched it, and came to the conclusion that the probabilities were that it could be climbed, that it would be a teaser, or that quite possibly the final rock face might turn us back defeated after the lower portions had been conquered. Clearly we must not attempt it with snow on all the ledges, and with that cruel and pitiless icy wind.

At 4.55 we reach the depression between the two northern peaks. As a steep tongue of glacier, perhaps 2000 feet in height, a portion of the great

Styggedalsbræ, comes nearly up to the gap, it is proposed to vary our route back by making a new glacier pass. Ole very truly points out the fact that there is a large bergschrund at the bottom of the tongue, in fact just where it ought to be, and that no bridge can be seen over it. Naturally this is an encouragement to proceed. Tons of rock are heaved over as pilot engines to try the character of the snow on the slope. It is all right, there is no fear of an avalanche. Some of the stones leap gallantly over the crevasse, others are swallowed by its capacious jaws:

"You can never get over that," says Ole.

"Oh yes; we can turn it some way or other. Nature is generally very good-natured, and if she bars one way she opens another."

Four of the party, fired with a laudable thirst for adventure, rope together and prepare to descend. The two others, with a prudence which is equally laudable, keep to the ridge.

"The boy" goes first and soon reaches the snow. It is uncommonly steep, though perfectly safe. In time the lip of the bergschrund is reached. It consists of a straight face, perhaps 35 feet in height at the lowest place, and it certainly has no bridges. It cannot be safely jumped, because the snow which fills it up to a level with the lower glacier is of much too unstable a character to put trust in.

To the right or south side is a chaos of tottering towers of ice which plainly says "No road, trespassers will be-" (the last word obliterated). These might probably be turned by making a traverse of about a quarter of a mile along the side of the steep glacier tongue, and one of the party suggests it, but, strange to say, no enthusiasm in favour of its adoption is shown by the others.

To the left are steep crags of schistose-rock, and at the base of these the schrund is passable in most places. At 5.40 the party step on the rocks, Hogrenning leading. A nasty corner is rounded, and a narrow ledge is reached which may or may not lead to a shallow gully 150 yards away, the nearest point down which it is even remotely possible to gain the glacier.

"One at a time please."
"Hitch the rope on that knob."
"Don't touch that stone, it's awfully loose."
"Throw your axes down."

Down they go, and the senders look with envious eyes on their axes on the snow below. Slowly, steadily, but ever forward. The ledge runs out into the face of the rock as ledges are in the habit of doing. "Up there and along," instead of down, is the order as the rock below is perpendicular.

"How lovely those flowers are!"
"Hang the flowers, and hold on!"

So the time passes. An unlovely boss of rock is climbed, another narrow ledge is traversed, and for the first time for an hour and a half there is good standing-room at the top of the shallow gully. Three men are lowered about sixteen feet. The last man throws the rope over a little spur, and with help from below he lands safely on the three-inch ledge, which, being on sound rock, is considered to be a real good place. A traverse, back this time on hard granite, is now made, then a crack is climbed down. Another traverse back again towards a snow-bridge. Three men are again lowered and their work is done. There is no hitch now, but it is barely twenty feet in height. There is only one hand-hold, and that is at the top. It is not a dangerous place, still it is not a nice thing for the last man to face. He lowers himself as far as he can, and then slides down on the head of Hogrenning's axe, which is placed for the purpose, and at 7.52 all are safely on the glacier. Two hours and twelve minutes of real hard work have been consumed in turning a crevasse of only thirty-five feet.

The Styggedalsbræ, a large glacier, is unusually denuded of snow, and its many crevasses afford ample scope for practice in the finest branch of the mountaineer's art – that of snow-craft – in circumventing the difficulties of an intricate glacier. Opinions vary as to the best main line to be taken, and the leadership is changed, with the result that a fine steeplechase course is followed, instead of a longer and more prosaic one.

A very large avalanche of ice is seen to fall from a hanging glacier on the face of Mellemste, and its thundering noise is very impressive.

An ascent of Mellemste was made from the head of this glacier in the year 1897 by H. Kempson and C.E. Ashford with Ole Oiene. They cut up a steep glacier arm and then followed the more northern of the two buttresses which strike the ridge a little south of the mountain. It was a first-rate expedition in every respect.

At 9.31 the lovely gentians on the moorland below the glacier smile a welcome to the party. A glissade alongside the waterfall is a pleasant change, and in an hour after leaving the glacier, Turtegrö is reached.

The new pass, which had been descended – not crossed – was named the Næbbe Skar. Earlier in the season, this pass, which had proved on this one occasion to be so difficult, could be crossed with ease.

Soon after our return, I had the great pleasure and honour of a visit from Herr Edvard Grieg, who was staying at the other inn, and I feel sure that much of the delightful music with which he has charmed the civilised world has been inspired by the grandeur of the mountains and fjords of his native land, for which he has the most intense love and admiration.

My friends Priestman and Baker could not spare the time for another attempt on the 'V', and went home, and though I had wished to spend the few remaining days of my holiday in another district, the 'V' proved too strong a magnet for me. So I retained Hogrenning and kicked my heels, impatiently waiting for bright sunshine to come and steal away the snow from the crags. Hogrenning did not find the time to hang heavily upon him, as he turned shoemaker. One day he soled nine pairs of boots and shod a horse as well.

Ole and I got up two mornings about four o'clock, but clouds and drizzle drove us to bed again. The second day we really ought to have gone, and would have done so but for "the boy," who hates snow-clad rocks, though in other respects he is an excellent climber. It was well for me that the company at Turtegrö was so charming, that the details of the moorland all around were so beautiful, the colouring of the mosses so exquisitely lovely and varied, and that many a favourite flower, and amongst them the *Linnaea borealis*, could still be picked in quantities near at hand. Had this not been the case, my impatience would have crystallised, and I should have been a general nuisance.

The last day which I could possibly spare for the expedition was Saturday, 4th August. Ole looked out at three o'clock, but as it was raining he did not waken me. However, I looked out about four. At 5.30 it was more promising, so I ordered Ole to rouse "the boy" out of his slumbers, and also Sundt, who was most anxious to accompany us. "The boy" talked about snow still left on the ledges, but agreed to come.

At 11.5 we stood once more in the 'V' gap. Snow lay here and there where we least wished to see it, but even if the sun were to come out brightly, it would not shine on these rocks until three or four in the afternoon, and as it was at best a doubtful day, we could not afford to wait. So an advance was ordered.

Ole was evidently wishful to lead, and being a local guide it was of more importance for him to do so than for anyone else. "The boy," big, strong, and capable as he was, was placed second so that he could back up Ole. Then I came, and lastly Sundt. We used an 80-foot rope, which proved to be rather too short for four men, as Ole needed about 35 feet clear. We had also a spare rope for an emergency. Not a moment was lost. Ole now knew the first stage and was helped up a long slab to a three-inch platform by "the boy," while I hitched well behind to a capital belaying-pin. Then I shoved up "the boy," and Sundt hitched in turn. Ole had now to move on. The place was a shallow gully of some twenty feet in height, in which there was one big knob which stood out exactly where it was most wanted. Unfortunately it was loose, and so was worse than useless, as it was in the way. Ole would have none of it, but, steadied by "the boy," he avoided it and just managed to reach a fairly good hold for the left hand. This formed a footstep too, and with great care he climbed out on to a broad but steep ledge directly over Sundt and me, as we soon found out when he shovelled away the snow and ice and gave us an unexpected bombardment. This is nothing unusual in mountaineering, but, for all that, it is a cold and cutting proceeding.

Now came my turn for the slab, easy enough with a rope above and a shove below. As there were only about a dozen feet of rope between Sundt and me, the former had to leave his hitch and spread-eagle himself for a minute on the slab, whilst I piloted "the boy" up to the ledge. Then Sundt, who is a promising young mountaineer, climbed up very nimbly, and we knocked away the objectionable big loose knob, and both climbed together up to the ledge, a gruesome place in a wind. A short, easy, but straight-up chimney came next, and Ole saying he had good hold, we hurried on, as the cold wind was numbing his fingers and we could not say what was yet in store for us.

Next came some steep slabs without any visible joints. To the left was a sloping ledge covered with snow, and under those conditions it was a sensational place. Still, it seemed to offer the best route. Ole advanced very cautiously over it, and after climbing a short chimney he returned to another ledge just above us and at the top of the slabs, which, with the help of the rope, we soon climbed. An easy traverse to the right was now revealed to us, followed by an interesting chimney, and we knew that we must be near the top crag, which we feared might perhaps be too stiff for us after all. "Can you climb it, Ole?" I called out when I was in the chimney but still out of sight of the crag. "Yes, I think so. Come on," was the cheering reply. Up we went, and at last stood on a roomy ledge. The top crag, perhaps 15 feet in height, was certainly straight up, but there was a crack up the face of it, invisible from below. Ole, however, followed the ledge to the right, and a still better crack appeared on the west side. We were soon up, and at 1.58, or in 53 minutes from the bottom of the 'V', we found ourselves on the top of this troublesome letter.

Much of the climb reminded me of the north side of the Ennerdale Pillar below the Stomach Traverse, but on the whole, the Cumberland climb is perhaps rather the more difficult of the two, although not so sensational.

On the top of the 'V' there is a remarkable flat rock platform of about 200 square yards. Seen from the neighbouring Dyrhougstind this platform resembles the seat of a huge easy chair, the crags above forming the back. This naturally suggested the name of Ole Berge's Stol, which it will doubtless bear for many a long year to come.

When the necessary cairn was built, we set off to complete the climb of Mellemste. Ole, encouraged by success, went straight at it up some nasty rock slabs where there was little to hold on by, although an easier way could have been found on the western side.

We reached the top at 12.14, and would have probably traversed the whole range as far as the Gjertvastind, a superb expedition, if it had been a fine warm day such as that which we had enjoyed exactly a week earlier on the same peak. It was, however, cold and clammy, and there was an icy wind blowing; so we descended by Hall's most interesting route, and reached Turtegrö at 4.20.

The Norse and English mountaineers at Turtegrö took a great interest in our expedition and gave us a very warm welcome. They seemed to think that it was peculiarly fitting that the man who in 1876 made the first ascent of Skagastölstind, should have been one of the party to cross the 'V' gap for the first time, and by doing so forge the last link in the chain which connects the whole of the Skagastölstinder. This new route is a welcome addition to the many fine climbs within easy reach of Turtegrö. Indeed, it is the nearest of them all. Though Mellemste Skagastölstind has now been climbed from each of the four cardinal points of the compass, I am glad to believe that there is no way which can truthfully be called an easy one.

I much regretted that Fröken Bertheau had not shared in our success, especially as I believe that her reason for not joining us was her fear that the addition of another member to the party might possibly endanger its success by making us go slower in the doubtful weather which prevailed. If anyone at Turtegrö deserved to share in so grand an expedition, it was certainly the excellent climber who had made the first lady's ascent of the great peak, and had, by so doing, set such an admirable example to her sex. Fortunately, Fröken Bertheau succeeded not only in crossing the 'V' gap, but traversed the whole range over to the Gjertvastind in 1901.

By waiting for this climb, Hogrenning and I missed the steamboat connection at Skjolden, and, oddly enough, it took him six days to reach his home in Stryn. I was driven to Dosen by Sulheim, and then had to take a weary boat row to Lærdal. Yes, but I would willingly have been rowed the whole 150 miles of the Songefjord rather than have missed this last grand climb.

Chapter 15: Arctic Norway: Two Ascents Of Strandaatind

"Round the shore where loud Lofoden
Whirls to death the roaring whale,
Round the hall where Runic Odin
Howls his war-song to the gale."
    CAMPBELL. Ode to Winter.

Many of us were introduced at an early age by Harriet Martineau, in her charming little book *Feats on the Fjord*, to that mystic Norse Northland within the Arctic Circle, and have been by fancy led to picture the glistening snows of the monarch Sulitelma, the shadows of its rugged rocks projected upon its glaciers and the pine forests and mountain pastures which insensibly lead the eye down to the romantic Salten fjord below. Others have had their imaginations stirred by the modest story of "Peter and the Bear," which treats of much the same region. Edgar Allan Poe has also invested Nordland with a halo of romance which will ever abide, and all have heard of the Maelström. Collie is right in saying "Personally, I consider that by far the most beautiful part of the journey to the Norwegian Northland is after one passes the Arctic Circle." His description of the scenery in this paper in the *Alpine Journal* is the truest and the best that I have read. [32]

Years ago I became the happy possessor of the best book which has yet been written on Norway by any foreigner, the mountain classic, *Norway and its Glaciers*, visited in 1851, by Prof. Jas. D. Forbes, F.R.S. During the last thirty-five years I have very often turned over its pages and have almost invariably been attracted by a somewhat flamboyant but yet an unexaggerated sketch of "Mountains near Folden Fjord."

Oddly enough, though I had made three mountaineering campaigns in Arctic Norway, I had only once come by this part of the coast in a coasting vessel, and that was in the middle of the night, but had always crossed the Vest fjord on an express boat between Bodö and Svolvær. Hence, I had only seen very distant views of these mountains, the existence of which seemed to me to be more or less mythical.

Early in the summer of 1912 I was invited by our fellow-members C.W. Rubenson and F. Schjelderup to join them and another excellent Norsk mountaineer, Harald Jentoft, in a mountaineering campaign on the mainland in Arctic Norway, principally near the mouth of the Sör – or South – Folden fjord, some 25 miles N. of Bodö and between Lat. 67° and 68°, i.e. farther north than any portion of Iceland.

I accepted this invitation at once, on conditions that I should be taken up the grim monolith Stedtind, which two of the party and Alf Bryn had ascended the previous year by the route discovered in 1904 by Collie, W.E. and A.M. Slingsby, but which at that time was rendered impossible by a gale of icy wind.
<33>

There were also two other good reasons why I should join the party. First, because the company was excellent; and secondly, because wet weather in England had engendered a little rheumatism, and, as I had on one occasion completed a cure for lumbago by making the descent of Gaping Ghyll (near Ingleborough in Yorkshire) and joining in the survey of some newly discovered passages, when we were nearly impounded by a flood caused by a thunderstorm, it was a fair assumption that camp life in Arctic Norway would be just what I needed. The result entirely justified the prescription.

Fortunately, I was able to get from Howard Priestman much valuable information about the district we intended to visit. He also gave me some photographs which proved to be a great help.

So far as I am aware, the first visit of any mountaineer with designs upon the weird peaks of that wild but beautiful region of Sör Folden was that of Herr Carl Hall of Copenhagen in the year 1889. With two guides from Romsdal, first-rate cragsmen, he climbed the Folden fjord Troldtind, and the western but lower peak of the Strandaatinder. Farther north he also ascended the Tilthorn, but failed, like so many other men, on Stedtind.

On July 23rd I left home and early on 25th reached Bergen where, in order to fit in with the arrangements of my comrades, I had to remain for two days and one night. The picturesque old city was as busy as ever, and bright sunshine, with corresponding deep shadows, intensified the beauty of the surroundings. I bathed twice at the headland, and so warm was the water that it seemed almost sinful to leave it. Only a few days previously I had shivered in the sea at Scarborough. At the new wireless telegraph station on the top of that high sunbaked hill I had a very interesting conversation on international politics with an official, who unbent when quite sure that I was not a "Tusker." <34>

Yes, such a jolly voyage north in golden sunshine and over rippleless waters! I even breakfasted whilst rounding that dangerous and generally most tempestuous headland, Stadt, the westernmost point of Scandinavia, and what is more I did not realise that we were so far until I said to the steward, "How soon shall we come to Stadt?" when he replied, "We are nearly round it now."

At Aalesund, Rubenson and his bride joined me. They had been mountaineering in Jotunheim and had ascended Skagastölstind. The following day Schjelderup, Jentoft, and a lady friend of Fru Rubenson's joined us at Throndhjem.

Such perfect weather and so little, so marvellously little, snow on the mountains! No need in these days to send a boat ashore and to buy a favourable wind from a Lap necromancer, however famous he might be. No need then to pay for such a wind the sum of "ten crowns and a pound of tobacco." No I these are the prosaic days of steam and not such as they were in the year 1653 when this bargain and most successful fulfilment were made. Perhaps we have the advantage, but who can tell?

On Monday afternoon, July 29th, the cosy little steamer *Salten* gently glided over rippleless water into the sound of Kjerringo. As it was low tide we had to land in a large boat.

We went to the merchant's house and were most hospitably received by Herr Gerhard Kristiansen and his wife. Here off and on we spent five whole days.

Across a narrow strait is a flat island strip which in early summer is the home of innumerable eider duck. The view from this island is superb. Across the silver water streak are the pier, the warehouses, and the pretty white-painted wooden houses typical of the *amt* or province of Nordland. Beyond, in rich meadows, are a small settlement and the church with its pretty spire which tells the tale that Kjerringo is the centre of the district. Above are gentle rolling wooded uplands and beyond these a forbidding range of black mountains including the Troldtind.

The great feature is the grand range of the Strandaatind, so much admired by Forbes, and, from the window in my bedroom, I had before me only four and a half miles away the view of this lovely range.

It consists of a double-peaked mountain of which both peaks rise on the south side with most forbidding ice-planed precipices from a low and partly wooded line of foot hills. At their base are smiling fields and many cosy little farms. For their upper two thousand feet both peaks are exceedingly narrow, and the two walls, northern and southern, have been planed by the glaciers of old to a complete absence of cracks, chimneys, or ledges. There are black streaks running down the smooth sides which on the north give the appearance of the inside of the frame and the ribs of a shipwrecked vessel. Not one of these streaks indicates a place which would afford the passage for a goat. The walls are indeed terrible, that of the higher peak being fully 2000 feet of smooth rock, but the lines of the mountain are exceedingly beautiful.

The western and lower peak springs from the shore or *strand*. The *aa*, or river, on the south of, and almost parallel with, the axis of the mountain probably supplies another syllable in the name of the mountain. This western peak has a broad base on the sea front which turns first into a Roman nose and then into a jagged ridge.

Between this peak and its loftier rival is a great gash narrow at the bottom. At the east side of this gash and on the side of the higher peak there is a great square-walled perpendicular crag, some 60 feet in height and easily visible from the farms below. Above this, though the ridge is narrow and steep, there is only one place – a notch and a high crag – which would be likely to stop a determined and skilful party. This much knowledge we gained during a lovely walk which Kristiansen took us in the evening after our arrival, when Rubenson and I studied the peak carefully through our glasses. East of the principal mountain, but detached, is a group of peaks the lines of which recall some of the loveliest in Söndmore.

Next day was Rubenson's birthday, and the day on which two years previously he had led his party up to the top of what Woolley describes as "that singular caprice of Nature, the smooth and naked Stedtind." [35]

We left the house at 9 o'clock with little if any intention of doing more than to prospect the route to be followed later. Indeed we thought we should return in the afternoon, so took very little food with us. For 4 ½ miles we followed a good road through smiling fields of potatoes, hay, and barley. Cosy little farmhouses, and men, women, and children at work in the fields, all added to the interest. Many peasants told us that they "had seen the Dane (Herr Carl Hall) on that very top," the lower peak. As we advanced, the higher peak put on a very ferocious aspect.

For an hour, we followed the coast line, sometimes on the coral and shell-besprinkled sands, at others along cattle paths. Most beautiful it all was. In time we rounded the blunt end of the mountain and for the first time we saw into the grand cirque, Laaterbotn, well shown in Prof. Forbes's sketch. Here through forest and ling, over the crags and up the beck courses in order to avoid the trees, we found our way.

Even at an earlier period I had discovered that the legs of two of my Norsk friends were abnormally long and those of the third were very muscular and strong. Now, the fact was more than evident, and I realised too that "Anno Domini" had something to say on my behalf. [36] There was one redeeming point – the moltebar (cloudberry) in golden ripeness grew in profusion. Still, if the Norskmen liked the delicious fruit, so too did the Yorkshireman; and it was hot, very hot.

Above the tree line the interest increased and the northern face of both peaks looked ever more and more forbidding. Hardly was there a place for a sea eagle to perch on that gruesome wall. Near the sea end of the western peak is a small northern buttress and a corner. Obviously this led to a gap on the main ridge. In ordinary summers the top of the cirque into which we had now arrived must hold an immense amount of snow. Now there were only patches.

Up to the corner we went with little difficulty though care was needed here and there. We knew from Hall's account that we could at least climb the lower peak. We reached a gap in the ridge, at a height of some 2000 feet. I was tired and went slowly. Rheumatism also troubled me in one knee. Still I could climb. I had tested this during a couple of hundred feet where we had some easy climbing. Moreover, the great interest had begun, the rocks ahead partook of the Chamonix aiguille character and were absolutely sun-dried and warm. I knew I could reach the first summit. Should I continue and keep back my companions, or should I return? This question was one which I had not often put to myself. I quickly realised that it would not be fair to the others for me to proceed, though they pressed me to do so. I told them that I would return. One other factor which led to my decision was that we had so small a supply of food with us. After handing some of my share to Rubenson I sent them off with my best wishes, and climbed a little crag behind so that I could see them the better. Yes, it is quite true my feelings were mixed.

For 200 or 300 feet I watched them closely, overcoming one obstacle after another under Schjelderup's skilful leading. When they vanished, I turned towards the Lofoten Islands, a serried line of gabbro peaks, clear cut against the deep blue sky some 70 odd miles across the Vest Fjord. This made me supremely happy.

With due care I descended into the basin of the high mountain cirque close to a tiny tarn where I sat on the sunwarmed rocks, watching my friends gain the first summit. Then they vanished for a long time but reappeared at the gap. Unexpectedly, a shower of rain came on, the only one which I saw in Norway that summer. I sheltered awhile; then, noticing that they were closely examining the great slab of rock at the foot of the higher peak, I realised that they contemplated the possibility of its ascent.

Meanwhile I studied with my field glass the north-east arête in profile. This was a route which I had advocated the previous evening, though, truth to say, I had not seen the arête itself, as it was at the back and then out of sight; but I was certain that one existed, and that it must start from a relatively high gap. Two conclusions were soon arrived at: first, that the gap between Strandaatind and the Laater fjeld could be reached, and secondly that some two thirds of the way up the arête there would almost certainly be much difficulty.

About two hours later I got to the hamlet of Strand, and looking up I saw a figure on the top of the great slab in the gap. A farmer came to me and pointed out the figure to me. Others came and their interest was intense. I think at first they looked upon me merely as a chicken-hearted foreigner but were pleased when they found I could speak Norsk. As was most natural they were mightily pleased when I told them that all the three men up there were Norsk, also that their success was almost assured.

> *"In cold laborious climes the wintry north*
> *Brings her undaunted warriors forth,*
> *In body and in mind untaught to yield,*
> *Stubborn of soul, and steady in the field."*

When I arrived at Kjerringo, I found Kristiansen standing on a little knoll above his house with a Norsk flag ready to hoist on the flagstaff. He had seen the party in the gap and was fully prepared for the result. At 8 p.m., a few minutes after my return, we were delighted to see the gallant trio reach the summit, and the national flag was duly hoisted and dipped in their honour. With Kristiansen's powerful telescope we noticed them building the inevitable cairn. Rubenson had therefore again celebrated his birthday on the summit of a maiden peak in Nordland and had successfully accomplished a bold deed, which he thoroughly deserved.

We went to bed as usual, well knowing that the party could not return for several hours, though there was no darkness to hinder them: but we were up betimes. Six o'clock came, and then seven and eight, when we became a little uneasy and prepared to meet them. Kristiansen, armed with a long Alpine rope, and I with food, set off at 8.30. We met them two hours later. They were desperately hungry and (shall I say it?) they were tired. When they reached Kjerringo, they had been 26 hours out. Truly a good training walk!

I would not like to say that the Yorkshireman could not have done it, even with a few twinges of rheumatism; but I will say that if he had done so, the length of the expedition would have been extended at least to 30 hours.

In the *N.T.F. Aarbok* for 1913 Schjelderup has given a graphic account of the ascent of Strandaatind. The traverse of the lower peak was sensational, interesting, and certainly difficult. When however they reached what from below we deemed to be the crucial point, a 60-foot slab, smooth and perpendicular, their hopes of success were faint.

At the foot of the slab they found a cairn built by Hall's guides in 1889. This plainly said,

> *"Thus far shalt thou go, but no farther."*

The three hardy Norskmen, with whom I would trust myself as readily as with any men living, were not the men to give up without a trial, even when damped by the one shower of the campaign. There was not a chance of turning the obstacle, as on each side was clear inaccessibility.

It was Schjelderup's turn to lead and he would have loved to have done so, though probably his reach would have proved too short; but, as it was the birthday of the hero of Kabru, Schjelderup, with rare self-denial, gave up his turn to his lifelong friend Rubenson.

The leader put on rubber shoes as the rock was as smooth as the bald pate of an alderman, and the slab was 60 feet in height. Fortunately, detached from, but near to, the great slab was a rock of some 20 feet in height. This gave Schjelderup an opportunity of giving a little support to Rubenson's feet. Jentoft lower down was holding Schjelderup in. The only chance of success lay in the remote probability of being able to traverse diagonally up the slab towards the south, where a flake of rock suggested the existence of a miniature chimney, or crack, up the edge of the slab, but yet out of sight.

A few mere scratches on the face of the slab afforded but little hold for hand or foot, and Rubenson's great length of arm and leg was none too much. He came down once, and all three took a good breath. In a couple of minutes "Jentoft the tall" held Rubenson's feet in and slowly yet surely the bold leader advanced, whilst Schjelderup took a photograph of him at work. As usually is the case, the tendency was to fall outwards. The miniature chimney did exist, but was of little service. The rain shower had wetted the rocks, the rubber shoes were unreliable and Rubenson longed for his nailed boots. The situation became critical, a hasty conference was held, and meanwhile Rubenson's fingers became cramped.

A small notch was noticed in the edge of the rock flake. Happy thought! "Switch a rope over it, if possible." After several trials this was done. Very gently, very firmly, it was held and Rubenson pulled himself a few feet up and behind the face of the slab and above a ghastly mural precipice many hundreds of feet in height. In due time he stood as a conqueror on the flat top of the slab, and there I saw him when I was talking to the farmers in the rich lowlands. Rubenson frankly admitted that this was much the most difficult climbing that he had ever done. This means much. The two others found the difficulties very great, even with the rope above them. The second great crag on the ridge, which Rubenson and I had examined very carefully through our glasses, proved to be more sensational than difficult. The climbing of the whole of this narrow ridge was really first-rate. In three hours from the gap the summit was reached. Mummery says "To set one's utmost faculties, physical and mental, to fight some grim precipice, or force some gaunt, ice-clad gully, is work worthy of men." Yes, this was a magnificent climb, and one which called forth the full powers of the men who undertook it, and it was worthy of them.

The descent was difficult enough, and, hanging down the faces of the two great crags, ropes will probably remain for many years to puzzle the inquisitive eagles or ravens which may chance to perch thereon.

At 10 p.m. they reached the gap. After a short rest they tried to descend due south between the two peaks. Some 1200 feet down their way was blocked by impassable crags, they were dog-tired, there was grass. Surely too, sleep would come! At 2.30 a.m. they got up and at 4.30 reached the gap once again. They recrossed the lower peak and at last were heartily welcomed by Kristiansen and myself at the little hamlet of Strand.

This brilliant success on a mountain which had been attacked on several previous occasions was duly recognised by our genial host and his wife, and I am sure that the remembrance of the first ascent of the mountain which ennobles the more placid beauty of the rich farm-lands at its base will be cherished by the farming-fisher folk, their wives, and families, for many years to come.

Without much difficulty I persuaded my companions to set aside a day for us to attempt the ascent of Strandaatind by the route which I had chosen, namely by the north-east ridge. I, on my part, offered to cancel the arrangement which had previously mainly interested me, that my friends should accompany me on an ascent of Stedtind. This was to follow some expeditions in Sör Folden.

We made two most successful expeditions from a sunny camp at the bend of the Sjunk fjord <37> and on returning from one had a very narrow escape from having our boat capsized in a sudden storm. My companions, excellent oarsmen, fought manfully against a head wind; but we were driven back and had a walk of many weary hours along the pathless shores of the fjord, in some cases over huge avalanche debris overgrown with alder and Scotch firs. I lagged terribly behind, and I shall ever remember seeing Rubenson awaiting me when I thought him a half hour ahead. Ultimately he got me a boat which brought us to camp. The two other men had wisely gone ahead to prepare a much-needed meal.

We had scored some successes in Sör Folden, but alas I had suffered one notable failure. Here we found ourselves in the lap of luxury once again at Kjerringo. The weather was perfect as it had been the whole time we were in Arctic Norway. Yes, we have every reason now to look back upon the summer of 1912 as ideal. What a contrast to 1912 in the Alps, practically to that of the whole Continent. The only weak point was crudeness and lack of the lovely half-tones of colour, which form usually such a distinguished feature of Nordland. This was due to the dry weather. At Kjerringo the thermometer often showed 88° to 92° F., and once 90° in the shade, and at nine o'clock in the evening!

My last available day for mountaineering this summer, August 10, arrived all too soon, but we were determined to make the best of it. For once we were up in good time and were rowed by an old fisherman to the coral cove, and enjoyed to the full the view from the sea which inspired Prof. Forbes with enthusiasm and led him to make his sketch of "Mountains near Foldenfjord." This sketch, which is from the west, well shows the lower part of the cirque, though not a wicked-looking buttress which divides it in two, the buttress being hidden by the lower peak of the Strandaatind in the centre of the view.

The highest peak is that on the right. Its summit is barely 3000 ft. above the blue waves.

The little journey by boat had been most enjoyable and I think we were all sorry to land. However we found the now well-known cirque, the Laaterborn, as beautiful as ever, the slopes as steep, and the cloudberries, though not quite so numerous as on our previous visit, if possible more delicious.

Camp life and plenty of exercise had not only driven away my rheumatism, but had put me into rather better training than when I toiled up through these woods and up the bare rocky hill slopes a short time before.

When under the northern walls of Strandaatind, we turned to our left instead of the right as before. My love of snow led me a little out of the way to two little snow-fields. To my mind the only disappointing part of climbing the grim aiguilles and horns on the mainland and near the coast in this part of Nordland arises from the absence of glaciers, or even of snow gullies in the summer. It is very different in the Lyngen peninsula and even at the head of the Sör Folden fjord where there are large glaciers.

Two or three hundred feet of rocks gave us a little climbing to reach our real starting point, a saddle between Strandaatind and the Laaterfjeld.

The view from this saddle of the northern wall of Strandaatind was most striking. Here could we see our work now fully revealed to us, and it was easy to realise that success could not be attained without a struggle. Indeed the issue was doubtful. Our feelings were probably mixed. A failure here could not possibly mean so much to my comrades as it would to me. Indeed, it would add a lustre to their mountain. Yes, surely it would be rather hard too, on the long-called inaccessible and unconquerable mountain itself if a second feasible route should be found up it? Herr Hall had declared it to be absolutely hopeless to try new routes, or apparently any route at all, as he had failed on the west arête.

I too was the one who first believed that there was a fair chance of success on this ridge, and I had brought Rubenson also into my way of thinking when we saw the peak from a hill above Kjerringo. The others with rare good nature were willing to help me to indulge in my idiosyncrasy.

From the saddle the ridge, or rather blunt but narrow end of the mountain, resembles the north face of the Pillar Rock, but is steeper and not a third of the width, and fortunately a Pillar Rock minus moss, bent grass, bilberry roots, and sedums.

As in the case of the other route there were manifestly two crucial places. A crag fairly low down, and a black chimney in the narrow face, both unavoidable. Lunch on dry moss. [No, we didn't eat the moss.] Then the inevitable pipes. Very suitable too. Delightfully warm and such a grand view of the Lofoten peaks across blue seas.

"Come along, you fellows! I want to see that black chimney."

We were soon hard at work, up and over, or under and through, a maze of huge blocks which had thundered down the mountain at a place where the ridge had become very narrow. A square-cut and partly overhanging crag barred our way.

"Hallo! Here's a cairn."
"Ah, yes! Only another 'Thus far shalt thou go, but no farther.' "
"Why, it's only 15 or 16 feet high at most."
"I wonder who built that thing. It was not many years ago."
"Evidently it was built by novices."

Schjelderup was hoisted up and on to Jentoft's head and steadied by an axe to where he reached a good hold. A few pulls and he soon stood on the top, saying, "This is the place for a cairn."

We had discussed the question whether we should use the rope before now or not, but agreed to wait a little. Now it was needed and for a couple of hundred feet we had really good rollicking fun. The rocks were mostly firm and gave excellent hold. Narrow ledges, some flat, others inclining upwards, alternated with little chimneys, then letter-boxes where we posted and delivered ourselves;

or as a change, came steeply inclined blocks up which we went astraddle. It was the orthodox Chamonix-aiguille type of climbing, barring one great feature – the presence of snow or ice.

We approached the foot of the black chimney, and the nearer we came to it the less we liked it. Rubenson prospected the ridge itself which we had left. It was very narrow, terribly steep, and altogether most unpromising, and he came down to us.

In order to get into the chimney it was necessary to traverse the plinth of a huge rough natural pilaster which formed one side of the portal of the chimney. There were no handholds and the diminutive ledges of which the plinth was formed sloped downwards at an angle of about 35°. Moreover they were wet or greasy. Below this was a ghastly precipice. Schjelderup led and was paid out by a long rope which, after all, was not long enough. Jentoft followed, and when he got into a position of rather less unstable equilibrium than usual Schjelderup advanced to the actual foot of the chimney, where he had the semblance of a handhold. Rubenson and I followed and the two others had to move up. The chimney was perpendicular and about 150 ft. in height from the place where we struck it. A mid-rib divided it in two for about 12 ft. in height, and this was the only easy place in the ghyll. Above this a tall man can go up by back and foot progression. A short-armed man has to do as best, or as little bad, as he can. As Schjelderup was too short in the limbs, Jentoft went first and climbed this horrid place brilliantly. Near the top the rocks bulged outwards and there was a well-nigh unconquerable inclination to fall out. It was certainly an unpleasurable place and we all disliked it. The view between one's legs downwards was not of the nature to stimulate any latent artistic tastes. Well! All of us have been in such places and most of us may again, but we only go there as a means to an end. For a few feet near the top I was hoisted up like a sack of potatoes. This mode of progression at least saved time.

How we enjoyed the bright sunshine when we reached a platform at the top of the ghyll can easily be imagined. From here the climbing was thoroughly enjoyable, neither too easy nor yet difficult. We reached the summit rather unexpectedly in 2½ hours from the saddle, and I had the pleasure of photographing the three gallant Norskmen who had made the first ascent of the mountain only ten days previously.

The view is inexpressibly grand. The recesses of numberless unknown fjords are unfolded. Smoke issues from cosy homesteads in many an unexpected comer.

East and south are several truncated pyramids, ugly enough in themselves, but which harmonise with their savage surroundings. Some of these we had ascended. Far, far away east, at the head of Sör Folden, are range upon range of snowy mountains, on or across the Swedish frontier. Sulitelma, that mysterious ice-girt mountain, invested with so charming a halo of romance years ago, was one of these. Kebnekaisse, explored and ascended by the Frenchman M. Charles Rabot, is there, white and glittering. Farther north are the ice-bound fjelde and nunataks of Frostisen, ascended by Hastings, but about which he has told us so little. Yes, that is Stedtind, and mellowed by distance it looks less ferocious than usual. South, the glaciers of Svartisen sparkle in golden sunshine. Nearer to us are dozens of sharp peaks. But look below the terrible precipice on which we are standing, see the smiling homesteads of the many farmer-fisher folk. They are now cutting the barley or leading hay, but see their boats in land-locked safety, ready for the herring in summer or for the cod in winter. See the forest lands and be thankful for the comparative absence of the pernicious goats, the ruthless destroyers of all young trees. That white-painted house is the school, wisely closed during the harvest months. In every direction there is something which fascinates us.

Yes, but look 70 miles away across the placid water of the Vest fjord! See that grand array of sky-piercing gabbro peaks, standing out clear-cut against the deep blue sky. Where but in the Lofotens can such a glorious line be seen? Deeply cut is this line in some places, because the Lofotens consist of many islands great and small. Still it is a chain, here and there a doubled or a trebled chain, of mountains 80 miles in length. Even at that distance, through the clear atmosphere which usually prevails in Nordland in summer we easily recognise many old friends in the serried ranks of peaks. First of all let us greet the noble Vaagekallen, the long-called "inaccessible aiguille," [7] which rises superbly out of the deep waters; nor must we omit to take off our hats when we see the island Skraaven, where lived the greatest of all Nordland mountain pioneers, Martin Ekroll. Naturally the twin-peaked Rulten claims my homage and the sight of it awakens many delightful recollections. Let us look too at the island Moskenesoen. The Maelström is only a mile or two away from its southern headland! Have we not had our sympathies awakened when we pictured the full-rigged ship – did we ever think of the crew? – or the ponderous whale being drawn into the vortex of the Maelström? Can we not in some measure also follow Kircher in his weird imagination and see the same ship and the same whale, possibly rather bruised, as they emerge from their subterranean voyage on to the placid waters of the Gulf of Bothnia?

A cold wind and the remembrance that we were to leave Kjerringö by steamer soon after midnight warned us to be off. In addition to this we wished to be below that most gruesome black chimney.

We had noticed, soon after regaining the ridge or nose of the buttress which ends the mountain on the south-east, that a little crack, or an undeveloped ghyll, existed just over the main axis of the buttress from the side of the black chimney. It was worth trying whether we could descend by this to some ledge along which we could traverse to a place below the mouth of the black chimney, but yet on our original line.

We started merrily and we got into a broad shallow gully; very steep it was too, and we saw that the steepness was approaching perpendicularity. Fortunately, we found a natural pillar, an Arctic milestone, on the side of this gully. It was perfectly firm and we knew that we could rely on its stability. The gully continued some 50 or 60 feet below the milestone and then ended at the top of a shoot.

Rubenson and I stopped at the pillar, and having anchored ourselves we lowered the two others down to the top of the shoot. Here there was an overhanging rock on the top of which was a notch which made a partial hitch, but only when the rope was held to its place. Jentoft was then lowered to a very small ledge, and guided by the rope above him to the main ridge. Then after I had come down to the top of the shoot, we lowered Schjelderup. Rubenson meanwhile discovered what he conceived to be an easier place to descend than over the shoot proper. With the help of a rope which I had hitched, he got down to the little ledge but could go no farther for want of rope. The Yorkshireman felt that he was "up a tree" and awaited developments.

"Now then, Slingsby; put your rope on to that notch on the overhanging rock, and climb down."

This was all very well in theory, but it would absolutely fail in practice because the notch was but a snare and a delusion. Very shallow it was and only one sided. Such in fact that the pull of a rope from below must inevitably cause the rope to slip off. True the distance to be descended to the narrow perch below was only some 50 or 60 feet; but many hundreds of feet below this, one looked down at a terrific angle upon a cheval-de-frise of sharp rock needles, and most fiendish and threatening they appeared. I have rarely, if ever, seen such truly savage rocks.

We were now perched in three places. Two were for the moment in perfect safety, but could not climb up to any position where they could help me. Rubenson could not proceed for want of rope, and he and I were sticking to the rocks like limpets as best we could. After a futile suggestion on my part that I should try to climb down without help from above, a short conference was held. The outcome of this was that Rubenson climbed up again to me with the aid of the rope and then up to the Arctic milestone round which, having cleared away a few stones, he ascertained that a rope could be drawn safely. I was then lowered, and drawn on to the ridge below. Even this process was not too easy. Meanwhile Rubenson was at the Arctic milestone and out of sight. An extra 60-foot rope was tied on to the long one we had been using. Schjelderup climbed up some 20 or 30 feet on the ridge and held on to the rope whilst Rubenson tied himself on the other end and began to descend. The rope ran beautifully round the smooth milestone whilst Rubenson descended to the top of the shoot. Then he swung himself carefully over the edge and according to Schjelderup, "he hung dangling like a spider at the end of a long thread, and swaying about in the wind like a pendulum." We drew him in carefully and the other end of the rope ran beautifully round the milestone and, we all stood in safety in a little gap on the ridge.

Although the descent of this formidable though short place had occupied two hours of hard and careful work, we had avoided the black ghyll which would have taken all our powers and care to descend safely, without giving us any compensating pleasure. Our new route on the other hand was very enjoyable.

The rest of the ridge or buttress gave us much interest, and though it was not absolutely essential, a length of rope was cut off at the rock above the "Thus far" cairn, and we used the now much too common "abseilen" method and soon stood on the great saddle and below our climb. From here we descended in a south-easterly direction by rocks, sheep lands, and down rock terraces covered with primeval forest which was hot and not too easy for quick walking.

In due time we gained a little hamlet and drank much delicious milk. A six miles' walk through rich pastoral lands brought us once more to Kjerringö, where, though it was 1 a.m., we found an excellent supper provided for us.

It was by no means an easy matter to leave so lovely and so interesting a place, and we parted from our kind host and hostess and other good friends with regret. My companions were bound for the Lofotens, whose peaks we could see clear against the blue skies. It was only 5 a.m. when we left, and at that time Strandaatind and the forest-clad hills below were suffused with a deep purple hue which, owing to the warm weather, had not been so general as usual.

"Farvel Kristiansen. Lev godt."

At Bodö our party broke up. Rubenson, taking advantage of the opportunity of getting a well-earned nap, was left on board the coasting steamer which quickly left the quay. We took a boat and found him fast asleep and chaffed him a good deal because the little steamer was soon to set off with a party of a hundred teetotallers for a day's trip up the Salten fjord. My friends left for Svolvær, to join Fru Rubenson and her friend, and ascended the Svolvear Gjeita.

There are still many grand and new mountain expeditions to be made in Arctic Norway. Of this fact the Norsk mountaineers are now fully aware, and year by year the number of maiden summits gets less and less. Let members of the Alpine Club note this fact.

Chapter 16: Farvel!

"Let us be grateful to writers for what is left in the inkstand;
When to leave off is an art only attained by the few."
LONGFELLOW.

All who are worthy of being termed mountaineers, in contradistinction to climbing acrobats, find that year by year their love of mountains increases, and so too does their respect and veneration. They feel more and more, as they gain experience, that the sport of mountaineering – the finest sport in the world – is to be treated seriously. They will not deny the fact that with this sport, as with all other noble sports, there is a certain element of danger; but they assert with equal truth that with forethought, prudence, and by putting into practice certain well-established maxims, these risks can be reduced to a minimum.

In Norway, probably the greatest mountaineering danger is that of climbing with so-called guides, or with inexperienced amateurs, who have no nails in their boots.

In some places the peasants use broad-soled rounded shoes of soft leather, called *snau-kopper* ("snau" meaning quick or nimble-footed, and "kopper" meaning cups). These afford a wonderful grip on the smooth glaciated rocks of the deep valleys, but they are useless for general mountaineering.

Up to a few years ago, there were barely a dozen really capable mountain guides throughout the whole length and breadth of Norway. The number is not great now, but every year some stalwart young fellows are added to the list, and are gradually gaining experience.

There are hundreds of peasants "born the wild northern hills among," who have toddled literally out of their cradles on to the rocks and who are surefooted and fearless before they learn their ABC. The best of them become excellent cragsmen, and they are in great request when a crag-fast goat or a sheep has to be rescued. These men are capital porters, though they seldom carry so much as their Swiss brethren. Many would make excellent guides if they had the opportunity of accompanying good leaders, but this is seldom their lot. As they are self-reliant by nature and habit, they rarely understand or appreciate the need of combined climbing; nor do they understand glacier work. However, owing to their general ability in the sport of running on ski, the Norse peasantry have a practical knowledge of the condition of snow which their class in other lands does not usually possess. The Norse peasantry are more strongly built, more intelligent, and better educated than most peasant folk. They are good material for guides. In the Alps it is comparatively rare to find a guide who can read a map correctly. In Norway, on the other hand, I have found the young fellows whom I have had with me on the mountains in one capacity or another take an intelligent interest in the *Amtskarter*.

Few Norsemen have acquired real snow-craft such as is understood and practised in the Bernese Oberland. The reason is this. The Oberland guide usually has been, and perhaps still is, a chamois hunter; if he will succeed, he must scale the lower precipices of mountains like the Jungfrau or Wetterhorn; when he sees his game or finds fresh spoor, he has at times to cross some chaotic ice-fall, to go, in fact, wherever his quarry may lead him. Chamois-stalking undoubtedly often makes him the fearless and self-reliant mountaineer that we find him.

In Norway, on the other hand, a man who is actually afraid of venturing on a steep glacier may, and often does, become an excellent bear and reindeer hunter. This is also the case with the chamois hunters in Austria and Bavaria.

It is, however, only fair to the bear and the reindeer to add that the bear is an excellent rock-climber, and will cross any glacier almost as well as a chamois, and that the reindeer takes readily to the ice; also, that I have on several occasions met with exceedingly difficult climbing on rock and ice when reindeer-stalking or bear-hunting. This, however, arose from the fact that I chose the wildest haunts of both animals, and possibly preferred to enjoy the grand scenery into which I was led, to taking the lives of the noble animals which led me. Let the scoffer go into Knuts Hullet or to the foot of Midt Maradal.

The sport of mountaineering is by slow degrees becoming popular in Norway, and the number of foreign climbers who go there is increasing rapidly.

On every mountain expedition there must be a responsible and an experienced leader whose word should be unquestioned. His ice-axe must be looked upon for the time being as the sceptre of an emperor. It is necessary that the leader, whether he be a professional guide or an amateur, should be a capable man, wise and discerning about the weather, cool and courageous. He must be a man of resource, a born pathfinder, able to read the face of the mountain in front of him, as the page of a book. Let him remember that according to the Duke of Wellington, "a good general is one that knows when to retreat and has the courage to do it." All mountaineers would do well to engrave this, metaphorically, on the handles of their ice-axes. Carlyle says, "Experience does take dreadfully high school wages, but he teaches like no other." This is very true with respect to mountaineering.

During my first five campaigns, I never met a Norseman who had acquired real snow-craft though I climbed with many good cragsmen. Since then I have generally been able to find a man or two who would take to glaciers as a duck takes to water. Still many a time, I have been obliged to climb with comparative novices if I would climb at all, and by doing so have probably acquired much mountaineering knowledge and experience, which otherwise would not have been attained. One learns to appreciate the difficulties which fall to the lot of an Alpine guide, if one has to act as a guide oneself, to carry a rucksack and two axes, and to help the man below with the rope at the same time; to watch one's companions like a cat watching a mouse, to hold the one extra taut when one sees him likely to slip out of the step in the steep snow, and to see at the same time that the other has his rope hitched properly round his axe. I maintain, without fear of contradiction, the theory that more practical mountaineering knowledge can be acquired by leading a novice and a third man up a mountain such as the Ober Gabelhorn, or even the Wellen Kuppe, than by traversing the Matterhorn in the company of two first-rate guides. However, though I have climbed without guides for many years both in the Alps and in Norway, I wish it clearly to be understood that I do not for one moment advocate the practice of guideless climbing until an apprenticeship has been served under the leadership of masters of the craft. It is true that my mountaineering knowledge was acquired without the help of guides, but it is equally true that the *only* reason for this was because at that period, though there were many good cragsmen in Norway where I wished to climb, there was no one in the country who really understood snow-craft, that highest and most interesting branch of the art of mountaineering, and hence, there were no good mountain guides. Had there been even one, I should undoubtedly have become his disciple.

A year or two before my first visit to Norway, my father gave me a copy of *Scrambles in the Alps*, which I read and re-read, each time with a greater and more absorbing interest, as so many mountaineers have done, and I here state my indebtedness to Mr. Whymper for having fostered my natural inclination to climb mountains, and for having, at least theoretically, taught me a considerable amount of snow-craft.

On two occasions I completed the first ascent of a difficult mountain alone, and feel certain that in similar circumstances most of my Alpine friends would have done the same, and that they would also agree with me in saying that the stupid practice of solitary climbing cannot be too severely condemned. I have also crossed scores of snow-covered glaciers in company of only one companion, solely because we could not get a third man. On another occasion I got a third man, and was benighted in consequence. However, I am, and always have been, a staunch supporter of the old-fashioned mountaineers' creed, that on a snow-covered glacier, no party ought to consist of less than three members. There are, however, I regret to say, some excellent climbers who aver that a party of two can traverse the snows in perfect safety by using a light double rope, and that in case one of them should fall into a crevasse, he could be liberated by the combined efforts of his companion and himself. I do not believe this for a moment, and have had many a strong argument on the subject. Of course, no one ought to fall into a crevasse, i.e. out of sight, and as a matter of fact, such an accident very rarely happens; but when it does, it is serious enough, and it is exceedingly difficult to extricate the man from his icy prison.

Nowadays there is no excuse for slipshod ways, as mountaineering is popular in Norway; there are a few good guides and porters to be obtained in most centres, and as many mountaineers are ready to go out in the holiday months, a genial companion can generally be found.

The sons and daughters of the grand old northland have every reason to be proud of their native country, and of their race. Surely too, we whose "forelders," barely ten centuries ago, were Norsemen, can share to some extent in this most worthy and justifiable pride? The mountains of Norway – probably the oldest in Europe – invite us all. Let us go then and learn amongst them the wholesome lessons which Nature never withholds from those who really love her. The musician, the artist and the poet will get inspiration amongst the purple, cloud-wreathed mountains. The philosopher and the politician will learn something of the sense of proportion. The schoolmaster, with the experience of the man, will for the time become the frolicsome boy again. The hard-headed business man will forget his worries and his money-bags, and will become imbued, for a time at least, with a wholesome air of romance. No man, however callous he may be by nature, can be much amongst the high mountains without gaining strength of character as well as physical strength. King David knew this when he wrote Psalm cxxi : "I will lift up mine eyes unto the hills, from whence cometh my help."

Go then to the mountains for all that is best worth having in life. Learn again in the mountain solitudes the lessons which you learned on your mother's knee, and perhaps have forgotten in the bustle of this noisy world. You will form friendships amidst the storm or sunshine, heat or cold, hard toil or well-earned ease, keen pleasure or danger and anxiety which are more reliable than those formed in the city or on the plain.

There are in Norway many virgin mountains yet to conquer. Woo them, as they deserve to be wooed, with an intense love and with a wholesome respect. Remember, when you are on the mountains, the friends at home. Be bold, but take no unwarrantable risks. Forget not the truth of the maxim, "Discretion is the better part of valour." Be boldest of all in your determination to turn back when, from your experience, you feel quite sure that to advance would be to court danger.

The high mountains are the natural playground of those who are endowed with health and strength. They are the resting-places for the weary. Then away to the mountains, away, away, and glean more health and strength of mind and body to enable you to combat the difficulties of life, and to lay up a rich store of happy memories from which you can always draw, yet can never exhaust.

Yes, go and worship in "these great cathedrals of the earth, with their gates of rock, pavements of cloud, choirs of stream and stone, altars of snow, and vaults of purple traversed by the continual stars."

Appendix A: Mountaineering in Norway Today

David Durkan drafted the following for the 2003 edition of "Norway the Northern Playground".

NORWAY – "Land of the Midnight Sun"
by David Durkan

A title that may conjure up mosaic images of Trolls, Vikings, valley farms and homeward bound fishing boats, of giant rock walls vibrating between sun and sea, and, of course, the always-distant snow-capped peaks.

My intention was to present an updated view of the areas Slingsby had visited, as an appendix to the re-launch of the book you hold in your hands. The intent, to show how Norway, the people, the land, and the sport of mountaineering had changed from the one Slingsby knew. On re-reading his book (my first read, like Tony Howard's, had been 30 years ago) I came to the conclusion that it would be sacrilegious to comment. For Slingsby's "Norway – The Northern Playground", is *the* "reference to the subject". Like Whymper's "Scrambles in the Alps", or Heinrich Harrer's "The White Spider" – all are in a class of their own. I realized to tamper would risk eternal damnation in the fires of Muspell.

Slingsby's climbing achievements inspired one. His work, and this book, is a magical-mystery journey of great proportions. He inspired the climbers of his time, and the generations that followed. I take the liberty to present a somewhat superficial overview of the main mountain areas, my intention: to encourage a wider range of mountain enthusiasts (than just the classical climber) to visit this diverse and exciting country.

For Norway has something to offer to all who seek the hills. From rolling moors set against a backcloth of a solitary peak and rolling clouds, to rock walls a mile high where the underworld people live, Trolls and Huldras. There is variation, from one-day walks to 20-day multi pitch climbs. There are endless valleys you can explore, and spooky ridges that lead you from one cloud to another. If you forget your map, you can even rename these peaks. For a short time at least – for in some areas a day or a week can pass before you meet another person to disturb your adventure. There is plenty of scope for new climbs, on the crags, the big walls and in the mountains. In winter Norway is more than ski-touring, with its countless waterfalls it is an Eldorado for ice climbing. So to, for the new sport of bouldering: "the art of climbing on your finger nails" on big steep boulders/stones, with a soft mini-gym mat placed below you to take the fall. What would Slingsby have thought of this development?

Norway – Its Mountains

At first glance Norway gives the appearance of a curving jagged backbone, with little in the way of substance. This is deceptive, for although never really wide throughout, it is a big country, with a landmass of 386,958 sq km, if we include Svalbard and Jan Mayen. The mainland coastline is several thousand kilometres long. Nearly 70% of this area is designated as "mountain range". Something to make one smile with glee. Unfortunately, much of this mountain range does not suit our purpose, so I suggest careful consideration as to which area(s) to visit. Areas called mountain are often heavily wooded, or with small hill groups isolated by wide or complex valleys, tundra, or seemingly endless tracts of high marshland.

Transport to Norway, and when you arrive.

There are regular flights from Britain, and with airline deregulation prices have fallen considerably over the last few years. A restriction with flying is the baggage allowance. Today's airport security are always on high alert so it is no longer easy to smuggle 20 kilos of climbing hardwear, including crampons, in your hand luggage. Or what we did, an ice axe down your trouser leg, and a rope wrapped around your body. Once in the country public transport brings the southern ranges within reach in one to two days, although the northern ranges will need longer. The recent privatisation of transport has led to a number of very efficient, comfortable and inexpensive bus services, which serve the country well. You can take a bus to one mountain area, walk across the range, and pick up a bus on the other side, that transports you to another area, or back to your start point. Or, the train system, somewhat limited, but this normally connects with local buses. There are often reduced priced summer domestic flights, which can bring the far north within easy reach.

However, a car does have its merits. Car hire and petrol are expensive by UK standards, although companies such as Rent-a-Wreck are reasonable (no break down service/guarantee).

A good alternative is to bring your own car. The country may be reached by car ferry from Newcastle or Harwich to Bergen, Kristiansand, Stavanger or Oslo. Some routes go via Denmark or Sweden. Your own car opens up other areas on route, serves as a useful base, and with food being more expensive than in Britain it means you can stock up. Especially, with beer, cigs and booze, for those who indulge. A half litre of beer in Norway can cost the same as 3 pints of best bitter at home. You have been warned. When desperate for a good night's sleep you can swap a bottle of unopened Malt Whisky for B&B...

Accommodation, there is a summer hotel pass system, offering reasonable prices, often including breakfast, at hotels noted in the pass book. There is one hotel in virtually every town. The mountain walker and climber will normally prefer huts, or camping. There is a well organized system of camp sites all over the country, usually by the side of main roads, often with their own shop, and some serve meals. Many of these sites have wooden huts/cabins with 2, 4 and even 8 beds, often bunk, self-catering, and usually with quilts. Showers, laundry and cooking facilities are all thrown in. In Norway, by law, you can camp on wilderness land, and even on farmland, but ask the local farmer for permission first as there are some restrictions. However, with the growth of tourism it is common practice to be referred to the local campsite.

If you intend to be based in one area it is also possible to hire a hut for a week or longer on a private basis. Another hut system is that run by the D.N.T., or Norwegian Tourist Association. The Association's function is rather like that of a sports council, they offer organized walking tours, with special themes, from bird watching, to geology, even to singles weeks. They have climbing and glacier courses, horseback excursions and dog sleigh tours. They have excellent programs for children, and youth camps. However, their main function is managing a comprehensive hut network system that is second to none in the world. There are hundreds of huts all over the country that you can stay at.

These are joined by normally well marked paths, and even in winter the ski trails are marked with giant "lollipop sticks" in case of dense mist.

Some of the huts are not manned, yet have a food store that you pay for on a trust system (remember to bring Norwegian cash). Others are manned, offering self-catering, and/or full meal service. Membership also grants good discounts at many private mountain hotels and lodges, also on some bus services. The real intention is to meet the needs of walkers or skiers on the move, with most people not staying for more than one or two nights at the same place. Longer periods can be arranged, and there is a growing interest in serving family groups. Members receive priority for beds, with substantial reductions. There are bunk and double room accommodation combinations – all from the spartan to near luxury standard. No one is ever turned away, even if you have to sleep standing up. Many visitors, especially climbers, like to use the huts for a base, and then use their tent for a few days, or longer, this combines price saving with the comfort of a good meal and hot shower.

The summer season extends from June to early September, but in the high mountain areas, or in the north, June is still early. With the climate being both high mountain and coastal you should prepare for inclement weather. I repeat, you should expect the worse: allow for high precipitation and sudden cooling. This is especially true in the high western ranges, no matter what the tourist brochures show. Here I touch on equipment, related to the weather. Locals often use Wellington boots for approaches over marshlands, or slightly stiff low ankle rubber boots that give some ankle support, and at the same time keep the feet dry. I prefer a spare pair of light leather boots with good gaiters (Yeti) when crossing wet glaciers or marshes, some extra woollen socks, and then change to climbing boots higher up. Waterproofs are a must, as is a good fleece or woollen jacket. Your standard UK summer and winter equipment is suitable for Norway. Bring some extra layers, and don't be afraid to bring your long johns. Once I met a British climber with one pair of leather gloves, on a two-day route. They were rather like last week's treacle pudding, left out in the rain: cold, sticky and soggy. *Use some time on the equipment list, as there are no Tisos or Brigham's at the bottom of the hill.*

Technical gear, depends on what you intend to do. Glacier walking and ridge traverses above the snow line require basic mountaineering equipment, from ice axes to crampons and ropes, plus helmets. Equipment often makes one look impressive, but it does not help to be roped up on a glacier if you do not know how to do crevasse rescue. Book theory, or attending Himalayan lectures at home is one thing, but to fall in a 40 metre crevasse, bang your head and bleeding, with companions who are tired and expect you to tell them what to do – and then find you have left your prussik slings in your mate's tent can be embarrassing. This is a true story. Norway is a sparsely populated country and help may not be close at hand.   Remember, DNT offer courses, or when in doubt, use a guide. Climbing on middle grade routes requires a standard rack of protection, from rocks to hex's. Long slings for rappels (abseils). There have been a number of fatal accidents from rappel anchors failing. Those brightly coloured nylon slings you find in-situ have often been there a number of years. Nylon deteriorates quickly, so the moral of the story is clear: put in your own anchors and remove/destroy the old ones found. Check the block, twice, and put in back ups. On pure rock routes, in the Lofoten or on the big walls of Romsdal, fuller racks, with Friends etc are recommended. Double ropes are more and more common, remember that many routes have complex descents. Big wall climbers know what they need.

Winter season, depends on what you want to do, and where. Whilst I call this article "The Land of the Midnight Sun", in the winter it's the opposite. In the far north they do not see the sun for many months – their winter is longer – and spring short. Basically, for ice climbing, skiing, and winter mountaineering the season begins around Christmas. With February to April being the best time, as the days get longer and lighter. A private tip, in the winter it is normally better weather five to seven days before the full moon, and three to five days after. Don't tell anyone, or the mountains will be crowded at these times. Also, in areas like Romsdal you are lower down and near the sea, so the Gulf Stream warms and the ice-falls melt at valley and mid level earlier, whilst in the Jotunheimen the winter stays until April/May.

Language is no barrier, with English being spoken by most. In fact, it is a very useful social introduction. Many a strong romance, and a few unexpected children, has started with the blond farmer's daughter teaching the "two-left-footed-show-pity-on-me" English climber how to do the local folk dance. So country dancing in the village hall is rewarding, and should be experienced to help social integration. The basic steps, moves, and throws are soon mastered to the tune of accordion and fiddle. Although often dry affairs, when held at the village church hall, many locals sport hip flasks of the famous home spirit, called Hjemmebrent. The local vicar turns a blind eye to all the bottles of coke that people clutch as they walk or stagger around the dance floor. With the high price of drink, take your full quota of duty-free on route. However, there is virtually a "no tolerance" attitude by the police to drinking and driving. Be warned, as it can mean loss of license, a fine, and 21 days "enforced holiday" (there is a waiting list of up to 9 months to serve sentence) and full damage responsibility. Your holiday budget for years to come has vanished...

The Southern Mountains

The Setesdal/ Aust-Agder Highlands are interesting in that as well as having the normal mountain features; the valleys are then crossed by almost linear crevices running up and down hill entirely against all topographical rules. This may appear as a hindrance to the walker, yet these vast tracts provide a fine blend of low mountain, wooded valley, and lake and fjord landscape. Most hut-to-hut tours take from six to nine days, although this may be tailored to suit party requirements. With villages being few and far between it is advisable to stay at some of the staffed huts, serving meals, so reducing loads. Backpackers travelling light may hop huts, so covering large areas, or allowing for diversions. Climbers will find the Setesdal valley one of the best rock climbing areas in Norway. There are giant slabs and walls, which are easy to find and approach, often bolted/trees for rappel descents. It is in a part rain-shadow, so late spring and summer days can be ideal, but the evenings bring blood-sucking midges. The Germans have led development here, and produced their own guidebook.

Rjukan, home of Hitler's Heavy Water Plant, and The Hero's of Telemark fame, is only three hours drive from Oslo. This is a winter sports area, for the average ski enthusiast, without the razzle-dazzle of the Alpine resorts. The town has seen a depression as industry closed down, and the youth have moved away. The town itself is so deep down in the valley (your guarantee for good ice climbing conditions) that they hardly see the sun there during winter. However in the surrounding area there are great cross country skiing trails, and reasonable downhill ski facilities. Rjukan is probably the best ice climbing area in, dare I say it,

Europe. Here one drives virtually up to the bottom of the icefall, and starts climbing from the car. There are over 100 falls in the region, from one to six pitches. There are numerous huts, on sites by the side of the road, for hire – 4 beds for £50 a night. They normally have a small kitchen, and shower/wash facilities. The youth hostel in the centre of town offers reasonable bunk accommodation, and is self catering. There is a cinema (normally English, with Norwegian subtitles), various eating places that revolve from being Chinese to Italian from year to year. Plus, a couple of almost English-like pubs. Steve Haston and I ate at "Gunn's Grill", a worn out shack in the middle of town where you get real greasy British fish and chips, with dashings of salt and vinegar.

Back to climbing, there is an indoor climbing hall, and each year, about March, there is an Ice Climbing Festival. The local club organizes this, with equipment testing, guide service, and non-serious climbing competitions. The waterfalls have been lit up with giant spot lights (reminiscent of Hitler's anti aircraft system) and people climb to well after midnight. The festival usually finishes with slide shows and party.

To the west is Folgefonna, a glacier covering 260 square kilometres and remote to the point that most groups visiting it must be pretty self-sufficient and experienced. Its northern end is a fantastic place which lies so close to the sea that you can approach it from the west with the whole Atlantic blowing in your back. On reaching the top it is only a matter of crossing a few hundred meters before you can look down into the Hardanger Fjord.

The Hardangervidda Mountain Plateau varies from mountain glacier to moorland terrain, with a number of small and not so small peaks, and deep valleys around its border area. It covers an area more than 15,000 square kilometres, at an altitude between 1060 and 1860 meters. Hårteigen, at 1690 meters, is the highest of the peaks, and a worthy grail. The plateau is crossed by over 1600 miles of cairned tracks. The trails usually take in some place of interest, such as animal traps from prehistoric times, or ribbons of small lakes. The hut situation is one of the best in Norway, and with large herds of wild reindeer, some 40,000 animals, rich flora, over 400 plant types, and varied wild life. It will suit most hill walkers' needs for many weeks. Additionally, a popular winter ski touring area, but not to be underestimated. It is a rolling hill moorland landscape that lacks clear physical features, and as it has a weather pattern that demands respect, and competence, take heed to the rolling mists.

The Stavanger area has blossomed to be one of the great climbing venues of Europe – with bouldering, crag and big wall climbing. Developments have been by both local and UK based climbers. It has its own guide book: Klatring I Rogaland (see Appendix C).

The Finse/Filefjell Ranges are popular with tourists, but the mountain walker benefits, for the mass leaves in its wake comfortable huts and well marked approach paths. Finse is the main starting point, allowing for a combination with the last area. The most famous route is the five day "British Route", which is, "incredibly grand...the track following a chain of small lakes, connected by a river, which sets off a series of wonderful waterfalls". Further, to the northeast, is an interesting traverse to the Hemsedal Valley, leading to a popular climbing area, with many one to five pitch rock routes, plus excellent winter ice climbing. Hemsedal is known for its cross-country and slalom skiing, and high tempo nightlife – for the young and strong of heart. In the summer it is a peaceful farming region, with many excellent open mountain landscape and moorland walks. An ideal area for family and youth groups, as there is fishing, canoeing, river rafting, horse riding. Only 3 hours from Oslo.

Mjølfjell Ranges are on the other side of the Oslo-Bergen railway, popular for one day walks from such centres as the Mjølfjell Youth Hostel. The experienced walker will be able to piece the two halves of this region together, producing longer routes, through and over impressive passes well laced with lakes and waterfalls. Get out your maps, and start planning.

Oslo and Bergen, the two main cities are also served well, with indoor climbing walls, and lots of quality rock within an hours drive. Oslo has as much rock as the Llanberis Pass, excellent climbing at all standards.

The Lillehammer Trail runs from the town of that name, and where the 1994 Winter Olympic games were held. A typical walkers' trek would be six days hut to hut across the vast moorland to reach the Rondane Mountains. The Rondane is a national park, visited by geologists and naturalists as well as by keen walkers. There are numerous huts, and although mainly a walking paradise there is some climbing, on unusual rock faces which consist of large square blocks. The numerous cirques are appealing, which with spooky peaks create images of long forgotten Troll strongholds, rising in grand solitude amidst peaceful surroundings.

Talking of Trolls, you are probably familiar with these mythological creations, made famous by Grieg's music: In the Hall of the Mountain King. They, like mountaineers, have their sub-groups. One is the Huldra, often seen as a beautiful woman, with long blond hair in pigtails, wearing a long flowing dress (where she conceals her cows tail). She entices the hunter or farmer deeper in to the depths of the valley – to have her wild way with him. If he satisfies her then they may marry, or be allowed to return to the world of the humans, where his hunting will be plentiful. If not to her satisfaction then he is never seen again. The young people who leave the low valley farms to take the cattle, sheep and goats up into the high pastures for the summer live in small huts, called sæter. When they enter they ask for permission from the Troll and Huldra people that they may live there, and show respect and courtesy to them throughout the summer, leaving bowls of cream out at night (which the supernatural folk eat with glee, as each morning the bowls are empty).

In the higher mountains there was once a famous hunter, who slipped when crossing a glacier and slid towards the crevasse. At the last second he drew out his knife and thrust it in the ice, and stopped half way over the edge. His body hanging above the black depths, he pulled himself up by his one arm, then waited until his leather pants froze to the ice. Held by the ice he drew out the knife and stuck it in higher, then ripped the leather free, pulled himself up and again waited for the leather to freeze fast. He continued this until he reached safety. As can be imagined, such a hero was popular with the Huldras, they always released him after a weekend in the mountains, and he always came back for more. Where folklore and truth cross paths there is always room for a warm smile.

To the east lie the Østerdal-Femund national parks, where five to ten days walks are possible along the characteristic pine covered highlands.

The Synnefjellvidda Plateau is a minor, but classical hiking area, affording serene undulating moors broken by the solitary peak. An anteroom to Norway's Alps.

The Jotunheimen: the country's finest mountain area. It has over 60 glaciers, some 250 peaks over 1,800 meters, and some rising to 2,400. This is probably the country's most popular walking area, and has been developed as such, with numerous huts, and well marked trails. Between each hut there is a time given on DNT hut maps, normally not more than 6 hours. Be warned: the Norwegians have long long legs, and the times given do not allow for rests. Within its borders are a number of individual and quite independent mountain groups – a real alpine area.

The most diverse of these groups is the Hurrungane. This massif of nearly twenty peaks affords well situated ridges, cairned approaches and reasonably safe glaciers, making it ideal for attaining basic alpine skills. From the hotel at Turtagrø one to four-day routes at all standards, on both rock and ice, may be climbed. It was here Slingsby and other pioneers stayed. The hotel is also a mountaineering school, offering courses and guide services. The gem is Store Skagastølstind, 2405m, the country's third and most coveted peak. Also called Storen, this is Slingsby's mountain – never doubt that. The approach is long, the way not always easy to follow, and the easiest route is grade III+/IV-. This involves a demanding approach, exposed climbing, and boasts a spectacular abseil. One drops down over Slingsby's Glacier (a good 500 meter free fall below your feet). The alternative is just as airy, but the view broken by a ledge called Hjørnet, before disappearing into space.

For those wishing demanding climbing on Storen, they can turn their attentions to the West Face for sustained grade V and VI climbing, on solid rock, varied and in spectacular positions. The approach is from the glacier on the way between the Tindeklubb (The Norwegian Alpine Club, a private hut) and the DNT refuge called Hytta på Bandet, on the via normal. At the top of the wall it's possible to reach the summit by various connecting routes, or traverse to the normal route to descend.

It is also worth considering the sadly neglected overhanging South Wall, a well situated 16 pitch route at grade III to V-, with a glacier approach leading to a somewhat imprecise start. The face is really S.E., it is big and complex, on a high mountain, and is suited for competent VS parties, with mountain experience. When I first climbed it I was in awe with the first acensionists, who had done this big wall back in the 1930's. I had to ask them how they had managed such complex route finding, up such a big and impressive (sometimes loose) wall with the equipment they had at that time. They were pretty relaxed about the whole thing, and talked about stopping to light their pipes, about how they had joked, and how they looked forward to the three course dinner at the hotel that night, with bottles of red wine. We talked for the rest of the climb, swapped stories, I found them full of humour, and always willing to lend a hand. They told me to go right when I thought I should go left. Just me and them (my climbing partner never saw them). They said goodbye, and flew away at the top. The top can often be iced up, and in the event of bad weather descent from over half height can be problematic. An escape up to Hjørnet may be an alternative (I have not tried). Descent can be by the normal route, but if there are a number of parties on the abseil you may like to take the traverse to the North towards the hotel, and endless draught beer. This I did once, following the beams of a warm sunset, and count it as one of the gem days in my 40 years of climbing. Allow 4 to 12 hours extra for this descent, depending on weather, and how tired you are. As a guide I climbed Storen over 60 times, and never once grew tired of it, but my favourite route I keep to myself.

The surrounding peaks, namely Midt Maradalstind (2057 m), Søndre Dyrehaugstind (2074) and Store Ringstind (2124m), provide excellent climbing and ridge scrambles, although even the easiest routes require mountaineering skills. The latter has a wonderful day's outing, a short 3 pitch route, One Step in the Clouds. This involves a glacier approach of 3 hours, 3 to 4 hours climbing, grade V-, reasonably exposed and varied, in wonderful situations. This is followed by a spectacular descent down to the valley (yes, you could carry your skis on your back while climbing, and ski down what is one of the worlds finest ski runs). The view is impressive – with the whole Hurrungane range in front of you. And don't forget its neighbour, the solitary and alluring Austabotntind, 2204 mtrs. Add swirling mist to this backcloth and you have an atmosphere to compete with both the Alps and Tolkien's fantasy world.

The other groups, namely Falketind, Smørstabtind, Bygdin / Gjende ranges, Leirvassbu and Raudalen, all have their devotees and are worth attention – but space limits us.

The heart of the area is Galdhøpiggen, (2469 m), and the true Home of the Giants. The country's highest peak, it may be reached by an easy though heavy ascent from the lodge at Spiterstulen. My preference is the easy snow gully on the south side, or a solitary traverse from the unnamed peak on the main ridge, from the northwest, a ten to fourteen hour day as taxing as it is enjoyable.

Parties going guideless should inquire as to present glacier conditions, this applies to the smaller glaciers as they too have the inherent dangers. Another centre is Juvasshytta, here large parties are roped together looking like Chinese New Year dragon parades on their way up to the top of the country's highest mountain. Don't knock it, as many a famous mountaineer started his career after a first taste through a package glacier crossing. They take children, properly dressed/footwear, over the age of 12 on these trips – that take about 6 or so hours. The last five years or so Ang Dorjee Sherpa, from Pangboche in Nepal, who has climbed Everest 8 or so times, has been a guide here. He has climbed the mountain each day for about 3 months, each year, possibly making him the person who has climbed the mountain the most.

Climbers visiting this region might turn their attention to the S.W. Wall of Veslepiggen (2369m), a seven pitch route with reasonable rock, sustained climbing but somewhat complex route finding. At grade VI it should be courted only by strong VS to HVS parties. Easier, but nicely exposed, is the S.E. Ridge of Skarstind (2363m), grade IV+, again comprised of seven pitches and of a mountaineering character.

A word about grades in Norway. They basically follow the UIAA European system, with the highest technical point of a given pitch being noted. In the introduction to most climbs there will normally be a description to the over all difficulty of the climb, with information on type of climbing i.e. loose or solid, and sometimes tips on equipment needed. I to II is heavy walking to steep scrambling, and often exposed, at III we are looking at UK Diff to V.Diff. There are also sub divisions of + and -. When we reach IV we are looking at Severe, V is about V.Severe, and at V+/VI- we reach the realms of HVS. On big mountain walls it is recommendable that you climb E1 when reaching grade VI. Above this grade, because of wet rock or the threat of bad weather, there has been a trend to use the occasional sling for aid, e.g. on the Rimmon Route on The Troll Wall, and AO or A1 is noted in the guide. Many of these points can actually go free. The harder grades, notably on the modern big walls and in the Stavanger area – go as far as VII on the UIAA scale, and VIII on the crags.

The Jostedal Glacier, a glacier walkers' paradise, lies between the Jotunheimen and the North Sea. Rising above the surrounding peaks, it resembles the ice caps of Greenland. At a height of approx 2000 meters, and covering 475 sq km, it is the largest ice field on the continent of Europe. A complete N. to S. or S. to N. traverse for experienced skiers in good conditions takes about twenty hours. Most parties prefer to utilize the well situated huts on both sides, so making a variety of glacier crossings.

The Sunnmøre Alps, is reached by travelling further north by steamer from Bergen, or from Oslo via Åndalsnes. It is here that the feeling of sea and mountain is first apparent. It is a high rain area, but rumour has it that the month of June is reasonably stable. It has a reputation of being suited for climbers only, based on an exaggerated feeling of isolation brought about by there being few high connecting ridges between peaks. But as the descents usually follow easy ridges keen walkers can follow these descents upwards, thus proving the area to be quite versatile. From the towns of Øye or Ørsta most routes may be completed in one day, with fine scrambling, in remarkably concentrated mountain surroundings. A traverse of the never ending ridge system of Skarstind (1500m), or the Kolåstind Pinnacles, or Staven (1518m) and Rana (1,593m) are fine outings.

Romsdal is probably the most famous climbing area in Norway, with the town of Åndalsnes being dominated by the majestic Romsdalshorn, 1555m, and laying subject to the mighty walls of the Trolltind (1795m). The main attraction in the valley is its big wall climbs, which are usually multi-day affairs at very high standards. There was recently a giant rock fall down the Troll Wall, changing a number of the central routes, climbers should therefore take contact with local climbers for up to date information.

I have been lucky enough to have climbed four routes here, all of which represent their particular epoch. The Fiva Route, first done by two local boys, Erik and Arne Randers Heen. An amazing effort when we realize that their knowledge was gleamed from a short chapter in a boys book of sports, and by watching visiting English gentlemen climbers. Arne told me that after a days climbing, "we lay down to sleep on a ledge, in the morning we awoke to find ourselves covered in snow, so we swept it off our tweed jackets, and continued. We placed some pitons, never above the shoulder, and never for aid."

Arne was to become Norway's most famous climber, and a decorated resistance fighter. He was the local gym teacher and a tailor, and one day he decided to climb Mt Blanc. So he got on his bike and cycled from Norway through Europe to Chamonix, climbed the mountain, and then cycled all the way back, without telling anyone. The Troll Pillar, was also an Arne Randers Heen route, and became the longest grade VI climb in Europe. This time Arne was jointed by the new generation's leading climber, Ralph Høibakk, who led the route. They repeated it ten years later as a jubilee ascent, when Arne was 60! 1800 meters of climbing, with pitches of grade VI – not bad for a local teacher/tailor. I did it with an American I'd met by chance. He said, "let's third class it", "ok" said I (not knowing what "third class" was). I turned my back, started to uncoil, sort out gear only to see him soloing off up the first half of the Pillar – I followed in silence, internally screaming for a rope.

The Rimmon Route, or The English Route made Romsdal (and Norway) famous in the world of mountaineering. It became the trade big wall route. With twenty-four pitches, half of them at sustained HVS/E1, in a steep and impressive vertical and overhanging landscape, it was a break through in Norwegian climbing. The climbing is varied and some pitches, such as on the Great Wall, are classic Cloggy Wall style: ...start up a slightly more than vertical finger crack, some god jugs, good protection leads to a heel belay. Hand and foot jams past a roof, bomb proof hex, smile, up and up to a one foot/bent knee belay with uncertainty above; an exposed escape, to where - ? - and there is more to come. Flake Crack, Narrow Slab and Exit Chimney (that was dripping wet), were names many of us grew up reading about. Tony Howard and Rimmon Climbing Club became household names after their 1965 ascent. Mountain Magazine wrote about it, Tony brought out the guidebook and the area opened up.

The next great classic was the Swedish Route, 24 pitches of E1 and E2 free climbing, with sections of 5c – this ranks as one of the best big wall routes in Europe. Additionally there are modern monsters such as Arch Wall, Trollkjeringa, and Strawberry Dreams for the hard youth of today.

Romsdal is famous for its big wall climbs, but there are many all round climbs to suite all tastes and standards. This makes it an ideal area for large parties with mixed ambitions. One group can do a big wall, another a classical ridge, and family members can go walking/exploring the many neighbouring valleys. It is well worth considering an ascent of Venjetind (1843m), or of course the Romsdalshorn (1550m) itself. Biskopstind tempts with a good route by the S.E. Pillar where competent Severe parties should find solid rock and interesting climbing just reward. Don't be shy about taking some bivi equipment on some of the area's peaks, as a little imaginative map reading can lead to all sorts of exploratory adventures, at varying standards – but let your friends know where you "expect" to be.

Dovre, this is a national preserve, offering strenuous walks, with the once isolated peak of Snøhetta (2286m), being a popular objective. It was once thought to be the highest mountain in Norway, as well as in Europe! The small herds of wild reindeer, imported musk ox from Greenland, various rare plants and birds go to make it an interesting area, which it is possible to extend to Trollheimen.

Trollheimen, or *The Home of the Trolls* – gives an intoxicated feeling of size, and is well sprinkled with huts, paths, glens and lakes. The main starting point is the valley of Sunndalsøra. Nordmøre, is the neighbouring area, and extremely popular with Norwegian climbers. This popularity is based as much on the warm hospitality received at the lodge in Innerdal, as on the fine rock climbing, and reasonable weather patterns. There have been all-lady climbing meets there, popular with both genders! Guides are available, with courses being run during the summer months. The mountains are splendid, with Dalatårnet (1394m), being the Tower of the Valley, and a mini Matterhorn to boot. There are numerous one-day climbs at most standards, with routes of quality to compare with most areas in the country.

The Northern Mountains

Earlier generalisations pale as we journey towards and past the Arctic Circle. Our approach marches become ones of involvement as paths disappear, cairns are few and far between, huts are few and spartan, and approaches terminate below vast unclimbed (unrecorded) walls.

The Okstind Glacier lies to the north of Mosjøen, a wild glacier area surrounded by alpine peaks. Further north, from the town of Mo i Rana, Svartisen (Black Ice Glacier) dominates, offering fine hikes and glacier crossings, with the western sector harbouring interesting ascents. Again, DNT course country. There are also a number of cave systems, with a lot of explorative activity from both local and visiting cavers. There are rumours of unmapped cave systems awaiting a finder.

The Sulitjelma region is of interest to those seeking isolation and who wish to explore, with glacier crossings into the lower Swedish mountains. Bodø has some excellent climbing in the region, opened up during the last ten years or so. It is an ideal starting point for the Folda region, but climbers and walkers have to be reasonably self-sufficient when exploring new routes and reaching the last of the lost valleys.

An increasingly popular area is Tusfjord. Here it is Stetind (1381m) that is the main attraction. Writers, like fishermen, tend to use superlatives, and here I admit that words do not do justice, but I try: "a magnificent and natural obelisk of sheer rock power." Here the most popular route requires good technique (or brawn for the hand traverse), and some nerve, as its not well protected, and very exposed. It has been designated: Norway's National Mountain. It also sports modern routes that would grace Super Extreme Big Wall Climbing (is Ken Wilson listening?). Slingsby described it as "nature's giant anvil." A true masterpiece of natural sculpture – the Gods and Trolls have a lot to be proud over.

At this point it seems appropriate to quote from the late Ove Skjerven: "Mountains are the basic resource of climbers; we should take good care of them and keep them clean." Ove did not just mean litter, he was propagating a deeper ethic. Perhaps we could re-discover the excitement of exploration, forming an emphasis on basic discovery in an ever-shrinking world; be we walker or climber.

How to do this? Leave the guidebook at home, and do new climbs that others have climbed before us! Ask ourselves to view the line, feel our feet touching the earth, and pretend that what is before us has never been climbed before.

Norway is such a land where one can still do this.

~

The Lofoten consist of over eighty islands; offers excellent climbing, and un-natural nature experiences. Here is the real land of the midnight sun, as in the summer it only grows dusky past midnight for an hour or so. Moskenesøy is a gem sporting numerous spires that grace complex ridges. Climbs here can be quite alpine and are worthwhile. Hinnøy Island is notable, and the island of Austvagøy was designed with climbers in mind. I steal from Per Prag: "Strip the Dent Blanche of its ice, double the number of its arêtes, making them more jagged, cut off all but the upper 1000 meters, plant it by the seashore, and a fair idea will be had of Vågekallen." Not bad for a peak that only reaches a height of 942 meters. Add the peaks of Kabelvåg, Svolvær, Rulten, Troll Fjord and you have unprecedented sport.

One famous climbing "tourist" outing is the ascent of Svolværgeita (The Goat) standing lofty at 569m. The summit consists of two 4.5 mtr high pinnacles known as "De to elskende", or The Two Lovers. They are separated like Adam and Eve on Tryfan by a narrow gap. However, owing to the difference in height a 1.5 meter leap is necessitated. All this conveniently situated 300 meters over the local cemetery. Good planning.

The North Norwegian Climbing School offers guide services, full week courses for novice and advanced climber alike, plus a café/pub called Den Siste Viking (The Last Viking). They can provide accommodation, and sell climbing equipment, if you forget/lose any. There is a guidebook to climbing on the Islands, written by Ed Webster, which is excellent, so I refer you to that for more information.

Langøy Island sports a spectacular peak, Reka (609m) – rather reminisant of Crib Goch, but by the seashore. Every area has it's local Matterhorn. In the Narvik region it is Rombakstøtta (1243m). There is plenty of scope in the surrounding area, with the island of Andøy being ideal for congenial parties who have no pressing ambitions. Here, like Lofoten, one can combine local living, by renting an old fisherman's cottage, with mountaineering. Further north we reach Tromsø, which has its devotees, two indoor climbing walls, and an active climbing club.

The Lyngen Peninsula is one of the least spoilt mountain areas in Europe, covering over 11,398 square kilometres. Here a number of ascents have been made and recorded, but very little information exists. The Tromsø Climbing Club was working on a guidebook, but that is probably still in the future. A traverse of Lakselvtind (1617m) is a joy for the proficient. Jægervasstind (1540m) is a most alluring peak first climbed by the British mountaineer, Elizabeth Main, in 1898. The more proficient alpinist may turn toward Jiekkevarri (1833m), a huge rock massif dotted with small ice fields and flaked by several glaciers. Its South Face resembles the Benva Face on Mont Blanc, and there have been British ascents of its East and South East Faces. With information scarce, you may be able to experience the joy of exploration, as the pioneer spirit is needed for this great beast of the north.

Our odyssey continues to reach the north of Lyngen, the Skjervøy region. The main islands are Arnøy, with peaks rising to over 1000 meters, which may offer climbing, and Vannøy, which is in the main unexplored. Access and weather conditions have probably deterred most people in the planning stage.

The Øksfjord region is an isolated part of Finnmark with low mountains offering pleasant expedition conditions – a number of schools/institutions have used the area for moral fiber building. They say the climbing is reminiscent of Skye, and while most peaks may be reached by gentle slopes, the opposite sides offer pleasant routes of passage on good gabbro.

Mountaineering may be defined as being: the art of moving safely in potentially dangerous places. Norway's mountain ranges are many, diverse, splendid and worthy of attention. But it is a vast country with limited rescue facilities and when these are mobilized the time, energy and costs can be staggering. So take the scale into consideration: choose your climbing partners with care, and the objectives you set yourselves. Be proficient in the art of partner-rescue, be it on rock or on the glacier, and respect the weather patterns, as there is no instant rescue.

The Origins of Norway...

In the beginning of his book Slingsby tells you of the origin of the country, it is here, and only here, I beg to differ with him. His version of Creation is local, originated by the hill farmer and the fisherman. They saw their valley or village as the epi-centre of the country. This was based on their lunar/solar rhythm and their natural nearness to the powers of Mother Nature. Plus a real fear, an ever-nagging doubt, that never quite removed their belief in the supernatural people, even after Christ came to Norway. Early and later Christian churches have their pre-Christ deity images to protect them, and those who pray there. The real Norwegian genesis has a wider view, it acknowledges that the supernatural was there, and is here. This fact of Creation is almost alien to present day thinking, I therefore offer you the *indisputable truth* to dwell upon.

Ginnungagap is the Almighty source of Creation, a concept of inner reality concealed by an outward appearance of total, all encompassing emptiness. Eternal, and in the abyss of "nothing" existed the potential of all life. The fiery realm of Muspell in the far, far South kissed the frozen wastes of the North. From the passion of fusion came Chaos, resulting in the birth of Ymir, father of the Frost Giants and ancestor to all. The Cosmic life energy.

Three gods slew Ymir, turning his bones to mountains and his flesh to soil, while his blood flowed to form Sea. Four dwarfs raised his skull above World, his brains forming clouds which in turn brought rain. The innate soul, or primal intelligence, of Rain kissed Earth, allowing hair to grow as vegetation. The Gods created Time, and allowed man to breath, giving life, senses and understanding.

There is another less probable (quite idiotic) genesis; that 5-600 million years ago, after the planet had cooled, sedimentation due to erosion lay in a deep sea basin. Under heat and pressure the metamorphosis of mud was rock – seemingly eons passed and the Caledonian earth-crust fold was reality. Ice covered and sculptured the land, and eventually receded to allow the mountains of Norway to rise from sea level.

Such people may also believe that agents such as wind, rain and sun completed the vegetation cosmetic make-up – allowing man to emerge from the sea. Whilst you and I know it was the Troll-people who formed and twisted the rocks to reflect their own needs and nature.

~

I lean once again on Ove Skjerven:

"Sometimes we must protect them from large-scale commercial tourism, sometimes abstain from writing about them – leaving them as a gift to future generations. But don't take any of this to mean that you should not come to Norway and climb our mountains. ...when the cold rain stops pouring down, you can make new ascents that have been made before."

~

Editor's Note:

David Durkan, from Holyhead, N. Wales, landed in Norway in 1971, and never left – except to trek/climb in most regions of the world, including 24 visits to Nepal. He was previously guide/instructor at Turtagrø (Norwegian School of Mountaineering), followed by managing a sports company. He has at the same time run his own courses and seminars in the Jotunheimen and in Nepal. Today he is a writer and travel guide.

Appendix B: Old Norse Names on British Hills

One of the themes regularly mentioned by Slingsby was how many place names of Norse origin could be found in the north of England. A glance at the map on a walk through the Lake District or the Yorkshire Dales will throw up a surprising number. I have listed a few common hill/land features below, which could perhaps add a bit of interest to an otherwise dull wet weekend in the British hills.

At any rate it answered a long wondered question of mine, namely why so many streams in the English Lake District were called "*Becks*", waterfalls called "something *Force*" and the hills themselves called – the Lakeland *Fells*.

English (or commonly used)	Scots	Norwegian
brook	burn	bekk
cirque, cwm	corrie	botn
cliff	craig	stup
col	bealach	skar
dale	glen	dal
fjord	sea loch	fjord
wide gap, hause	nick	band
farm		gard
headland	ness, mull	nes
mountain	ben, beinn	fjell
See note 1 below.	shieling	sæter
tarn	lochan	vatn
waterfall		foss

For those interested in a detailed examination of old Norse names in Scotland and the so-called "Danelaw" in northern England, "Scottish Place-Names" by W.F.H. Nicolaisen *, is worth a read.

For those who are after a more comprehensive list of mountain features in Norwegian, Tony Howard's "Romsdal" guide gives a good list – see *"Links"*.

Ian Robertson, March 2003.

* Publ. John Donald, Edinburgh, 2001. ISBN 0-85976-556-3

Appendix C: Useful Information

The Slingsby Trust

The Slingsby Trust was established on May 17th 1993 in Årdal, Norway. One of its most important goals is to ensure the continuance of Cecil Slingsby's legacy: his passion and practice of exploratory mountaineering; as well as the greater appreciation of natural history, ethnology, folklore and the living mountain environment. The Trust works in establishing mutual connections and co-operation between Norwegian and foreign mountaineers, philosophers and environmentalists.

Chairman: Erling Eggum E-mail: post@klingenberghotel.no

Address: The Slingsby Trust, P.b. 28, N-6882 Øvre Årdal

Guide Books and Other Books

English Language Books

There are not many English language books on the Norwegian mountains that are available – "Norway the Northern Playground" is one of the very few. Some others are:

"Walking in Norway", Connie Roos.
        Published by Cicerone. ISBN 1-85284-230-X

This book is mainly aimed at trekkers and gives some good "hut-to-hut" routes. It also serves as an introduction to various areas for those interested in day walks.

"Walks and Climbs in Romsdal", Tony Howard.
Published by Nomads. ISBN 1-871890-04-7

As well as describing the many classic rock routes around Romsdal, this book also covers some walks and scrambles in the area. It is available from the Nomads website (see links).

"Jostedalsbreen, Norway's Largest Glacier", Bjørn Wold, Leif Ryvarden.
Published by Boksenteret A/S, Oslo. ISBN 82-7683-092-7

This is a good "coffee-table" book for various parts of the Jostedals-breen. There are some good photographs of the route Slingsby took during his "epic" descent into the Kjenndalsbreen (see Chapter 11 of "Norway the Northern Playground").

"Climbing in the Magic Islands – Lofoten", Ed Webster.
Published by Nord Norsk Klatreskole. ISBN 8299319900

This book is now out-of-print and is quite difficult to get hold of.

Norwegian Language Guidebooks

Various walking guidebooks are published in Norwegian, and are available in good book shops in Norway. They have useful maps that show walking routes, and approx hours walking between huts. The majority are published by the D.N.T., their website is listed in Links below.

Some climbing guidebooks are listed below. Most are available in local (Norwegian) sport shops or via the climbing local club. A useful bookshop is Fjellsport, Christian Kroghsgt 16, 0186 Oslo. They have, or can obtain, most guidebooks.

Norwegian guidebooks have useful topos and international signs.

Norse Guidebook	Publisher
Hurrungane – Jotunheimen	Norsk Tindeklubb.
Innerdalen	Norsk Tindeklubb
Klatring i Romsdalen	Anne/Grete Nebell/Bjarte Bø.
Buldrefører for Romsdalen	Lars E Roald/Dag K Næss.
Klatring i Rogaland	Vegard Aksnes/Arne Gjessing.
Klatrefører for Kristiansand	Kristiansand Klatreklubb.
Klatring i Bø	Eilef Gran.
Klatrefører – Nissedal	May be purchased at Nisser Camping.
Klatrefører – Oslo	KKK – Kolsås klatre klubb (KolsåsClimbing Club)

Links

www.RippingYarns.com	Ripping Yarns.com website
www.turtagro.no	The home of Norwegian mountaineering
www.nomadstravel.co.uk	Tony Howard's website.
www.stonedonkey.co.uk	The Aberdeen Mountaineering Club website (see acknowledgements). The AMC have trips to Norway almost every year.
www.stanfords.co.uk	Stanford's map shop (for ordering Norwegian maps from the UK)

www.steepstone.com	A discussion site – in Norwegian. Has useful links to local clubs. You can ask concrete questions, and maybe get some good answers/info.
www.klatring.no	Norwegian. Overview of climbing clubs. Norsk Klatreforbund is the Norwegian semi-version of BMC. Good info and contacts.
www.headwall.com	In English. Various guide pages, including Oslo, Dokka, Romsdalen – and a link to Bjarte Bøe's guide in Romsdal.
www.krimp.no	New-wave magazine, which has links to guides in Tromsø and Tvedestrand, and a boulder guide in the Oslo area.
www.nordnorskkklatreskole.no	Climbing school in Lofoten – with café, shop, courses, and even their own pub: *The Last Viking* – recommended.
www.ntk.no	Norwegian Alpine Club - sells their own guidebooks.
www.turistforeningen.no/codeland/default.asp	The Norwegian Tourist Assosiation (Den Norske Turistforening – DNT, Storgaten 3, 0101 Oslo)

NOTES

This section contains Slingsby's original footnotes from "Norway: the Northern Playground". Any additional comments from the editor are in italics.

1. *In Slingsby's time a "sæter" was a hut occupied during the summer months, for people to tend livestock on high summer pastures. The Scottish equivalent would be "shieling". I don't know of a direct English equivalent. Ed.*
2. *The capital was renamed Oslo in 1925 which was the ancient name of the city. Ed.*
3. This only refers to visits up to 1903. Slingsby made six or more expeditions mostly to Northern Norway, the last in 1921.
4. *Whilst the above was in press, two others and I have had a month's mountaineering in Lofoten under Professor Collie's leadership, and I feel sure that the preceding paragraph is strictly true. In addition to most pleasant reminiscences of other grand expeditions, the memory of three glorious days on the rugged rocks of Rulten will always be recalled by us with intense pleasure and satisfaction. Note: Collie's account of mountaineering in Lofoten can be found in his book "From the Himalaya to Skye", available from Ripping Yarns.com. Ed.*
5. These are supposed to have been formed by sub-glacial rivers. Some, no doubt were, notably the large cauldron above Meraak. We have excellent examples at the Strid, near Bolton Abbey; some are ancient, others are being formed to-day. Two little ones are being formed in a beck about one hundred yards, distant from my garden.
6. The Cenomyce rangiferina, the genuine lichen; the Cetraria nivalis or "gold-beard"; the olive-green Cetraria Islandica, and two or three other varieties all go by the general name of "Renmos," or Reindeer Moss.
7. Alpine Journal, vol. iv, p. 23, and illustration p. 24.
8. *Slingsby's first ice axes were always made in the village where he lived, Carleton-in-Craven, Yorkshire. Ed.*
9. *Edith Slingsby. Ed.*

10. In years when there is an exceptionally heavy snowfall, it is the belief of many persons that Glitretind is higher than Galdhöpiggen. This I can readily believe, as the snow domes of the former must vary in depth, whilst on the relatively narrow ridge which forms the top of the latter the wind never allows much snow to accumulate.

11. *Author of "Tent Life with English Gipsies in Norway". Ed.*

12. Norsk schoolmaster and scholar.

13. A fælæger is a cattle-drover's hut; and a fækarr or fækarl, is the cattledrover.

14. On two occasions I have been within a few feet of an eagle. Once, when I was stalking a herd of reindeer, an eagle rose up barely three or four yards away. Though it was a remarkably easy shot I did not pull the trigger, and consequently succeeded shortly afterwards in securing a reindeer. The other occasion was in a pine forest near the Grand Paradis in the Graian Alps, when our party surprised an eagle which was looking down a precipice. It hardly deigned to turn round to look at the intruders, but quietly soared away amongst the crags below. I have often seen these noble birds comparatively near, but only on these two occasions have I surprised them close at hand.

15. Alpine journal, vol. xiii, p. 153

16. Ibid., vol. xiv, p. 508.

17. See "My Climbs in the Alps and Caucasus" by A.F. Mummery. *Note: Mummery's book is also available from Ripping Yarns.com. Ed.*

18. In that best of all books on mountaineering, "Scrambles amongst the Alps, p. 287", Mr. Whymper shows how much depends on the dip of the strata when difficult rocks have to be climbed.

19. The few climbers who have followed this route have all been impressed with the fact that this portion of the ascent is not easy. One writer says: "There was no snow on the rocks, but they were wet and cold. We found several little varde (small cairns which I had erected twenty years before) still standing. In two or three places, notably at one corner near the top, it was a solid satisfaction to know that one was on a good rope well held."

20. In the year 1895, we Yorkshiremen, especially the members of the "Yorkshire Ramblers' Club," felt a similar disappointment when we heard that Gaping Ghyll Hole, a most gruesome pot hole, on Ingleborough, 360 feet in depth, had been successfully

descended by a gallant Frenchman, Monsieur E. A. Martel, who most richly deserved the success which he attained, and for which we most heartily congratulated him, though it was by the merest chance that he was not forestalled. Vide Alpine Journal, vol. xviii, pp. 120 and, 185

21. Sixty feet. At this period, 60 feet was considered to be ample for three climbers, now (1903) 80 feet is considered to be the proper length, besides which a light rope of 100 feet is often carried for use in emergencies.

22. Næver, the outer bark of the birch-tree, is used for roofing buildings and for lighting fires. It ignites readily, blazes away most brightly, and is invaluable at a sæter and when camping out.

23. *Slingsby is understating his contribution here – see "My Climbs in the Alps and Caucasus" by A. F. Mummery, also available from Ripping Yarns.com. Ed.*

24. Emmanuel Mohn.

25. *In 1882 Slingsby had married Alizon Ecroyd who accompanied him often in his later mountaineering. Ed.*

26. *Later the same season Cecil and Alizon Slingsby made the second ascent of the Romsdalhorn (the first time by a lady).Ed.*

27. Why not call the latter "pot-holes," which they would be, if they occurred on a plateau of carboniferous limestone instead of on a glacier?

28. Alpine Journal, vol. xix, p. 604.

29. This summer, 1903, when climbing within the Arctic Circle, we saw mountains quite clearly which, measured on the map, proved to be 180 to 200 miles distant from us.

30. Since writing the above I have received corroboration from Herr Petersen, who says he is certain that in 1878 my route, on the south side of the Skar, was the only possible route, and he agrees with me in thinking that a large fall of rock must have taken place after our ascents.

31. Alpine Journal vol. xviii, P. 254, and Nor. Tur. For. Aarbog for 1897, p. 54.

32. Alpine Journal vol. xxi, p. 91.

33. Alpine Journal, vol. xxii, p. 624.

34. Tusker = German.

35. Alpine Journal, vol.. xxv, p. 375.

36. *Slingsby was sixty-three at this time. Ed.*

37. Alpine Journal, vol. xxvi, p. 466.

Acknowledgements

The following people must be given a special mention for the help they gave in bringing "Norway: the Northern Playground" back to life. In alphabetical order:

Dr John Baddeley: Norway enthusiast of the Aberdeen Mountaineering Club and former Spitzbergen polar scientist; for proof-reading the final copy. John also supplied many of the colour pictures inside the book and I am due him a great thanks for that.

David Durkan: member of Turtagrø Venner ("friends of Turtagrø"); for the Appendix and for incredible enthusiasm in assisting the republication of "Slingsby..." from the Norwegian side of the North Sea.

Tony Howard: Troll Wall pioneer and author of the Romsdal guidebook (amongst many other things); for the introduction.

Krystina Lotoczko: for many hours slaving over the computer typesetting "Slingsby..." – and for dragging *me* away from the computer when the weather on the Cairngorms was too fine to be sat indoors!

The 2003 edition of "Norway the Northern Playground" was published with the assistance of Turtagrøs Venner.

About Ripping Yarns.com

There are a lot of classic adventure books which are undeservedly now out of print and unavailable to the general public. In today's mass-market publishing world they would be likely to remain that way.

Ripping Yarns.com was started in 2002 to publish out-of-print adventure books on the internet in e-book form. This will ensure that these classic tales are once again available and not forgotten.

The more popular titles are also being republished in conventional soft-back form – the proceeds from these will be used to cross-subsidise the website.